THEATRE, COURT AND CITY, 1595–1610

Drama and Social Space in London

JANETTE DILLON

CAMBRIDGE
UNIVERSITY PRESS

PUBLISHED BY THE PRESS SYNDICATE OF THE UNIVERSITY OF CAMBRIDGE
The Pitt Building, Trumpington Street, Cambridge CB2 1RP, United Kingdom

CAMBRIDGE UNIVERSITY PRESS
The Edinburgh Building, Cambridge CB2 2RU, UK   http://www.cup.cam.ac.uk
40 West 20th Street, New York, NY 10011-4211, USA   http://www.cup.org
10 Stamford Road, Oakleigh, Melbourne 3166, Australia

First published 2000.

Typeset in Monotype Baskerville 11/12½[SE]

A catalogue record for this book is available from the British Library

ISBN 0 521 66118 8 hardback √

Transferred to digital printing 2004

This book explores the vital and interactive relationship between city and court in the drama of Shakespeare's time.

The growth of purpose-built playhouses in late sixteenth-century London began to shift the focus of performance for many companies away from provincial touring, making the city a more conspicuous presence in drama. Janette Dillon looks at relations between drama and city through the wider lens of fashion and commercialism, examining in particular the developing 'west end' area along the Strand. She argues that the drama is oriented towards both the city of London and the court, rather than to one or the other, as previous studies have assumed.

The book is organised around physical and social forms of theatre space. It ranges from analysis of well-known plays, such as Shakespeare's *Love's Labour's Lost* and Jonson's *Epicoene*, to lesser-known drama by Heywood and the newly discovered Jonsonian entertainment *Britain's Burse*.

Janette Dillon is Reader in Drama at the School of English Studies, University of Nottingham. Her previous books include *Shakespeare and the Solitary Man* (1980), *Geoffrey Chaucer* (1993) and *Language and Stage in Medieval and Renaissance England* (1998).

Contents

Illustrations

Acknowledgements

I wish to thank the people who helped to make this book possible. I am especially grateful to Andrew Gurr, Simon Shepherd and the anonymous readers at Cambridge University Press, who read all or part of the manuscript and made numerous helpful comments and suggestions. James Knowles generously made his text of the New Exchange entertainment available to me before' publication, and Felicity Riddy and Douglas Tallack also shared unpublished work on the city with me. Ian Archer willingly answered questions about the complexities of city jurisdiction, and Alex Werner of the Museum of London helped me to locate papers and publications. Sarah Stanton and Hilary Hammond of Cambridge University Press have been helpful and supportive throughout.

I am grateful to the British Library, the British Museum, the Museum of London, the Royal Institute of Architects and the Provost and Fellows of Worcester College Oxford for their kind permission to reproduce illustrations. I would also like to thank the editors and publishers of *Medieval and Renaissance Drama in England* (John Pitcher and Fairleigh Dickinson University Press) and *Research Opportunities in Renaissance Drama* (David Bergeron and the University Press of Kansas) for permission to adapt and reprint material from existing published work for chapters 5 and 6. Thanks also to the participants in the SCAENA Conference at St John's College, Cambridge in August 1997, for their discussion of a paper which contributed to chapter 3.

Lastly I would like to thank the University of Nottingham for a grant towards travel and expenses and the School of English Studies at Nottingham for research leave. Without that stretch of uninterrupted time this book would still exist only in the imagination.

Conventions and abbreviations

Elizabethan and Jacobean texts are cited in modern spelling throughout in an attempt to eradicate the apparent discrepancy between citations from writers whose work is available in good modern editions and those whose work is either unedited or available only in older editions. Where the edition cited is an old-spelling edition, I have therefore silently emended spelling. (In verse quotations, however, I retain the apostrophe in elided 'ed' verb endings, and substitute 'd' for 't' where appropriate.) Quotations from plays are regularly taken from the collected editions listed in the bibliography except where otherwise noted. Where no collected edition is listed, quotations are from the individual editions cited in the bibliography.

Jonson's texts represent a particularly difficult case, since he revised so thoroughly for the Folio edition of 1616, on which most modern editions are based. Since I am discussing plays first performed from 1597 onwards, it might seem that the Folio text is unlikely to represent the text as performed at the earlier date. On the other hand, the early quarto texts do not necessarily give a version of the text closer to that publicly performed. In the case of *Cynthia's Revels*, for example, the Quarto text probably gives the text of the play's court performance rather than that of its earlier public performance, so that the Folio text, which includes whole scenes of satire against the court omitted from the Quarto text, may well supply a text closer to that performed in 1600. *Poetaster* also provides an example of the Folio text supplying material (here, most importantly, the 'apologetical dialogue') suppressed by the authorities at the time of first printing. I have therefore chosen to quote from the Folio texts throughout, except in the case of *Every Man In His Humour*, where the Quarto text, with its Italian setting, does seem to represent something closer to what was played in 1598. I have used G. A. Wilkes' modern-spelling edition, based on Herford and Simpson, for all citations except those from *Every Man In His Humour*, which is cited from Herford and Simpson, and *Epicoene*, where I use L. A. Beaurline's separate edition.

The only abbreviations in use are *OED*, for the *Oxford English Dictionary*, 2nd edition; *CSPD*, for the *Calendar of State Papers, Domestic*, 12 vols. (London, 1856–1992); and *CSPV*, for the *Calendar of State Papers, Venetian*, 9 vols. (London, 1864–98).

Prologue

This is not another book on city comedy. It is an attempt to explore across a more disparate range of plays a broader and more dynamic engagement between theatre and the city; and it is also a plea for the need to look at the city in conjunction with the court. Though so many studies separate the two environments for the purpose of analysing plays, their relationship is inextricably symbiotic, and no study of theatre and the city in this period can afford to ignore the court. The period in question here broadly coincides with that of city comedy, which is especially strongly associated with the first decade of the seventeenth century, though I look back also to the last five years of the sixteenth century. Yet although the theatre–city dynamic becomes especially marked during this relatively short period, its roots go back to the establishment of permanent playhouses in and around the city of London from the 1570s onwards, and to their increasing prominence in London life.

As scholars have often pointed out, these new playhouses tended to cluster outside the city boundary, but up to 1595 companies also performed within the city limits, notably in city inns, despite the city's consistent hostility to players performing within the area of its jurisdiction. Nevertheless the rigorous provisions of an act of the city's Common Council regarding commercial performance, issued in December 1574, probably contributed to James Burbage's decision to build the Theatre outside the regulated space of the city in 1576.[1] The players, however, were protected by powerful patrons who gave them their backing against the city's opposition. Such protection was vital, given the provisions of the Act Against Vagabonds. This statute, issued in 1572, five years after the building of the Red Lion and four years before the building of the Theatre, made it mandatory for players to be attached to a noble patron. Without evidence of such attachment they were liable to be treated as vagrants and subject to the rigours of punishment routinely meted out

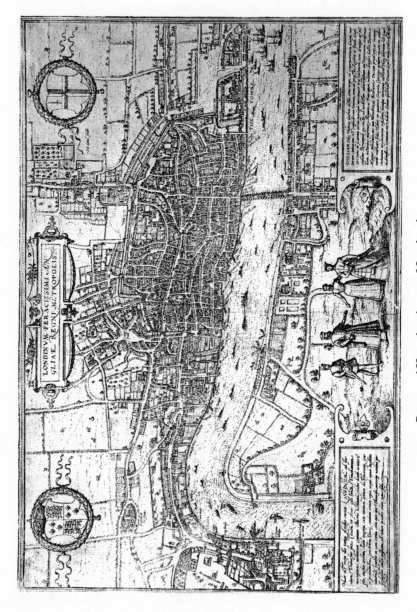

1. Braun and Hogenberg's map of London, late 1550s.

to masterless men. With it, however, they could be very strong indeed. A royal patent issued to Leicester's Men in May 1574 licensed them to perform 'as well within our city of London and liberties of the same, as also within the liberties and freedoms of any our cities, townes, boroughs etc. whatsoever as without the same, throughout our realm of England', the only reservations being that the plays should be approved by the Master of the Revels and that there should be no performances at times of prayer or when the plague was in London (Chambers, *Elizabethan Stage*, vol. II, pp. 87–8).[2]

Conflict between court and city over public performance was especially fierce in 1580–4 (Gildersleeve, *Government Regulation*, p. 160). Three notable stages mark the lines of battle: the new patent issued to the Master of the Revels in 1581; a city ordinance of *c.* 1582; and the founding of the Queen's Men in 1583. The first struck a blow for the crown against the powers of all local authorities by granting the Master of the Revels extended powers over public performance throughout England; the second showed the city taking a much harder line than in 1574 by prohibiting all public performance within the city, with 'like prohibition . . . in places near unto the city';[3] while the third established an unprecedentedly large and distinguished company of twelve sharers and gave them a degree of status and protection exceeding that of any previous professional company.[4]

It is clear, then, that the story of theatre and the city cannot be told without repeated recourse to the court. The monarch, the Privy Council and individual noble patrons all took an active role, usually in opposition to the city, in determining the place of plays and players in and around London. The Master of the Revels was keen to invite professional players to court as a way of avoiding the huge expense of staging in-house court entertainments, and the Privy Council was quick to remind the city authorities that the players needed to be allowed to 'rehearse' their plays before staging them for the queen. (Though the 'rehearsal' argument was certainly to some extent a mere pretext for commercial performance, there was enough force behind it to cow the city authorities.) And of course Privy Councillors were often the patrons of playing companies themselves, which gave them an added private interest in protecting the players. Even when the Privy Council finally backed the city in agreeing a total ban on performance in city inns in 1594, the lord chamberlain wrote to the mayor later in the same year asking for special permission for his own company to play at the Cross Keys during the coming winter (though the ban does seem to have been properly imposed from 1595 (Gurr, *Shakespearian Playing Companies*, p. 78)).

Hence, despite increased antagonism from the city, it is during this period, especially in the decade following the founding of the Queen's Men in 1583, that some companies (not including the Queen's Men) begin to consolidate the 'massive shift from habitual travelling to habitual residence in London' (Gurr, *Shakespearian Playing Companies*, p. 29). For all the city's urging of complete and final suppression of all plays in 1595 and 1597, and even the Privy Council's apparent agreement to tear down all playhouses on the second occasion of the mayor's plea for closure, the players continued to establish themselves ever more firmly in the wider area of London, if not within the city boundary itself, after 1595.[5] This strength was confirmed on the accession of the new king in 1603. James not only adopted the Chamberlain's Men as his own company within days of his arrival in London, but also made payments to the players thereafter not merely for performances given at court but during times of plague, when they could not perform at all. This was protection and status to a degree beyond even that of the Queen's Men in the 1580s.

Thus, at the same time as the theatre was consolidating its commercial urban, or suburban, presence, it was also strengthening its ties with the court. There is no pattern of court prominence falling as city prominence rises, or vice versa. At the heart of relations between theatre and city there is therefore a paradox: despite being taken under royal protection by Elizabeth in 1583 and by James in 1603, and despite the city's prohibition of players playing in city inns from 1594, the players never developed an exclusive allegiance to the court and against the city. What plays and players endlessly renegotiate is their double orientation towards these two locations, themselves necessarily in dialogue with each other as well as with the theatre. It is this phenomenon that is particularly noticeable at the turn of the century, as plays begin to create a larger and more explicit space for the city and city concerns while at the same time retaining a courtly orientation sometimes in overt tension with those city concerns and sometimes scarcely distinguishable from them.

The rise of the city as an especially palpable presence in plays written for public performance effectively begins with the rise of the Queen's Men.[6] Though plays of the 1580s are notoriously difficult to date with any precision, the earliest extant play to include London in its title seems to be Robert Wilson's *The Three Ladies of London* (c. 1581). If the dating is correct, this play predates even the foundation of the Queen's Men, but Wilson was to become a founder member of the new company in 1583, and his linked London play, *Three Lords and Three Ladies of London* (1588–90), was not only written for the Queen's Men but also incorporated a lament for the death of their star player, Richard Tarlton, who died in 1588. The moralising aspect of *Three Ladies* tends to make London stand in for all England, but there are occasional moments when the scene becomes localised in a way that is very specifically aimed at a London audience: Usury visits the Exchange, Simony is seen in Paul's Walk and Mercatore describes the practice of driving up rents by overcrowding and overpricing property leased to 'Frenchmans and Flemings', a problem that was particular to London at this time (Dodsley, ed., *Select Collection*, vol. VI, pp. 364, 305–6).[7] *Three Lords and Three Ladies*, however, has a much stronger sense of localisation about it and displays a marked civic pride that is closely tied to its nationalism. Written in the aftermath of the Armada, its prologue is spoken by a personification of London, represented as a lady richly attired and guarded by angels, whose closing line adopts the third person in order to tell the audience that 'London bids you welcome'. The direct address to a London audience is unmistakable. Throughout the play Wilson seizes opportunities to glorify both the pomp of London and the generosity of its citizens in paying for such pomp, and the great Tarlton is praised in terms that highlight his roots in the London guild system (Dodsley, ed., *Select Collection*, vol. VI, pp. 397–8). Local references also help to emphasise a strong sense of place in the play.

The other Queen's Men's play that speaks very directly to a London audience is *The Famous Victories of Henry the Fifth* (1583–8). With its familiar reference to 'the old tavern in Eastcheap' in the first scene (i.74) and its tradesmen keeping a look-out at Billingsgate and Pudding Lane End (ii.3–6), it anchors the prince's unprincely activities firmly in a material urban world that the audience recognises. Indeed, so recognisable is the reference to the old tavern in Eastcheap intended to be that it is not even named as the Boar's Head. And the reference, furthermore, is wholly targeted at a contemporary London audience, since the Boar's Head did not exist at the time of the play's setting (see note 74 to this passage in Corbin and Sedge's edition of the play).

This same low-life setting, of course, passed on to Shakespeare's *Henry IV* plays of the 1590s, by which time the London focus was well established in different ways in various plays of the earlier 1590s. The alien riots of *Sir Thomas More* (c. 1590–3); the linking of the coneycatcher to the

Royal Exchange in *A Knack to Know a Knave* (1592); the specificity of London locations in *A Warning for Fair Women* (1589–99);[8] and the repeated insistence in the opening of *The Four Prentices of London* (1594), which is not about London at all but about heroic adventures overseas, that the four sons of the Earl of Boulogne are proud to be London apprentices ('Even kings themselves have of these trades been free', says their father (1.i.134)), together demonstrate something of the range of dramatic genres that might carry this specific attention to the desires and concerns of a London audience.

The dramatic focus on London in plays from the late 1580s, then, needs to be linked to the increasingly firmly established status of players and theatres in and around London from about this time. It is also important, furthermore, to recognise the extent to which the psychic and the physical dimensions of the London environment as mediated in the theatre are interwoven. What we see in the plays is not a neutral or purely material place, but a representation of material place apprehended as a space occupied and understood in particular and changing ways. A further difference, then, between this study and existing studies of city comedy is that this one seeks to understand physical environments as 'produced' by those who occupy them, and the subjectivities of those occupants as in turn 'produced' by the spaces they inhabit. My thinking on space is greatly indebted to Henri Lefebvre, whose work insists on the material dimension of the psychic. 'Spatial practice', he writes, 'simultaneously defines: places – the relationship of local to global; the representation of that relationship; actions and signs; the trivialized spaces of everyday life; and, in opposition to these last, spaces made special by symbolic means as desirable or undesirable, benevolent or malevolent, sanctioned or forbidden to particular groups' (*Production of Space*, p. 288). Ideology, he argues, is to be understood only through its practical operations in social space, operations which are specific to time and place and are thus historical as well as geographical. Every place in time has its spatial code, which is 'not simply a means of reading or interpreting space: rather it is a means of living in that space, of understanding it, and of producing it' (pp. 47–8).[9]

The concept of 'place', then, germane to the chapter divisions of the present book, needs to be understood as both topographical and conceptual. Particular locations in London may emblematically represent particular activities (the Royal Exchange, for example, may stand for commercial transaction), but the inhabitants of the city do not experience those aspects of city life only within those special locations.

They carry their experience of the city in all its aspects with them, experiencing their own subjectivities as the sum (and conflict) of those various locations and activities. The book is therefore organised around ways of experiencing space rather than by physical locations, as chapter titles indicate, though physical locations of course play a crucial part in determining the nature of urban experience. Time and space, furthermore, as Lefebvre implies, are crucially interwoven. Individuals experience time in and through space, and their sense of changes in the world around them is necessarily linked to the places that feature in their everyday lives, from the home and the workplace to the larger structures of church, palace and civic institution, which function as both material and symbolic points of reference. New build-ings, especially buildings that initiate new categories of building in a given location (like the theatres or the Royal Exchange) produce new ways of being, new social orientations.

Theatre space is of course a special case. In Lefebvre's terms, though he does not discuss theatre in any detail, it is both a 'representational space' and a 'representation of space' and yet neither of these (*Production of Space*, p. 188). But underpinning the present book, which is centrally concerned with theatre, is the concept of theatre as a place to play. On the one hand theatres are real, physical spaces, architecturally and symbolically different from one another, constructing different spatial relations between performance and audience, and this needs to be taken seriously. On the other hand, they are all also places of 'virtual reality', literally staging in material form fictions and fantasies which offer an audience vicarious experiences. Their relationship to the wider physical space that surrounds them is therefore both mediated and provisional. This book seeks to consider only the London theatre, yet at the same time as investigating what the two elements of that phrase mean in the period chosen for study, it also seeks to break down that monolithic conception into its very different and oppositional parts. The public amphitheatres built outside the city limits, in Shoreditch or the Southwark liberties,[10] for example, must be understood to be very differently placed from the Blackfriars Theatre, built inside the city walls but outside city jurisdiction; the Blackfriars, situated within a liberty based on the ancient ecclesiastical privilege of a now dissolved monastery, must in turn be recognised as different from the Paul's theatre, located within an active ecclesiastical precinct that included the whole of Paul's churchyard and Paul's Walk (see figure 8), free of the city but subject to the authority of the Dean of St Paul's; and all of these are

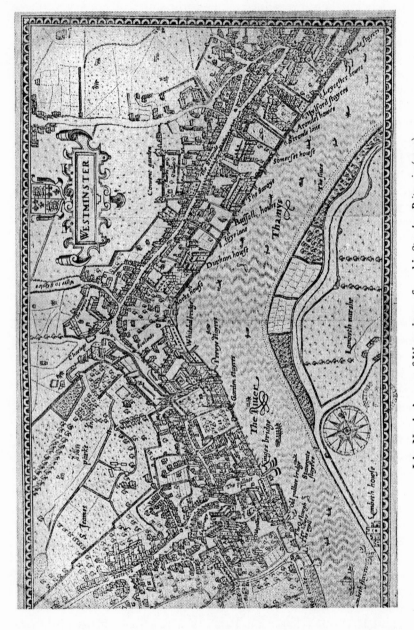

2. John Norden's map of Westminster, from his *Speculum Britanniae* (1593).

different again from the later Whitefriars Theatre to the west of the city boundary, the Banqueting Hall or the Great Chamber at Whitehall, or the New Exchange on the Strand (discussed as a performance location in chapter 6 below). And just as each theatre stands in a specific complex and contradictory physical relation to the city and the court, so the impressions of court and city that are mediated on any of these stages stand in complex and contradictory relation to the actual court and city. It is not my intention to try to reconstruct either the court or the city as they lie beyond the plays, but rather to look at how and why the plays play in the particular way they do with the concerns of both.

It may be useful to subject to brief scrutiny some of the recurrent terms and concerns of the chapters that follow before proceeding to more specialised discussions. What and where, for example, are the city and the court in this period? The city, as is well known, has many meanings. The most restricted of these is the use of the term to refer to the area within the old city walls, which still had powerful symbolic force in the way the inhabitant or visitor experienced the space of London. Since the early thirteenth century, however, the area governed by the city of London authorities had extended beyond the walls to what were known as the 'bars' (marked by posts or gates on the main roads). Other areas had been added since then: the city gained possession of the borough of Southwark, for example, in 1550, and further significant changes were part of the city's new charter of 1608, discussed in chapter 5 below.[11] Beyond the boundary of the city jurisdiction were the suburbs, fast expanding and encroaching on the fields and villages that surrounded the city.

Part of the city's encroachment extended in the direction of Westminster and the court. Technically the court could not be conceived of in a particular location, since it moved around with the monarch, but under James, though he personally spent more time than Elizabeth had done out of London, the court tended to become both physically and conceptually more fixed at Whitehall, in the city of Westminster. Yet the fixing was fluid in other ways. Several historians have emphasised the polycentric nature of the court, which was really not one court but three (including the separate households of the queen and the prince), and which centred too on the great West End palaces of some of the wealthiest courtiers.[12] It was during the period selected for study in this book that the gradual increase in fashionable building along the Strand, running between Westminster and the city of London, began to create an area that would eventually need a new name: 'the town'. Though the term is not in common use until later in the seventeenth century, one of its earliest occurrences is in Ben Jonson's *Epicoene* (first performed in 1609–10; see chapter 7 below), and its first use in the sense of 'fashionable London society', as cited by the *OED*, is in Francis Beaumont's 'Letter to Ben Jonson', from about the same date (Riggs, *Ben Jonson*, p. 157). City and court came together in many ways in this area, which was at one and the same time a place of aristocratic palaces, gentry houses, the Inns of Court and expensive shops.[13] Sir Robert Cecil's New Exchange, opened on the Strand in 1609, represented the coming together of courtly and business interests in one man's enterprise. Cecil himself was the product of more than one milieu: the son of Elizabeth's first minister, William Cecil, but not born of an old aristocratic family, he was by 1609 King James' lord treasurer, and one of the wealthiest men in England.[14] The conjunction of court and commerce was given expression in an extraordinary opening entertainment, staged before the king and his family, but not, as was usual with courtly shows, performed on courtly, or at least aristocratic, territory, but rather inviting the court into the new location of what was effectively a high-class shopping centre in order to celebrate the luxury commodities for sale in this new and ostentatious building (see chapter 6 below).

Since the conception of space underpinning the discussion here is one that understands it to be dynamic, a coming together of physical place and social life in ways that are always in process, all of these usages will come into play at different points. Maps are reproduced in order to help the reader recognise the topography of city and court from different perspectives (see figures 1, 2, 3, 4 and 5). The discussion itself will have to be the guide as to which meanings of 'court' and 'city' are uppermost at any given point. Since one of the central arguments of the book is that the interplay between these two entities makes distinction between them often arbitrary or problematic, and that social practices and discourses of the time themselves sometimes seek to blur the distinction between them, it is neither possible nor desirable to reduce either term to single or stable definition. As Frank Whigham has emphasised, in his book, *Ambition and Privilege*, early modern attempts to produce firm and exclusive definitions of particular social classes or institutions typically emerge from groups under pressure, seeking to insist on boundaries that have already been crossed. The very exploration in the present book of concepts that might go under such names as the urban, the suburban, urbanity, metropolitanism, civility, courtesy, courtliness, and so on demonstrates the need to retain a flexible understanding of the etymological roots at issue. In a sense the whole book could be said to be an exploration over a short period of theatre's play with changing definitions of court and city and the shifting sense of separation or convergence between them.

A further concept important for the book, one which is associated with particular places like the New Exchange and its predecessor, the Royal Exchange, but is also placeless, is that of the market. Jean-Christophe Agnew's work is seminal here for its exploration of the difficult adjustment that had to be made in the early modern period to the invisibility and liquidity of capital. A market, as Agnew argues, 'was emphatically a *place* in antiquity' (*Worlds Apart*, p. 18), and it retained this primary sense in medieval England. But by the sixteenth century the word referred to 'the acts of both buying and selling, regardless of locale, and to the price or exchange value of goods and services' (p. 41), and contemporaries found it hard to come to terms with this new liquidity, a liquidity which also finds an analogy in the fluidity of social relations. The main point of Agnew's argument, however, is that the mobility and polymorphousness of the market render it deeply akin to theatre, which began regularly to reflect on its own theatricality around the same time, leading it to address the same problems of 'authenticity, accountability, and intentionality' (p. 11) as are at issue in the concept of the market. As Lars Engle, developing Agnew's arguments in particular relation to Shakespeare, has shown, the theatre of this period, understanding itself to be market-like, a place where values may be tested in relation to one another, 'gives a local window on the larger economy of which it is part' (*Shakespearean Pragmatism*, p. 1). And, Engle emphasises, the word 'economy' signals a newly pragmatic understanding of what the world is. Economies are dynamic; they recognise values as mutable and contingent, continually reacting against one another. Representing the world as an economy signals the erosion of a tradition of fixed structures and beliefs.

There are more practical reasons for the prominence of the market and market-related systems in this book, moreover, besides their affinity with performance and even a broad understanding of everyday life. The trade guilds, for example, controlled not only all city commerce and organised labour, but also the government of the city. The Court of Aldermen was by definition made up of men who had reached their position through business, and the lord mayor was always either selected from or translated to one of the twelve so-called 'Great Companies'. Even the more popular assemblies of Common Hall and the Court of Common Council were based on recognition of some affiliation to a guild, though at a lower level.[15] The London business world had close ties with courtly magnates whose financial interests needed the import–export trade for their profitability. As Robert Ashton has demonstrated, relations between commercial and government business were mutually profitable in numerous ways: 'Capital from orthodox commerce flowed into customs farms, collectorships, the acquisition of patents and other concessions, and the fruits of this investment in turn flowed back into commerce' (*City and the Court*, p. 27). The select oligarchy who governed London were those most likely to have interests in overseas trade or domestic concessions, besides being those with sufficient wealth to lend money to the crown when it needed it; and both these factors gave the city some influence over court expenditure and national government. London's status as an international market grew fast, particularly after the fall of Antwerp in 1585, and the expansion of commerce and of overseas trade had immediate effects on both the quantity and quality of commodities available in city shops as well as on prices. Materialism was singled out by the popular preacher Henry Smith as 'the Londoner's sin' (Wright, *Middle-Class Culture*, p. 286). That trade expansion, furthermore, was perhaps the single most important factor in setting London apart from the rest of England in terms of both size and nature (the uniqueness of its luxury market contributing, of course, to its immense and rapid growth).

The word 'commodity' is another word in regular use here which requires attention. Douglas Bruster's study of drama and the market, which draws on Agnew's work, calls attention to the changing meaning of the word at the end of the sixteenth century (a change which is discussed further in relation to the writing of John Stow at the beginning of chapter 3 below). Bruster abbreviates the older meaning to 'something like "convenience"', but 'convenience' now has a rather weak and reduced force compared with the more strongly positive senses of 'benefit', 'advantage' or 'good' which were available in the sixteenth century, as Stow's usage confirms. Bruster's main point, however, is that the word began to refer more frequently to material objects, and this is undoubtedly so. He also quite rightly situates this change in usage within the context of a contemporary preoccupation with luxury objects (*Drama and the Market*, p. 41; cf. Minchinton, *Growth of English Overseas Trade*, introduction).

Any reader of late Elizabethan or early Jacobean texts is familiar with the discursive phenomenon of the list. A sense of the overwhelming material life of objects is regularly produced by the interruption of continuous prose by a catalogue of nouns, juxtaposed for no good reason other than their contiguous physical presence. Such a list can have a precise, almost fetishised, particularity about it (as in Thomas Platter's numbered list of exactly fifty selected items on view in Sir Walter Cope's collection of exotic objects, see chapter 1 below) or a tumbling, breathless speed (as in the Shop-boy's account of his goods for sale in the New Exchange entertainment, see chapter 6 below). In both cases, however, there is an emphasis on disconnectedness, on the independent life of objects.[16] The list form highlights the lack of any inherent connection between items. Their only connectedness comes from the discursive chaining together of the list itself. The independent, fragmentary presence of the commodity is underlined at the same time as its connection by definition with other commodities is revealed.

The further question then arises of what defined any particular commodity as a luxury, and here the discourse of usefulness comes into play. Louis B. Wright has shown how signally reliant on a utilitarian ethic are many of the middle-class texts of Renaissance culture. 'Usefulness', in his view, 'is always the criterion of value in bourgeois civilizations' (*Middle-Class Culture*, p. 295). The work of Thorstein Veblen allows this brief remark to be extended. Where Wright's focus is on what he calls 'the middle class', Veblen refers to the target group of his study as 'the leisure class'. Though the leisure class extends to the top of the social hierarchy, there is some overlap between the two categories, since both represent groupings well above subsistence level. The point about the leisure class, according to Veblen's analysis, is precisely that its consumption is not only in excess of the minimum, but that that consumption also undergoes a specialisation with regard to the quality of goods consumed. In order to display his 'pecuniary strength' (Veblen's term), the gentleman of leisure needs to have luxuries about him.[17] Conspicuous leisure and conspicuous consumption go hand-in-hand, and both are characterised by the element of waste. Veblen laments the unavoidably deprecatory overtones of the term 'waste', which he claims to be using neutrally for analytical purposes, yet points out in passing that the very fact that the word 'waste' in everyday usage implies deprecation is significant in itself. 'This common-sense implication', he argues, 'is itself an outcropping of the instinct of workmanship' (*Theory of the Leisure Class*, p. 98). 'Waste', in other words, is the term that reveals most clearly the extent to which the definition of luxury items demands to be understood within a binary framework that conceives of luxury from within a work ethic. It is the notion of the useful that allows non-functional and novelty items to be defined as luxuries.[18] The preoccupations with functionality and wastefulness are symbiotic.

A further point which neither Wright nor Veblen makes is that these preoccupations are likely to become particularly visible in specific economic conditions, so that their prominence in late sixteenth- and early seventeenth-century texts needs to be related to changes in trading practices, developments in the domestic and overseas markets, urban growth and other factors, more fully outlined in chapter 1 below. Thomas Gainsford, writing in 1618, notes the relative cheapness of luxury pursuits and commodities, assuring his readers that it is possible 'to wade through the current of pleasure, although it run to voluptuousness' even on a very moderate income (Wright, *Middle-Class Culture*, p. 40). For later historians, too, the period is recognisable as 'an age of exceptionally prodigal living', in which high levels of consumption are fuelled by the ever-increasing quantity of luxury imports (Stone, *Crisis of the Aristocracy*, p. 184). Again and again the texts of the period reveal either a singular attachment to material objects or an anxiety about the process of commoditisation.

A logical paradox follows: while the word 'commodity' was coming increasingly to refer to concrete individual *things*, the process of commoditisation was felt to be pervading all kinds of practices, activities and entities that could not be defined as objects. John Wheeler voices this sense of creeping commoditisation in 1601:

The prince with his subjects, the master with his servants, one friend and acquaintance with another, the captain with his soldiers, the husband with his wife, women with and among themselves, and in a word, all choppeth and changeth, runneth and raveth after marts, markets and merchandising, so that all things come into commerce, and pass into traffic (in a manner) in all times, and in all places. (Quoted in Bruster, *Drama and the Market*, p. 41)

Hence it becomes possible, and on occasion even necessary, to talk about other aspects of the period (from texts, to social personae, to theatre) as 'commodities'. Frank Whigham, for example, argues that courtesy books 'function as commodities, in two ways. First, each offers a specimen of its author's worth, epideictically . . . Second, each offers itemized concepts that may be traded anew by its consumer.' Furthermore, the tacit understanding of self as performance underpinning such handbooks produces the self as a product or commodity (*Ambition and Privilege*, pp. 29, 33). Agnew too talks about a 'commodity self: a mercurial exchange value or "bubble" floating on the tides of what attention others were disposed to invest' (*Worlds Apart*, p. 13). Both Whigham and Agnew, like Engle, are concerned to convey a sense of how the dominant world-view of fixed categories and essences (or recognised 'truths') is beginning to give way in this period to a view that perceives the world as more like a market, in which values are understood to be relational.

Such a worldview, as already pointed out, is necessarily dynamic, perceiving change rather than fixity as the dominant framework of human existence. The focus of this book is on the visible mobility of relations between court and city, as influenced by the development of the market and as represented within the domain of theatre, itself a place for testing and playing with different ways of seeing, estimating and valuing. The social backgrounds and professional activities of playwrights themselves offer a window on the way affiliations to a variety of locales and social classes may come together and contest one another in a range of complex ways. David Riggs, in discussing the unclear social status of the *arriviste* profession of playwright, notes that the first generation of professional or semi-professional playwrights (between 1572 and 1597) divides fairly evenly between the literate artisan and university-educated classes (*Ben Jonson*, pp. 25–6);[19] but closer attention to the status of individual playwrights shows up some of the tensions and anomalies around these categorisations. Shakespeare, for example, though the son of a glover, does not appear to have followed his father into that or any other trade, though the activities of his early years are far from clear. He is also an anomaly in the London theatre by virtue of having no previous connection with either London or the universities. In 1596, however, his father was granted a coat of arms, which entitled him to call himself a gentleman. Given that John Shakespeare was in debt at the time, it is likely that his son was primarily responsible for obtaining the coat of arms.

Ben Jonson mocked Shakespeare's pretensions in *Every Man Out of His Humour* (1599),[20] but was himself subject to mockery in the opposite vein. His scorn for Shakespeare's upward mobility is in tune with his own pride in his supposed origins in the ancient Scottish Johnstone family, whose arms he adopted. Unfortunately for him, however, his father died shortly before his birth, and his mother remarried a bricklayer, who later forced Jonson into apprenticeship in this trade. Although his stepfather was no poor artisan, but became a master of his trade and a man of substantial means, other playwrights knew that the way to needle Jonson was to joke about his bricklaying connections, and Jonson, for all his sense of shame about this aspect of his youth, knew the value of being a freeman of the city and went to considerable lengths to become a citizen of London through the Company of Tilers and Bricklayers (Miles, *Ben Jonson*, pp. 1–8; Riggs, *Ben Jonson*, pp. 53–4).

Thomas Middleton, also the son of a bricklayer, does not seem to have been the butt of this kind of joke, perhaps because he laid no claim to ancient or landed lineage. His origins were much more closely tied to the city of London, though his father represented that further anomaly, a city gentleman, having a coat of arms besides his trade.[21] He also owned considerable property, which became the subject of prolonged litigation following his wife's remarriage, and part of Thomas' share went towards funding his education at Queen's College, Oxford (Heinemann, *Puritanism and Theatre*, pp. 48–9).

John Webster, like Middleton, was the son of a wealthy man of business. His father was a coachbuilder. Where Middleton's father's marriage and Middleton's own baptism in the city church of St Lawrence Jewry tie them to the city proper, however, Webster's father spent all his working life in the parish of St Sepulchre's, just outside the city limits. Like Middleton, Webster continued with an academic education rather than becoming apprenticed to his father's trade; and the record of his admission to the Middle Temple in 1598 describes both himself and his father as gentlemen.[22] Like Jonson, however, he chose to claim membership of a city company, becoming eligible for entry to the Merchant Taylors Company by patrimony in 1615, following his father's death; and he too became the butt of jokes about his background in trade, perhaps as a result of taking up citizenship, or perhaps because of an active interest in the business at this point.[23] Henry Fitzjeffrey labelled him 'the playwright, cartwright' in a satiric verse of 1617. The social world of the theatre, then, was a melting-pot in terms of both playwrights and audiences, bringing together a mix of social classes and taking the instability of that mix a stage further through its own agency.

Yet instability, change, mobility, fluidity, and so on, are all words that describe social process impersonally, almost as if it occurred without agency. There is another word directly relevant to understanding the relations between theatre, city and court which offers a different, and very important, emphasis. That word is 'fashion'. By putting the concept of fashion into the discussion of shifts and realignments in early seventeenth-century London it is possible not only to highlight agency, but to begin to understand the place of the theatre within those social relations. The theatre is above all a place of show, but one with a high degree of agency. The stage can display what is already current and give it wider currency, but it can also display something new and

create new currency. In other words, it is a powerful maker and dis-
perser of fashions. It is also likely to pursue and create new fashions
with especial avidity because it stands to profit commercially by its
capacity to attract an audience. As audiences knew then, and still know,
theatre has something to sell; and though some of the shows that sell
will be old favourites, Henslowe's Diary makes clear that the London
theatre, itself still a relative novelty, fast expanding, in the 1590s, created
an audience with an enormous appetite for the new. New plays, and
indeed new playhouses, appeared at an astonishing speed, and
Henslowe's record of the performances of the Admiral's Men makes
clear that the company was performing a different play almost every
day of the week, and a high proportion of these were new plays.[24] The
invention of new genres is also a notable feature of the period, often
linked to the establishment of new companies: the formation of the
Queen's Men, for example, created the circumstances for a vogue for
large-cast plays, while the revival of the boy companies in 1599–1600
stimulated a fashion war between companies, with the development not
only of specific genres characterising the different repertories of each
boy's company, but different responses from the established adult companies (see further chapters 3 and 4 below).

At its most basic level, an appetite for plays about the city and the
court reflects the locations of the audience, given that these were the
two primary places of performance.[25] But the audience's interest in
one or other type of play is more than a matter of mere navel-gazing.
In the first place, it is evident that London audiences were as fascinated
by the doings of the court, to which they stood in such close proximity, as they were by the activities of their own environment (though the
same is not true in reverse for a court audience). Secondly, the demand
for a particular kind of play is a fashion, subject to change as material
circumstances in court and city (or beyond either) change.
Furthermore the concerns of the two environments were closer than
the court in particular was likely to admit. The matter of fashion itself,
for example, brought court and city together in ways that did not
simply display the predictable model of city aping court. Fashions in
dress and material objects may have looked as if they originated with
courtiers, but were in fact heavily dependent on what city merchants
could and did supply. Supply did not (and does not) simply follow
demand, but created (and creates) the conditions for demand in the
first place. So when new fashions emerged, they were often linked to
the availability of new items on the market; and it is perhaps pointless

to ask whether city money or aristocratic taste first made them fashionable. The point is rather that city and court were bound together in ways that were often suppressed by the courtly need to draw a firm line where there was in fact no such line.

New fashions were of course not only a matter of material objects, but also of speech and behaviour, and subsequent chapters frequently return to language as an indicator of shifting fashions. Commodification, for example, as I have argued above, is visible not just in the way material objects are apprehended, but in ways of being and speaking. It is a process that affects city and court alike, though it may appear in very different guises, masquerading as either specifically urban or specifically aristocratic. Hence the earliest play I discuss, *Love's Labour's Lost* (*c.* 1595), is the first play to show the obsessive concern with fashionable language that characterises so many plays around the turn of the century, but in this first instance the play concerned is dedicated to presenting linguistic extravagance as a characteristically courtly aberration. Yet there is no reason why we should take the play at its word, as it were. Though it places its excesses within a 'little academe' remote from any urban environment, Shakespeare's interest in those excesses is more likely to arise out of urban developments than out of courtly ones, of which his experience was much less direct (though again the point is partly that the two should not be separately conceived: commodification is precisely an area in which the interests of court and city are indivisible). Though it may have looked to Shakespeare, and probably also to his audience, at this early date, as if such cultivation of the word as object was a practice most properly represented not even in a realistic courtly environment, but in an absurdly segregated and elitist courtly hothouse, within two years Jonson was putting this kind of linguistic absurdity into the mouth of a city cobbler (Juniper in *The Case Is Altered* (1597–8)). Indeed, in slightly later plays Jonson shows the same kind of linguistic affectation within both city and courtly environments in a way that suggests, first, that the choice of environment should not always be read as a realistic one, and second, that there is a degree of affinity between these two social settings. Just as Milan or Venice or any number of foreign cities can stand in for London in the plays of this period, so, on occasion, can a courtly setting have wider application. The following chapters take up the various issues outlined here in more detail, with chapter 1 providing an overview of general issues of relevance for subsequent chapters. The sequence of chapters below is both synchronic and broadly chronological; that is to say, chapters explore aspects of court or city that are present throughout the period selected for study (and in some cases present by definition in courts or cities), but they do so in relation to specific plays in specific times and places. Thus, while it is self-evident that the city of London, or any city, must always be understood in relation to its boundaries, there can be moments when the question of boundaries becomes particularly pressing. One such moment for the city of London was the year 1607, and that moment is the subject of chapter 5. Despite this kind of continuity across chapters, however, I am nevertheless also making a broad chronological argument that there is a recognisable shift in ways of conceiving the court and the city between 1595 and 1610, though there are contradictions at both ends of that spectrum. The impulse towards retreat visible in *Love's Labour's Lost* stands in contradiction to the impulse towards celebration evident in *Edward IV*, but both conceive of the city as an entity separate and different from the court, however much that conception may be seen to be under pressure from different directions. A decade later, however, both *Britain's Burse* and *Epicoene* focus on the place where the two converge, though displaying markedly different attitudes towards this convergence.

As is already evident from this introduction, I have drawn on terms developed in later theoretical discourses where they seem to me to offer illuminating ways of conceiving the historical configurations in question. Though 'early modern' is increasingly the current, almost neutral, designation for the period under discussion here, it is one I find problematic for routine use because of its implicit subordination of the period in question to later developments. It is not, I think, helpful to summon such a perspective automatically, so that it becomes naturalised. On the other hand, summoning it intermittently and by design can facilitate ways of thinking about the earlier period which open up fruitful comparisons with the present. Both that term and other potentially anachronistic terms from later discourses may suggest potential affinities between the moment of writing and the moment under study, both poised at the turn of a century.

CHAPTER ONE

City, court and theatre

Every town is and wants to be a world apart
(Fernand Braudel)

In a speech to Star Chamber in 1616 James I inveighed against a change that seemed to be affecting the whole country as a result of London's growth:

It is the fashion of Italy, especially of Naples (which is one of the richest parts of it) that all the gentry dwell in the principal towns, and so the whole country is empty: even so now in England, all the country is gotten into London; so as with time, England will only be London, and the whole country be left waste: for as we now do imitate the French fashion, in fashion of clothes, and lackeys to follow every man; so have we got up the Italian fashion, in living miserably in our houses, and dwelling all in the city: but let us in God's name leave these idle foreign toys, and keep the old fashion of England: for it was wont to be the honour and reputation of the English nobility and gentry, to live in the country, and keep hospitality: for which we were famous above all the countries in the world. (McIlwain, *Political Works of James I*, pp. 343–4)

For James, as this speech makes clear, the expansion of London was evidence of a rejection of social duty and of a lamentable tendency to imitate foreign fashions. Writers at a more popular level agreed with him. Stow's tone is sternly moralistic: 'the gentlemen of all shires do fly and flock to this city, the younger sort of them to see and show vanity, and the elder to save the cost and charge of hospitality, and housekeeping' (*Survey*, vol. II, p. 212); while Dekker's is more sardonic: 'And thus we that mock every nation, for keeping one fashion, yet steal patches from every one of them, to piece out our pride, are now laughing-stocks to them, because their cut so scurvily becomes us' (*Seven Deadly Sins of London*, p. 44).

The dual focus on fashion and duty, and the moralising cast of mind that sees devotion to the first as evidence of neglect of the second, will be central to the discussion of relations between court, city and theatre in this book. The opposition pinpoints a set of tensions: between the governors and the governed of the city; between the individual and collective impulses which are part of the necessary undertow of city life; and between the city and all that is not the city, whether that other is conceived in any given context as the suburbs, the country, the nation or the rest of the world. Crucial though boundaries are, however, to the production of space, their demarcation is never absolute. Social spaces interpenetrate one another:

They are not *things*, which have mutually limiting boundaries and which collide because of their contours or as a result of inertia . . . Visible boundaries, such as walls or enclosures in general, give rise for their part to an appearance of separation between spaces where in fact what exists is an ambiguous continuity. The space of a room, bedroom, house or garden may be cut off in a sense from social space by barriers and walls, by all the signs of private property, yet still remain fundamentally part of that space. Nor can such spaces be considered empty 'mediums', in the sense of containers distinct from their contents. (Lefebvre, *Production of Space*, pp. 86–7)

As Fernand Braudel states in the epigraph to this chapter, 'Every town is and wants to be a world apart' (*Capitalism and Material Life*, p. 382). In order to define its integrity and apartness it has to construct boundaries (city walls are common to most medieval and early modern cities, and both Stow's *Survey of London* and Fitzstephen's description of London, which Stow incorporates, place accounts of the city wall close to the beginning of their works). It has to conceive of itself as different from, though standing in important forms of relation to, those elements that surround it. Thus, for Stow, to whom this book repeatedly returns, London is first and most fully described in relation to its own components, the twenty-six wards (see figure 4 for Steve Rappaport's map, which is based on Stow); this is followed by a description of the suburbs, summarised together under that one heading rather than itemised like the wards; and London's relationship to the realm is conceptualised through a mixture of self-congratulation and due, if somewhat token, humility ('in respect of the whole realm, London is but a citizen and no city'; *Survey*, vol. II, p. 206).

At the end of the sixteenth century, when Stow was writing,[1] London was having to come to terms with one of the most marked population expansions experienced anywhere in Renaissance Europe, and the king was not the only one who wanted to hold back the tide of its tremendous growth; contemporaries regularly wrote about its growth as a symptom

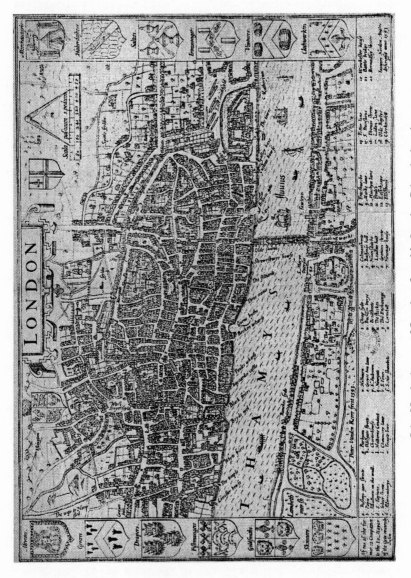

3. John Norden's map of London, from his *Speculum Britanniae* (1593).

of disease rather than health.[2] Its population had more or less tripled in the course of the century, with most of that proliferation concentrated in the last twenty years, 1580–1600; and it continued to expand at speed throughout the Jacobean period. That expansion, furthermore, was entirely due to immigration. London, according to John Norden, 'as an adamant draweth unto it all the other parts of the land' (*Speculum Britanniae*, p. 9). Its population would actually have declined during the same period, given the comparative birth and death rates, had it not been for immigration.

'To understand the extraordinary fascination of London in the sixteenth century', Lawrence Stone argues, 'one must realize that it was not merely the only city but also the only substantial town in England . . . It was not merely a difference in degree, it was a difference in kind: London was unique in a way which it is not today' (*Crisis of the Aristocracy*, p. 386). As King James remarked with bitterness in the speech quoted at the opening of the chapter, 'the new fashion is to be had nowhere but in London' (McIlwain, *Political Works of James I*, p. 343). Stone goes on to discuss London's attractions under the headings of business, pleasure and the lure of court office. His discussion is of course focused on the aristocracy, but it was the gentry and aristocracy in particular who were responsible for the development of the West End. The huge expansion during the sixteenth century of legal business and of the royal court and the central administration necessarily led not only to a rise in those employed within the legal profession or the Elizabethan equivalent of the civil service, but also to an influx of gentry and nobility pursuing lawsuits, court office or men of influence. They were also, of course, in pursuit of pleasure, as were their wives and families, and Stone remarks on the speed with which the London 'season' developed over a relatively short period between about 1590 and 1620 (*Crisis of the Aristocracy*, p. 387). Even seasonal visitors, however, needed places to stay, and this demand stimulated an extraordinary increase in building to the north of the Strand (as well as the subdividing and subletting of many of the Strand palaces). By the 1630s more than three-quarters of peers had permanent or semi-permanent residences in or around London, and several of those peers were developing fields and gardens into fashionable residential areas. The king, meanwhile, reissued in vain proclamations insisting that visitors to London leave when their business was finished and that the landed classes return to their country seats to keep hospitality. Not until 1633, when the government began to prosecute those disobeying the most recent proclamation of 1632, was any notice

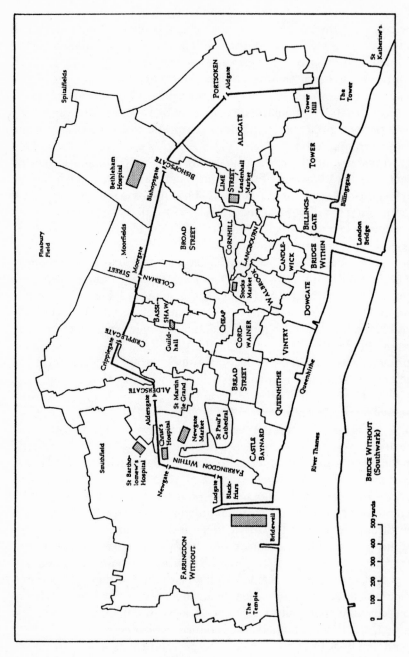

4. Steve Rappaport's map of London's wards and administrative boundaries.

taken of the repeated instruction to clear out of London (Stone, *Crisis of the Aristocracy*, pp. 385–98).

By the early seventeenth century, then, the majority of London's population was composed of first-generation immigrants, most of whom were from other parts of England, though foreign immigration had also increased during the sixteenth century, reaching its most significant level during the last third of the century. Population estimates for this period vary, of course, because the sources from which the figures are taken may be limited to the twenty-six wards of the city, or may include more or less of the expanding suburban area. Despite the expanding size of the metropolitan area, however, especially to the west of the city, there is evidence to suggest that even to the end of Elizabeth's reign most Londoners lived within the 'bars', the limits of the city's jurisdiction, covering little more than the square mile contained within the walls.

The pressure of the population within that small area was accordingly intense. Stow's laments for the building on and swallowing up of open spaces are well known, but he is not alone in protesting.[3] Both the government and the city authorities were also concerned. In response to a remonstrance from the lord mayor, a royal proclamation attempting to limit new buildings was issued by Elizabeth in 1580. This was then followed up by an act of Parliament in 1593 and repeatedly reinforced by further proclamations throughout James' reign. The Court of Aldermen, besides actively co-operating with these royal directives and making regular searches for breaches of the proclamation, also issued its own directives along similar lines.[4] One of the effects of these repeated directives, however (which by virtue of their very frequency indicate continued defiance of their edicts), was 'to encourage the dividing-up of existing houses and secret construction-work of poor brick in courtyards of old houses, away from the street and even from minor alleys . . . a whole clandestine proliferation of hovels and shanties on land of doubtful ownership' (Braudel, *Capitalism and Material Life*, p. 430).

Within the city limits, order was maintained through several intersecting structures, mainly those of ward, parish and company. Though these structures might be individually identified as those of city, church and occupation respectively, they were in fact much more closely interrelated than such a division would imply. The companies, for example, controlled city government: the Court of Aldermen was composed of men elected to office via their companies, and the lord mayor had to belong to one of the twelve great companies.[5] Guilds also took their religious duties seriously and scarcely distinguished between charitable benefactions and civic duties. Relieving the deserving poor, for example, was simultaneously a spiritual and a political act.

The 'undeserving' poor, however, presented an increasing problem as the population expanded. Church, state and city were united in their hostility to masterless or unattached individuals, 'sturdy beggars', as they were known, physically fit but unemployed. The ideal, from the authorities' point of view, would have been to erase such a category altogether; in practice the steps taken were expulsion and punishment. Vagrants were driven out of the city, sometimes whipped out, in an attempt to return them to the parish of their birth so that they could not become a burden on any other parish's poor relief. The statute of 1572, for example, ordered whipping, burning through the right ear, or serving as an indentured labourer for one year for a first offence. A second offence might incur the death penalty, and a third offence, according to the terms of the statute, undoubtedly would. Though the poor laws of 1597 and 1601 moderated these punishments, they were essentially based on this statute and its successor of 1575 (see further Beier, *Masterless Men*, ch. 9; McMullan, *Canting Crew*, pp. 36–41). Yet the particular circumstances of London's expanding labour market drew the masterless irresistibly towards London. It offered greater opportunities for casual labour than anywhere else in England; its sheer size provided relatively easy accommodation and the possibility of evading the authorities; and its organised poor relief, despite attempts to debar recent immigrants from claiming it, positively attracted vagrants to the capital (McMullan, *Canting Crew*, p. 10).[6]

London's expanding population, then, was a mobile and volatile one, including a relatively high proportion of potentially riotous and disorderly components. Vagrants were not the only group likely to provoke disorder. The ratio of immigrants to native-born Londoners was another destabilising factor, as were the numbers of aliens and apprentices.[7] While several recent historians have stressed the notable orderliness of the city as compared with the riotousness of other European cities, this is not to suggest that tensions were not present or that riots never broke out.[8] Roger Manning, under the heading of what he describes as a 'Late-Elizabethan Epidemic of Disorder', notes thirty-five outbreaks of disorder in the city between 1581 and 1602 (*Village Revolts*, pp. 200–10).

The conspicuous regulation of London's self-government might be read as indicative of anxiety regarding the perceived imminence of disorder rather than as pointing to a simple absence of disorder. City walls, especially when their defensive role ceases to be significant, can become, as Braudel notes, 'a system for supervising the townspeople themselves' (*Capitalism and Material Life*, p. 383). Valerie Pearl, stressing the essential orderliness of London, describes the high numbers of citizens who participated in city regulation at the local level of ward and vestry. Londoners lived in small, tightly controlled units within units: household, precinct, parish, ward and livery company all contributed to regulate the life of the inhabitants.[9] Constables and beadles were required to keep lists of householders, noting any 'inmates' (lodgers) and aliens, with the date of their arrival and the length of their stay. Householders were responsible for controlling the members of their household, and were under specific obligations to their community. They had to attend the meeting of the wardmote to elect its officers, and a significant number could expect to be elected to one or more of these offices in their lifetimes.[10] They were further obliged to help maintain order and could be required to arm themselves in order to assist in policing outbreaks of disorder. 'In some ways', Pearl comments, 'sixteenth-century London suffered not from too little government but from too much' ('Social Policy', p. 117). But too much government need not be seen as in contradiction with incipient disorder. London's orderly self-regulation and its outbreaks of riot may be seen as two sides of the same coin.

Amongst these outbreaks of disorder, the most serious disturbance was the sequence of riots of 1595. These constituted, according to Manning, 'the most dangerous and prolonged urban uprising in England between the accession of the Tudor dynasty and the beginning of the Long Parliament' (*Village Revolts*, p. 208). And most historians are agreed that the 1590s was a time of crisis in England. A sequence of bad harvests caused severe dearth and hardship and accelerated a rapid increase in prices already underway since the late 1580s. By the first decade of the seventeenth century prices were 47 per cent higher than they had been in the 1580s, and real wages had fallen significantly (Rappaport, 'Social Structure and Mobility: Part I', pp. 126, 131). More important than the scale of actual crisis, Ian Archer has argued, was the extent of perceived crisis: 'as far as the nature of social relations is concerned, it is people's perception of their situation, rather than the relativities in which historians so often deal, that matters. Londoners in the 1590s would have given short shrift to historians who pointed out that their suffering was not as acute as that of people on the continent, or that their tax burden was relatively low' (*Pursuit of Stability*, p. 14). That sense of perceived crisis is most evident, as Archer shows, in the aftermath of 1595, when the city declared martial law, executed rioters and appointed two marshals to contain any further disturbance. A permanent provost marshal was appointed to the city in 1603.

The influx of people into London at the end of sixteenth century was linked, of course, to significant economic changes. Population expansion both responded to and stimulated economic growth. London's status as 'the largest labour exchange in the country' was inextricably tied to its status as 'the largest single consumer goods market in England, probably in Europe' (McMullan, *Canting Crew*, pp. 9–10). Though bad harvests produced food shortages in the 1590s, the market for commodities was generally an inexpensive and expanding one, founded on an increasing demand for, and capacity to supply, imported foreign goods. New joint stock trading companies, formed from 1553 onwards, represented a form of business organised along lines very different from those of the old merchant companies. Far from restricting their membership to those who had worked their way up from apprentice to master craftsman over a period of years, these companies were open to anyone who had the capital to invest in them. New ways of getting rich quickly thus came into existence alongside more traditional practice linking wealth to work and to established citizen status. London embraced both these forms of business and emerged as 'the focal point of conspicuous consumption' in England (McMullan, *Canting Crew*, p. 12; see also Fisher, 'Development of London as a Centre of Conspicuous Consumption' and Stone, *Crisis of the Aristocracy*, pp. 184–8 and ch. 10).

The building of Sir Thomas Gresham's Royal Exchange in 1566–8 and the subsequent building of Sir Robert Cecil's New Exchange in 1609, set up to rival and outstrip the Royal Exchange, span a period notable for the increasing prominence, self-confidence and self-regard of economic enterprise in London. The Royal Exchange, first called the 'Bourse' in imitation of the Antwerp Bourse, was named the Royal Exchange on the queen's authority in 1571. It was an ambitious and self-important edifice, comprising covered arcades surrounding an open square and incorporating 120 shops selling, according to Stow, 'all kind of rich wares, and fine commodities, as any particular place in Europe, unto which place many foreign princes daily send, to be best served, of the best sort' (*Annals*, p. 869). As Thomas Platter describes it in 1599, it was 'a great square place like the one in Antwerp . . . where all kinds of fine goods are on show; and since the city is very large and extensive merchants having to deal with one another agree to meet together in this palace, where several hundred may be found assembled twice daily, before lunch at eleven, and again after their meal at six o' clock, buying, selling, bearing news, and doing business generally' (*Travels*, p. 157). It was located in the city, in Cornhill, one block north of Lombard Street, where the old open-air 'bourse' had operated informally since the fourteenth century.[11]

As Platter's comparison with a palace makes clear, the Royal Exchange had aspirations rivalling those of a royal court. It represented the city's expression of its own status in the same way as palace building expressed the court's power and magnificence. Elizabeth's authorisation of its 'Royal' title combined courtesy with necessity. Given her political and financial reliance on the city, she perhaps stood in greater need of its wealth than it did of her blessing; yet the obvious and politic route for both parties was to enact their mutual dependence in ceremonial terms which represented it quite differently, as a matter of mutual obligation, benevolence and respect. Thus were material realities most appropriately dressed up to enhance the status and respect both parties craved.

When Robert Cecil's New Exchange was built, over forty years later, its location expressed a significant shift in relations between city and court. It was built in the area of new, fashionable development on the Strand, alongside the great town houses of the nobility and very close to Whitehall. The Strand location seems to give symbolically appropriate geographical expression to the combination of separation and interdependence between the royal court and the city of London. It marks both the distance between them and the route that joins them. At a time when the ceremonial perambulation of space pervaded every form of public pageantry from the royal entry to the lord mayor's procession, contemporaries could scarcely fail to be aware of the symbolic geography underpinning the relative locations of city and court and the placing of institutionalised commerce between them.[12]

As the opulent splendour of both Exchanges demonstrates, one of the most prominent avenues of relationship between city (in both the narrow and the wider sense) and crown was through money, and the monarch was often dependent for loans on either the city as political entity or wealthy individuals within it.[13] Even Stow, nostalgically idealist as his perspective is in many ways, recognises the wealth of London as one of its singular strengths. It is with pride that he reports the city's capacity to relieve the poor, give money to the universities, yield a greater subsidy to the crown than any other part of the kingdom and lend money to the monarch. 'It only', he writes, 'doth and is able to make the prince a ready prest or loan of money' (*Survey*, vol. II, p. 214).[14] Merchants, Stow recognises, are 'necessary and serviceable' to both city and nation; but the only good merchants are rich ones, 'for beggarly merchants do bite too near, and will do more harm than good to the realm' (*Survey*, vol. II, pp. 209, 213). Rich merchants were expected to do their duty towards the city, both in endowing civic institutions such as schools and hospitals, and in taking up service in city government at high financial cost to themselves, but in taking up these burdens they thereby inserted themselves into the hegemony of London.

It was Thomas Gresham, in fact, builder of the Royal Exchange and a merchant himself, who was primarily responsible for persuading the merchant-adventurers of London in 1570 to lend the queen money to pay off her overseas creditors so that at least the interest fed back into her own realm rather than into foreign coffers. Despite the company's initial unwillingness, based on Elizabeth's previous high-handedness when demanding loans, Gresham negotiated terms that satisfied both parties, and loans from the city to the state became more frequent thereafter (Burgon, *Life and Times of Sir Thomas Gresham*, pp. 340–44; Blanchard, 'Sir Thomas Gresham', pp. 15–18). Official loans from the city to the crown totalled £120,000 in the years 1575–98, and unofficial loans from individual wealthy citizens were over and above that total (Manley, *Literature and Culture*, pp. 5–6). James I's demands, however, put considerable pressure on that financial relationship, since his expenditure was so notoriously in excess of his income. In 1610, when fiscal relations between James and his parliament were sorely tested in the matter of the 'Great Contract' (a proposal to abolish the monarch's rights of wardship and purveyance in return for an annual income of £200,000), even the richest citizens of London refused to lend him any more money.[15]

Relations between court and city were more than just a matter of money, however; and all forms of relation were also mediated through a variety of discursive representations. It was scarcely possible to conceive of political or economic relations other than through powerful myths and metaphors that carried their own ideological baggage. (One only has to compare the Dick Whittington story (which became popular in the 1590s; see Barron, 'Richard Whittington') with the conceit of the monarch as head of the body politic, for example, to see how the chosen image puts a particular bias in place.) Money, furthermore, was only one material expression of power and status; though the direction in which the money flowed, from city to crown, was an important index of the monarch's dependence on the city. London, besides being the nation's greatest market and financial resource, was its legal and administrative heart and its seat of government. When a king or queen died, the mayor of London became, briefly, the highest authority in England, since all royal offices were vacant until reappointed by the new monarch. On Elizabeth's death the mayor exercised this authority by closing Ludgate (the gate that led into the city from Westminster) until he received a promise that James was to be proclaimed king.

The mayor, styled 'lord mayor' from about 1545, was revered by an increasing attention to ceremony through the course of the sixteenth century.[16] The gradual rise of the lord mayor's show in tandem with the decline of the midsummer watch has been widely noted, as has Stow's studied silence on the subject of the lord mayor's show.[17] While Stow waxes lyrical on the former glories of the now lapsed midsummer festivities, which for him represent the community's celebration of 'familiarity' and 'good amity' (vol. 1, p. 101), he has nothing to say on the more recently introduced civic ceremony. It is difficult to resist the impression that he is passing judgement on the latter as a trumped-up novelty unworthy of serious attention; and his silence on the subject may be compared with his erasure from the second edition of his *Survey* of his already brief references to theatres in the first edition.[18] If he did feel any hostility towards the lord mayor's show, however, the emphasis was on the show rather than the office or person of the lord mayor, to whom the *Survey* is dedicated.[19]

Despite Stow's conservatism on the matter of public ceremony, his own work can be seen alongside the development of the lord mayor's show as part of a growing civic self-awareness in sixteenth-century London. The impulse to map and record the city is not entirely separable from the impulse to honour civic office: both aim to represent the city to itself, and both do so in a way that is either implicitly or explicitly celebratory. Both Stow's *Survey* and the lord mayor's show find their place within the context of a range of activities designed to consolidate the city's sense of its own definition:

The office of the Remembrancer, charged with the maintenance of customary practices and ceremonies, was created in 1571. The City had begun to issue its printed ceremonial calendars in 1568, and in 1596 the Court of Aldermen required "notes to be set down in writing and hanged in the Guildhall what things appertain either by charter, usage, Acts of Common Council or by custom to be yearly done." In the later sixteenth century the Corporation was involved as well in extensive efforts to consolidate its archives, ordering the recopying of the *Liber Albus* and other custumals, the sequestering of records, and the search for lost registers and papers. (Manley, *Literature and Culture*, p. 271)

Even as late as 1620 the city created the office of city chronologer to record notable acts of the city and to supply it with appropriate entertainments. Projects such as the paving of Smithfield or the rebuilding of Aldgate were part of the same drive as was represented, at a less institutionalised level, by the outpouring of popular literature on London (Knowles, 'Spectacle of the Realm', p. 162).[20] As Ian Archer points out, 'one could hardly claim that such civic self-consciousness was a new development' at the time Stow was writing, but the period is notable nevertheless for 'the range of media involved and the sheer density of representations' (*Pursuit of Stability*, p. 17).

This increasingly insistent self-representation has been linked to growing friction between city and crown, in the shape of various threats to the city's independence from sixteenth-century monarchs (Manley, *Literature and Culture*, p. 267), and this may be part of the explanation for it. But more evidently and simply it would seem to be a response to the speed of change in the city itself. A rising population was putting pressure on the boundaries of the city; new economic enterprises were challenging the traditional structures of labour; greater social mobility was putting traditional social divisions under pressure; and the more the shape of the city seemed to change, the more important it became to define and make sense of that shape. Telling stories about London, whether in official pageants, popular pamphlets or plays, was a way of making particular social relations visible. Material and psychic space are interdependent. The inhabitants of London produce its meanings by the ways they occupy it: by living within or outside its boundaries, working within or outside its structures of labour, operating within or outside the terms of its government, attending or not attending its civic ceremonies, worshipping or not worshipping in its churches, and so on. Representing the city on stage, in street pageantry, or in print is also a way of occupying its space, though a more mediated and self-reflexive way, in that it meditates on, as well as participates in, cultural practice.

Plays performed in fixed playhouses were one of the most popular and accessible forms of representation available in late sixteenth- and early seventeenth-century London, and were a characteristically urban phenomenon. As Michael Neill has noted,

the early modern ambivalence towards the city is nowhere more marked than in attitudes to the theatre. One the one hand, theatre is promoted by apologists like Heywood as the proper ornament of any metropolis that seeks to emulate the splendours of Greece and Rome; on the other, it is identified by its enemies – and sometimes, surprisingly, even by its own practitioners – as a place of disorder, a bastion of the unruly mob, a leveller of proper distinctions, and a source of moral and physical disease. (*Issues of Death*, p. 24)

Playhouse building in London may be said to begin with the construction of the Red Lion in Stepney in 1567. After that comes a steady stream: the Theatre in 1576, the Curtain in 1577, the Rose around 1587, the Swan in 1595. Around the turn of the century there is a surge of activity, and one that indicates increasing confidence on the part of the players, who are now building upgraded premises: the Chamberlain's Men, driven out of the Theatre by the expiry of their lease, build the Globe on the Bankside in 1599; the Admiral's Men, now uncomfortably threatened at the Rose by the proximity of the Globe, build the Fortune north of the river in 1600, contracting with the builder for conscious imitation of certain features of the Globe. Two children's companies, furthermore, become established around the same time at indoor theatres in St Paul's and the Blackfriars.

The open-air playhouses, as has often been pointed out, are all located either outside the city boundary or within liberties inside the boundary, and hence outside its jurisdiction, though playing at inns within city limits continued until the 1590s.[21] Theatres therefore stand at a crossroads between the city and the non-city. They are not simply 'marginal', as Steven Mullaney's argument would have it (in *The Place of the Stage*). Their location and status is more complex than that, and different playhouses stand in different relation to the city. The Blackfriars Theatre, for example, positioned in a liberty inside the city walls and discussed more fully in chapter 5 below, occupies a different position from either the theatres in the northern suburbs or the Bankside theatres across the river.

The word 'liberties', it should be noted, has contradictory meanings in this period, as seen by comparison of its use here with its meaning in the patent granted to Leicester's Men (quoted on p. 3 above). It can be used to denote the rights and privileges of a city and hence, by extension, its geographical and jurisdictional limits; or it can be used to denote precisely those areas that fall outside the authority of the city on account of their own hereditary rights and privileges.[22] The playhouses, whether situated in a suburb or a liberty, were free of city controls, but crucially determined by the city. They were simultaneously a city and a 'not-city' phenomenon, desired by, and paid for out of the pockets of, its inhabitants, yet banished by its governors.

The legal status of players and the economic foundations of playing companies together confirm their position on a cultural threshold at which city, suburbs and court all meet. The Act Against Vagabonds of 1572 defined players as vagrants, liable to the various punishments noted above, unless they 'belonged' to 'any baron of this realm or . . . any other honourable personage of greater degree' (14 Elizabeth I, c. 5). Hence the various titles of the companies, linking them to powerful noblemen. The Theatre was built with the protection of a patent granted to James Burbage and his company by the Earl of Leicester in 1574 which gave them highly protected status. Others less fortunate than Burbage's company simply pretended: the Common Council of London complained in 1584 that the city was full of players calling themselves the Queen's Men (Gildersleeve, *Government Regulation*, p. 41). After performance at city inns was banned, the players continued to need to show their documents with especial frequency when they were on tour, as they were required to produce them before being allowed a place to perform.

This system of licensing, then, seemed to formalise the old patronage relationship between great lords and players; but the terms of Burbage's letter to Leicester, asking for confirmation of his protection, make clear that the relationship did not extend to financial support. The letter specifically affirms that Burbage and his men do not intend 'to crave any further stipend or benefit at your lordship's hands but our liveries as we have had, and also your honour's license to certify that we are your household servants when we shall have occasion to travel' (Gurr, *Shakespearean Stage*, p. 29). At precisely the same time as the law was demanding that players provide evidence of a fixed affiliation to a noble patron, they were actually establishing themselves as self-supporting economic units. In this respect they also straddled a dividing line between the organised labour of the city companies and the casual labour of the suburbs. The fact that players worked virtually by definition outside city limits by the end of the century and that they were therefore not subject to the regulations that bound city companies into an integrated structure fixing prices and wages was what enabled players to make their fortunes. Not restricted by a powerful, institutionalised hierarchy, as most workmen and businessmen were, actors could become shareholders as and when the opportunity arose. As James Forse has demonstrated, 'being "masterless" is just the point. The theatre business represented one of the few avenues of free enterprise open to an Elizabethan of modest means. Acting took small capital investment, and, at least until after the turn of the century, there was no long period of apprenticeship required of one who entered the Players' profession. Success depended solely upon one's own effort, talent, craft and thrift' (*Art Imitates Business*, p. 14). Yet, as Forse also shows, playing companies borrowed in many ways from the practices of established city companies. The hierarchy of sharers, hired men and apprentices was clearly modelled on that of master-craftsmen, journeymen and apprentices, and the price of sharer-status (about £70) was the same as that of full status in a craft guild.[23]

The players were therefore operating in conditions that constructed what they did as simultaneously a trade and a service. Even as they played to paying audiences in purpose-built playhouses, the polite fiction was that they were rehearsing for more important performances at court. The argument featured regularly in the Privy Council's responses to the city's pleas for restrictions or outright bans on playing; and though the notion of 'rehearsal' may have been something of a fiction, performance at court certainly was not. The players made their reputations and their profits out of both court and city, and knew how to play one off against the other. They could successfully flout the authority of the city by invoking the support of their patrons, several of whom were members of the Privy Council. William Fleetwood, the recorder of London, wrote to Lord Burghley in 1584 to express his outrage at the insolence of a player, who had refused to submit to Fleetwood's attempt to discipline him and sent word instead 'that he was my Lord of Hunsdon's man' (Gildersleeve, *Government Regulation*, pp. 169–70).

It was not just a matter of players needing both court and city, however. Both court and city, including the city authorities, also needed the players. The city used those same players and commercial playwrights whose public performances were such a thorn in its flesh to write its pageants, just as the court later used them to write its masques. Men like Peele, Munday, Jonson, Dekker, Heywood, Middleton and Webster knew how to write for different audiences and, some of them, how to present material offered satirically in one venue for celebration in another.[24] Jonson, who received commissions from both court and city as well as writing for audiences at both public and private theatres, maintained a strong, even rigid, sense of distinction between his different modes of writing, and discarded his writing for the city, while carefully preserving his entertainments for the court.[25]

The fact that the same writers moved between the court and the city meant too that fashion travelled quickly and that the theatre became a central transmitter of new fashions. Courtly mores had always set high fashion. Now that the court was more firmly fixed in and around

Whitehall, with the Strand palaces stretching eastwards towards the city, and London was spilling over its boundaries to edge ever closer to the court to the west, the physical gap between court and city was less distinct. Architecturally, too, there was some closing of the gap: civic institutions like the Royal and the New Exchanges consciously cultivated a classical, courtly style. Lewis Mumford has argued that the baroque city should be viewed as 'a collective embellishment of the ways and gestures of the palace', a more pervasive cultivation of a lifestyle given over to luxury, leisure and display. The luxury goods displayed in the Exchanges' shops, Mumford argues, are a monument to the 'exquisite uselessness' that he identifies as the mark of the baroque (*City in History*, p. 429). Yet the value judgement underpinning Mumford's thesis here derives from a discourse of usefulness and thrift which might equally well be seen as a mark of the baroque city. Literature produced by and/or for the business classes repeatedly emphasises the need to work diligently, to guard against idleness and to contribute useful service to the common good, and this is a discourse long recognised as supported by a developing moderate Puritanism, also characteristic of London in this period. The emergence of a lifestyle dedicated to leisure, fashion and shopping is inseparable from a moral framework that judges those pursuits as luxurious, wasteful, useless and excessive; the conjunction is not just part of Mumford's critical discourse, it is also part of the 'baroque' moment. Stow's observation that the Londoners of his time privilege 'show and pleasure' over 'use or profit' (chapter 3 below) functions within the same conceptual framework as Mumford's bringing together of exquisiteness and uselessness.

It might also be argued that the interaction between city and court was rather less monolithically court-dominated than Mumford suggests. The cultivation of display surely need not proceed in one direction, starting at court and filtering down to the city. It is more likely to be produced by a combination of court and city influences. Which comes first: the demand for luxury goods or the capacity to supply them? Or, to put the question in a contemporary form: 'How would merchants thrive, if gentlemen would not be unthrifts? How could gentlemen be unthrifts if their humours were not fed?' (*Eastward Ho*, I.i.38–40). The expansion of the market, and its relation to such developments as the colonial enterprise and the establishment of the new joint stock companies, shape the craving for the exotic as surely as do courtly wealth and leisured extravagance. The shopkeeper's display is precisely not useless;[26] its function is quite consciously to produce consumer desire, and this is what makes it so morally problematic for those who represent it. The semi-darkness of the shop, where goods are both seen and not seen, on display but creatively (fraudulently?) obscured, quickly becomes a standard element in the satiric representation of buying and selling. (Shopkeepers in the Royal Exchange were ordered to get rid of any blinds or canvas that deliberately darkened the shop; see Saunders, 'Organisation of the Exchange', p. 94.) It is also, however, a practice acknowledged without either irony or outright condemnation in moral handbooks. William Scott's *Essay on Drapery*, alternatively titled *The Complete Citizen*, recommends a qualified honesty to the tradesman, advising him to keep his shop neither too light nor too dark: 'it is, or should be so ordered, that lest commodities be sold too dear, shops shall not be too dark; and lest they be sold too cheap, they shall not be too light' (pp. 41–2).

The craze for the *Wunderkammer*, or cabinet of wonders, in the late sixteenth century demonstrates the symbiosis of court and city in creating the conditions for the collection and display of exotic objects to flourish. Though the earliest collections, such as those in Vienna and Dresden, were dependent on royal or aristocratic wealth, the interest in curiosities was stimulated by travel to distant lands, underpinned by both commercial interest and an urge towards adventure and discovery. Merchants and citizens thus contributed to determining fashion just as much as dukes and emperors, and the fashion was one followed by court and city alike. Thomas Platter's diary, recording his visit to London in 1599, presents the *Wunderkammer* as a primarily urban phenomenon. He devotes considerable space to listing fifty items of special interest in the collection of 'Mr Cope a citizen of London who has spent much time in the Indies', and notes that Walter Cope is not the only such collector of 'strange objects' in London (*Travels*, pp. 171–3). Platter's own pleasure in inspecting the collection, as well as his indication that there are other collectors in the city, offer evidence of the interest in exotica as an established urban fashion in late sixteenth-century London.[27]

Social mobility tended to reinforce the blurring of distinction between court and city. While the sons of tradesmen were rising stars in the new professions of writing and theatre, the sons of gentlemen were becoming apprenticed to trades. The expansion of the educated, 'professional' class extended a social territory which was neither trade nor court, while the growth of literacy and the production of social handbooks supposedly for different classes contributed to the conditions for class mobility. The urban economy was instrumental both in facilitating that mobility and in confounding rigid class distinctions. While the guild system enabled an apprentice to rise to an alderman, even a lord mayor, new ventures like the joint stock companies attracted subscribers from all social levels and brought the interests of different classes together in colonial enterprise. Men like Sir Thomas Gresham became attached to the court without relinquishing their business activities, while books in praise of the city might conceive of themselves as 'pleasant for gentlemen, not unseemly for magistrates, and most profitable for prentices'.[28]

Social mobility encouraged precisely the consumption and display that made it difficult to read distinctions of birth. As Lawrence Stone points out, it is new money that needs to spend ostentatiously in order to advertise a status that is uncertain by virtue of being tied only to wealth and not to birth (*Crisis of the Aristocracy*, pp. 184–8). Fashion changes swiftly too, because the need to keep up the advertisement and the expenditure stimulates an increasing demand for novelty, for endlessly new ways of signalling one's good taste and spending capacity. It is therefore not surprising that court and city come closest to merging in the arena of fashion, so that a fashionable figure like the gallant is scarcely attributable to either single environment. The *OED*'s first definition of a gallant as 'a man of fashion and pleasure; a fine gentleman' pinpoints fashionable leisure as the area where court and city meet. Indeed Dekker's *Gull's Hornbook*, instructing the city gallant on how to behave, parodies the social handbooks that teach the courtier how to behave. Nor is it coincidental that visiting the theatre is portrayed as one of the pursuits of Dekker's gallant, since theatres were not only new and fashionable haunts in themselves, but places where different social classes came together. Courtiers and gentlemen went to the theatre alongside professionals and apprentices, and the young men of the Inns of Court who are so often identified as forming a significant proportion of private theatre audiences might equally well be progressing towards court office or city employment.

What made possible the mixing of ranks in theatre audiences was the commoditisation of theatre. Once playhouses became established and plays were offered for the consumption of paying customers more often than they were commissioned for private performance, anyone could buy entrance to a performance. Apprentices could see what courtiers saw: the same actors, performing in plays by the same playwrights, and often the same plays. Although patronised performance persisted, both at court and in aristocratic houses, the very fact that these performances were offered by the same companies as offered their plays for sale to a different audience changed the nature of the product. This is particularly clear in cases where the same play moved between different venues; but it was also true of works specifically commissioned for particular audiences. The Alleyn who played his part in the king's royal entry to the city in 1604 was the same Alleyn who had thrilled audiences at the Rose with his portrayal of Tamburlaine, Faustus and the Jew of Malta. The Jonson who wrote part of the text for that royal entry in 1604 and *The Masque of Blackness* for the Jacobean court in 1605 was the same Jonson who had been imprisoned for his part in *The Isle of Dogs* in 1597 and who was again to be imprisoned for satirising the king and the Scots in *Eastward Ho* later in 1605.

What was on offer in playhouses, in city streets, at court revels and, afterwards, in bookshops was a commodity both popular and fashionable, though of course some venues were more or less popular or fashionable than others. Plays offered at the Blackfriars, with its higher prices and more select clientele than at the amphitheatres, consciously set high fashion, while plays at the Red Bull went for popularity even at the cost of seeming old-fashioned. Even the same play performed by the King's Men at the Blackfriars, the Globe and Whitehall had different resonances, and a different fashion status, in each.

As the market for printed play texts expanded, title pages emphasised their functioning first and foremost as commodities for sale. And as Jeffrey Masten has argued, these title pages remind us that the plays they advertise stand 'at the intersection of two interconnected media markets': they are both 'theatrical commodities much like the props and costumes, valued for their ability to draw paying crowds into the often highly successful business places of the theatres' and 'print commodities, marketed by publishers who attempted to capitalize on the popularity generated by theatrical performances' (*Textual Intercourse*, p. 114). Even private patrons were selecting what they wanted from the market that was theatre; and the equation between theatre and the market was one made by contemporaries, as Douglas Bruster's excellent discussion demonstrates (*Drama and the Market*, ch. 1). What was on offer in both, he points out, quoting Stephen Gosson, was 'choice without shame' on payment of the right money (*Drama and the Market*, p. 6).

The new spaces of purpose-built market and theatre were conceived in relation to each other and to changing and developing conceptions of other, wider and more familiar spaces, notably those of court and city. The open courtyard and grandiose pillars of the Royal Exchange translated the architectural values of the palace to a building designed specifically for the expanding city. London had no central public square for civic display; St Paul's, unlike St Peter's in Rome or St Mark's in Venice, was tucked away amongst narrow streets (Cheapside excepted) with no large forum for assembly extending before it; and such open spaces as the city had, as Stow points out, were continually under threat. Gresham's Royal Exchange attempted to create a space for civic display, though it was a display primarily related to one aspect of the city: its commerce. Civic pride was thus particularly closely associated, for Londoners, with commercial success. The classical composition of the internal facade, furthermore, made the building 'unique in the City in 1566 and for many years to come and, save for Somerset House, with few comparisons in London as a whole' (Saunders, 'Building of the Exchange', p. 41; cf. ch. 3, pp. 61–4 and epilogue, n112 below).

Yet the architecture of the amphitheatres had associations similar to as well as different from those of the Royal Exchange. The pillars seemed to contemporaries to speak from within an elite and classicist architectural vocabulary, and just as John Norden singled out the 'pillars of marble' in the Royal Exchange (*Speculum Britanniae*, p. 35), so Johannes De Witt remarked on their presence at the Swan. Even though De Witt recognised that the Swan pillars were not marble, but wood painted to look like marble, the overall effect for him was still one of magnificence, not tackiness, and he assumed that the construction of the playhouse consciously imitated ancient classical precedent.[29] John Stockwood, like De Witt, emphasised magnificence as a characteristic of playhouse construction when he attacked the Theatre as a 'gorgeous playing place' in a sermon preached at Paul's Cross in 1578 (Ordish, *Early London Theatres*, p. 64).

The yard, on the other hand, was clearly not aiming at a similar effect. Whereas the 'quadrate' (Norden's term) construction of the Royal Exchange around a central courtyard was seen as part of its elegance, the pricing policy of the public theatres linked the central open space with the lower classes. Thomas Platter, another European visitor to London at around the same time as De Witt, admired the decorativeness and comfort of the galleried seating at the Curtain but emphasised the lowliness of the yard, with its one-penny admission and standing room only (*Travels*, pp. 166–7). The spacious open courtyard of the Royal Exchange, designed as a showpiece, inviting free movement and removed to a degree from the shop displays (which were on the upper storeys and would presumably have faced inward into the building),[30] was visually and symbolically quite distinct from a yard packed with paying customers, which was itself the mere surround to a different central focus: the stage.

What both new forms of building most importantly shared, however, was a foregrounding of display. Both the Royal Exchange and the theatres had products for sale and aimed to display both themselves as buildings and their products to the best possible advantage; but both also created the conditions for the consumers who came to inspect the saleable products to gaze on their fellow consumers, to display themselves and to revel in the pleasures of mutual showing and looking (what Stow sharply labels as seeing and showing vanity, p. 20, above). As Platter pointed out in 1599, the advantage of the galleries over the yard in an amphitheatre was that there the spectator 'not only sees everything well, but can also be seen' (*Travels*, p. 167). Both merchants and actors would have acknowledged, of course, that there were considerable differences between the modes of looking. Amongst these differences, two seem paramount. One is the economic implications. Where goods on display in the Royal Exchange shops aimed to stir consumers' desires to the point where they would put their hands in their pockets, plays were already paid for before they were displayed, nor could they be owned by individual consumers or taken home after purchase. They were by definition ephemeral pleasures. Yet, as the antitheatrical lobby kept saying, they stirred desires to a dangerous degree. Wherever the spectators looked, whether at the show, at the other spectators, or even at the building, their looking was likely to stimulate desires, erotic, immoral, materialistic, or all of these.

The second significant difference between theatre and shopping is also importantly related to matters of desire. It is the playfulness of theatre. Window-shopping may be playful to an extent, insofar as consumers imagine owning the various goods on display and play with notions of possession, of self-creation, of manufacturing a particular persona via particular purchases; but the act of purchase is a real transaction, one that transfers the purchased object from one place and person to another. The display of commodities helps to construct what is fashionable, and the moment of purchase puts the buyer in possession of the fashionable object of desire. In the theatre, by contrast, the spectator participates imaginatively in what is bought. He or she buys entrance to a space where what is on offer is the chance to play in imagination at being someone or something else, the chance to look not at objects for sale but at modes of being. But theatre can equally help to construct what is fashionable, since fashion is not just a matter of owning the right accessories, but of knowing what to do with objects, how to move, speak or stand still, what to put on show; and theatre in the latter part of the 1590s was especially preoccupied with the fashionable persona. Plays may not themselves be commodities in the sense of objects that can be bought and taken home, but they are learning how to offer commoditised behaviours, pieces of display that can be taken outside the theatre and possessed by way of imitation. Dekker is explicit about this in *The Gull's Hornbook* when he advises his gull to 'hoard up the finest play-scraps you can get' (p. 96). The plays that first create this kind of theatre in the 1590s, offering up their fragments for acquisition and reassembly, are the subject of chapter 3; but chapter 2 first turns to the problems encountered by a play that seeks open celebration of its loyalties to court and city. Though this chapter has sought to demonstrate the numerous points of overlap and interaction between the two, there remains an irrefutable ideological distance between them, and it is the negotiation of allegiances and resistances that emerges as the central focus of the next chapter.

CHAPTER TWO

The place of exchange

EDWARD IV

Towards the end of *1 Edward IV* (1599), Hobs the tanner comes to court and makes a significant mistake:

HOBS. What's he in the long beard and the red petticoat? Before God, I misdoubt, Ned, that is the King. I know it by my Lord What-ye-call's players.
KING. How by them, tanner?
HOBS. Ever when they play an interlude or a commodity at Tamworth, the King always is in a long beard and a red gown, like him. Therefore I 'spect him to be the King.[1]

But the man Hobs mistakes for the King is in fact the Lord Mayor; and the mistake is an emblematic one, occurring at a climactic moment in a play that is deeply concerned with relations, equivalences and mutual obligations between monarch and mayor and, at the broader level, crown, nation and city. It is also a highly self-reflexive moment, reminding a watching audience that ordinary people throughout England, and especially outside London, form their images of the monarch via representations such as the interludes Hobs describes or the play they now view. Theatre, the remark reminds us, makes powerful and memorable images; and out of such images ideology is formed. Theatre, as Hobs' terminology highlights, is a 'commodity' in several senses: it seeks to please, to offer something suitable, advantageous and timely on a particular and 'convenient' occasion; and it confers 'benefit' on both parties, bringing entertainment to its audiences and financial gain to the players. Like a market, it is a place of exchange, where pleasure is offered in return for payment; but because the pleasure consists in providing representations of the world the paying audience inhabits, what is exchanged is more than just a commodity for money. The commodity incorporates a view of the world, and the price to be paid for maximum pleasure

43

consists of more than the ticket price: it includes a willingness to celebrate what the play celebrates and reject what it rejects.

What, then, do the two parts of *Edward IV* put forward for celebration or rejection? At one level, they offer precisely what Hobs the tanner finds memorable: the spectacle of the elite in ceremonial mode. The plays are full of stage directions specifying stately entries in formal dress: '*Enter the Lord Mayor, M. Shore, and M. Josselin, in their velvet coats and gorgets, and leading staves*' (p. 11); '*Enter the Lord Mayor, in his scarlet gown, with a gilded rapier by his side*' (p. 57); '*The trumpets sound, and enters King Edward, Howard Sellinger, and the train*' (p. 58); '*Enter King Richard, crowned, Buckingham, Anne of Warwick, Lovell, Catesby, Fogg, and Attendants*' (p. 184). As these examples show, however, the display is as likely to attach to the civic elite as to the monarchy; and this is especially so of Part I.

One might argue that Hobs' mistaking of the Lord Mayor for the King is prepared for from the opening of the play, which shows the King putting his private interests before the safety of London and the well-being of England. The play begins with Edward's announcement of his marriage to Elizabeth Woodville and his mother's outrage at this folly, but the scene is immediately interrupted by a messenger bringing news of a huge rebel force marching on London. Edward's decision to spend the coming night 'in feast and jollity / With our new Queen and our beloved mother' (p. 8) and postpone the commission to raise troops until the next morning proves crucial. The rebels reach London before the King and his troops, leaving the city to mount its own defence without aid. The heroism of the city and its governors in these circumstances is of course heightened by the fact that it is victorious over the rebels single-handed, and the title page of the play, with its reference to 'the besieging of London, by the Bastard Falconbridge, and the valiant defence of the same by the Lord Mayor and the Citizens', makes clear the attractiveness of this content to a London audience.

Effectively the King's delay puts the Mayor in the position of governor of the realm, since the play makes clear that if London falls, England falls. More precisely, the Mayor is at the apex of a chain of command that shows all of London (or metonymically, all of England, with the exception of the King) working together to protect their common interest. The Mayor's first appearance in the play, by contrast with the King's, shows him already making preparations for defence, and doing so in conjunction with two of his aldermen, Master Shore and Master Josselin.[2] Pointedly, too, he seeks the advice of the Recorder, whose absence from this scene is explained by virtue of the fact that he is busy fortifying the bridge. What the scene seeks to highlight is an ideal-ised harmony between civic leaders appointed respectively by the city (the mayor) and the crown (the recorder). On the other hand, in tension with that idealisation of good government, of crown and city working together, is the fact that the King himself is absent without good reason, and this has the effect of making the King seem to resign his authority to the Mayor, forcing him to take responsibilities that are rightfully the monarch's by way of failing to take them up himself. The Mayor's speech to the London troops before battle is reminiscent of Henry V's speech before Agincourt in Shakespeare's play of the same year. Since both plays are attributed to the year 1599, it is not certain that the influ-ence was Shakespeare's on Heywood rather than the other way round; what is clear is that the speech is a kingly one, and that the Mayor's utter-ance of it emphasises the King's absence as well as his own nobility.[3]

Criticism of the King is unmistakable at several points. First, the Mayor's response to the crisis contrasts markedly with the King's. The play highlights the Mayor's devotion to duty by expressing his refusal to take rest in terms of his refusal to bow to the constraints of age and weakness: 'I tell ye, masters, aged though I be, / I, for my part, will to no bed this night' (p. 12). Meanwhile the young and lusty King, as we have seen, feasts in the company of women and plans to spend the night with his new wife before turning his mind to the matter of rebellion. Secondly, the Mayor's withering response to Josselin's question as to why it is thought the rebels are so near also implicitly targets the King's post-ponement of raising troops till morning. The rebels come, says the Mayor, 'neither . . . from Italy nor Spain; / But out of Kent and Essex, which you know / Are both so near, as nearer cannot be' (p. 12). Thirdly, when the victory is won, the term 'his majesty' is used, with irony not perhaps here intended by the Mayor, but certainly intended by Heywood via the Mayor, to foreground the absent place of the King that God must supply:

> And how much is this city fam'd for ever,
> That twice, without the help either of King,
> Or any but of God and our own selves
> We have prevail'd against our country's foes.
> Thanks to his majesty assisted us,
> Who always helps true subjects in their need! (p. 31)

The deliberateness of the irony is confirmed by the fact that the King's entry follows immediately after these words, and Edward's apology does nothing to mitigate it:

> You may condemn us
> Of too much slackness in such urgent need;
> But we assure you on our royal word,
> So soon as we had gather'd us a power,
> We dallied not, but made all haste we could. (p. 32)

This is true, but evasive. The dallying, as the first scene made clear, took place before the troops were summoned.

Despite this implicit criticism, however, all the rhetoric of the scenes where London prepares for and fights the rebels depends on an equation of loyalties: just as London and England are one and indivisible in the eyes of good governors, so they are for good citizens. As Matthew Shore says, when his wife Jane asks him why he fought so desperately, it was 'First to maintain King Edward's royalty; / Next, to defend the city's liberty' (p. 23); and when Jane pleads with him not to return to battle, his response is absolute:

> Envy shall never say that Matthew Shore,
> The goldsmith, stay'd, when other men went out
> To meet his King's and country's enemy.
> No, Jane; 'gainst all the rebels on Mile End,
> I dare alone King Edward's right defend.   (p. 25)

His reply brings together the play's concern with three modes of naming: personal names, the naming of occupation and the naming of specific parts of London.

These three concerns also come together much more prominently in the Mayor's long monologue on his origins and progress towards his present rank (pp. 57–8). He enters dressed in his robes of office, and begins his speech by offering to decode his ceremonial dress for the audience. He wears a gilded rapier with his scarlet gown, he tells them, because he was knighted in the field for service to his king; but it is precisely this rise to greatness that prompts him to remind himself, and hence the audience, of his humble beginnings as a foundling fostered by 'the Hospital / Of London' and apprenticed by the Hospital governors to the grocer's trade.[4] Again in this speech, the city is visible as a place of exchange: what the city invests in a penniless foundling, that foundling returns with interest. John Crosbie, named by the citizen who found him after the location where he was found ('Cow Cross near Islington') and supported by the charity of the Hospital, now gives the Hospital £100 a year in perpetuity and founds in his turn a poorhouse named 'Crosbie House'. The speech, as Alexander Leggatt has argued, shows a characteristically popular tendency to moralise from the individual to the universal, a tendency which confirms the solidity of the viewing community (*Jacobean Public Theatre*, pp. 32–5, 81). Its very specificity is exemplary, aligning John Crosbie with any other lowly Londoner, who, by implication, is equally capable of rising to the top of the hierarchy by personal merit. But the point of the speech is to highlight the civic context that supports this meritocracy: it is only through the combination of individual charity (the citizen who finds him and names him), institutionalised charity (the Hospital) and the structure of the companies (through which he is apprenticed and thereby empowered to rise through the ranks of journeyman, freeman and alderman to that of mayor) that he reaches the heights of knighthood and direct service to his king.

The occupational hierarchy of the city is underlined at every opportunity in the play and celebrated at every level from the 'velvet jackets' (the wealthy elite) to the 'flat caps' (apprentices). This terminology, like the Mayor's exposition of his scarlet gown and rapier, signals the play's emphasis on social categorisation and visual readability. The ceremonial entries of the elite are important not just for their inherent spectacle, but as a framework within which other kinds of entry can be interpreted, from the entry of the rebels marching with drums (p. 8) to the entry of the two young princes '*in their gowns and caps, unbuttoned, and untrussed*' (p. 153), the entry of Jane Shore '*in a white sheet barefooted with her hair about her eares, and in her hand a wax taper*' (p. 165) and the entry of Mistress Blage '*with her basket and clap-dish*' (p. 169). The company structure evidently underpins the efficiency with which the governors of London can muster troops in its defence. At least 200 men in arms are mustered from every hall, Shore reports (p. 11), and at certain strategic points, 'whole companies / Of Mercers, Grocers, Drapers, and the rest, / Are drawn together, for their best defence' (pp. 13–14). The importance of naming individual companies here is striking. Just as individual names and occupations must be formally rehearsed at particular moments, such as the knighting of the city's leaders after the victory:

> Arise Sir John Crosbie, Lord Mayor of London and Knight.
> Arise [up] Sir Ralfe Josselin Knight.
> Arise Sir Thomas Urswick, our Recorder of London and Knight, (p. 32)[5]

so it is on occasion important to name those companies that have given especially notable service.

Elsewhere, the social grouping is more important than the individual company, as in the case of the apprentices. Though the interest of the

preparation scenes centres on the governors of the city, from the point
of the rebels' arrival outside the city gates the on-stage presence of the
apprentices is prominent. Spicing (Falconbridge's closest associate) beats
on the gates, '*and then enters the Lord Mayor and his associates, with prentices*' (p.
14). When the Mayor delivers his speech of encouragement to the
assembled Londoners, he specifically addresses the apprentices as a
group ('And, prentices, stick to your officers, / For you may come to be
as we are now'), besides including them in the general appellation of all
together as 'brothers' (p. 17); and Heywood puts the responses to his
speech into the mouths of two unnamed apprentices, who assure him of
their loyalty and courage:

> FIRST APPRENTICE. Then fear not us; although our chins be bare,
>   Our hearts are good: the trial shall be seen
>   Against these rebels on this champion green.
> SECOND APPRENTICE. We have no tricks nor policies of war,
>   But by the ancient custom of our fathers,
>   We'll soundly lay it on; tak't off that will:
>   And, London prentices, be rul'd by me;
>   Die ere ye lose fair London's liberty. (p. 17)

When Spicing taunts them with the term 'flat-caps', they take it up
with pride, embracing their civic status, however low, as a mark of their
place in the community, while, significantly, putting the rebels outside
the boundary of the imagined community by associating them with the
suburbs:

> You are those desperate, idle, swaggering mates,
> That haunt the suburbs in the time of peace,
> And raise up alehouse brawls in the street;
> And when the rumour of the war begins,
> You hide your heads, and are not to be found. (p. 18)

There is a revealing inconsistency about this. Earlier statements have
identified the rebels as coming from Essex and Kent; but here this narrative element is simply overridden by the need to identify the rebels
specifically as outsiders to the city. To name them as Kentishmen or
Essexmen would lack the symbolic charge of the suburbs, with their
simultaneous closeness to, yet difference from, the city, their connotations of vagrancy, disorder and the anti-city. By contrast, the apprentices, in identifying themselves with London, identify themselves also
with England. Just as the Mayor is mindful of historic instances of
mayoral devotion to king and country (he reminds the men of William
Walworth's stabbing of Wat Tyler, the rebel leader of the Peasants'

Revolt; p. 17), so the apprentices call on 'the Chronicles of England' (p. 18) to testify to the historic achievements of apprentices.

The audience is also called on to identify with England's greatness through the specific topography of London. Like Stow's *Survey* and other chorographical works of the period, the play gives expression to political identity and civic and national pride through the mapping of place. London, of course, as the capital and seat of government, is an especially significant and recurrent focus of this mapping. The play first expresses the symbolic status of London through the aspirations of those who are outside and powerless, wanting to be inside and in control. For the rebels, marching on London and seeking to reinstate Henry VI on the throne of England, the landmarks of London represent the fixity, the familiarity and the continuity which they need to give political stability to their own project, which at this point, while they are merely men of Kent and Essex alien to the city, looks like upstart folly. It is Falconbridge, leader of the rebels, who gives utterance to the first of many celebratory inventories of London:

> We will be Masters of the Mint ourselves,
> And set our own stamp on the golden coin.
> We'll shoe our neighing coursers with no worse
> Than the purest silver that is sold in Cheap.
> At Leadenhall, we'll sell pearls by the peck,
> As now the mealmen use to sell their meal.
> In Westminster, we'll keep a solemn court,
> And build it bigger to receive our men.   (p. 10)

This speech gains its purchase by presenting Falconbridge as simultaneously familiar with the significance of various parts of London and insolently determined to wrest that significance into new forms. For a London audience, two important effects follow: the threat to the city is made real (a rebellion led by one who can read the topography of the city with such ease cannot be dismissed as an instance of ignorant provincialism), and civic pride and patriotism are called into place to intensify hostility to the rebels. The glory of London is summoned up more sentimentally in the speech of Smoke, the smith of Chepstead, one of many speeches in the play that seek to make the audience 'see' London:

> Look, lads; for from this hill ye may discern
> The lovely town which we are marching to:
> That same is London, lads, ye look upon:
> . . .
> Look how the Tower doth 'tice us to come on,

To take out Henry the Sixth, there prisoner:
See how Saint Katherine's smokes; wipe, slaves, your eyes,
And whet your stomachs for the good malt-pies. (pp. 10–11)

Meanwhile, within London, places are named with more immediacy and less sentiment as preparations for defence are put in place. Sometimes the sense of London as a whole and bounded entity, strong and well defended, is summoned up through general rather than specific reference, as in the Recorder's announcement on his first entry:

Good ev'n, my good Lord Mayor. The streets are chain'd,
The bridge well mann'd, and every place prepar'd. (p. 13)

Elsewhere, the city is evoked through its specifics, as when the Recorder, a few lines later, thinks through the possible points of entry and urges the fortification of Aldgate and London Bridge. Throughout the preparations and the actions, the staging as well as the speech seeks to highlight the stable and bounded specificity of London as a world apart from the rebel/suburban world that seeks to penetrate it. Scene after scene centres on the walls or the gates of the city, not just incidentally, because that is where the confrontation must happen, but symbolically, because that is the threshold where the city defines itself and where it meets but resists the intrusion of those who it seeks to outlaw. Stage directions call attention to the physical boundaries of the city – '*Spicing beats on the gates, and then enters the Lord Mayor and his associates, with prentices*' (p. 14); '*Josselin on the walls cries to them*' (p. 19) – and the climactic point of the action comes when the Lord Mayor finally gives orders to open the gates, not to let the rebels in, but to let Londoners out to pursue the fight more closely:

Set open the gates! Nay, then, we'll sally out.
It never shall be said, when I was Mayor,
The Londoners were shut up in the city.
Then cry King Edward, and let's issue out. (p. 20)

Characteristically, the play does not let pass the opportunity to bring together the names of 'London' and 'King Edward' in its glorification of courage and honour.

Perhaps the most deliberately rousing roll-call of famous London names is a speech of Falconbridge's spoken '*marching as being at Mile End*', towards the end of the battle:

We hear the Londoners will leave the city,
And bid us battle here on Mile End Green,
Whom if we vanquish, then we take the town,

And ride in triumph thorough Cheap to Paul's.
The Mint is ours, Cheap, Lombard Street, our own;
The meanest soldier wealthier than a king. (p. 26)

Not only is Mile End the location of Walworth's famous slaying of
Wat Tyler in 1381, mentioned by the Mayor in his speech to the troops,
but the triumphal ride through Cheapside to St Paul's was the most
stable and symbolically invested part of any ceremonial progress
route. As Lawrence Manley has shown, civic processional routes and
royal entry routes for uncrowned English monarchs, English monarchs previously crowned abroad and foreign monarchs differed from
one another in their beginnings and endings, but all shared the central
and climactic progress along Cheapside to St Paul's (*Literature and
Culture*, pp. 221–9). In anticipating this triumphal progress, then,
Falconbridge is striking at the ceremonial heart of London. These
civic ceremonies were also occasions for reaffirming the special relationship between the monarch and the city. The city took an important and visible role in royal entries, while the inaugural shows for the
lord mayor traditionally celebrated the monarch as well as the city.
Reference to the ceremonial route is therefore another way in which
the metonymic practice of the play underlines the threat to London
as a threat to the nation.

Though the King is shown to fail the city in its hour of need,
Heywood cannot let go of the desire to demonstrate an ideal unity
between the two. This unity is expressed not only through ceremony, but
through its opposite: unadorned plainness. The scene in which the King
finally arrives in London begins with his knighting of those who have
done great service to city, king and country (conceived as indivisible) and
ends with the King telling them as friends that he is newly married and
asking them to keep him company a little on his way. When the Lord
Mayor and Josselin next appear, the function of their dialogue is to
convey to the audience that this king is a man of the people:

MAYOR. Sir Ralph Josselin, have you ever seen a prince more affable
   than Edward is? What merry talk he had upon the way!
JOSSELIN. Doubtless, my lord, he'll prove a royal King. (p. 36)

Rendering the King approachable is as important as ceremonialising citizens' virtues: if the audience is to understand an identity of interests
between the two, the King must be shown to participate in common
humanity just as the citizens, and even the apprentices, participate in
nobility.

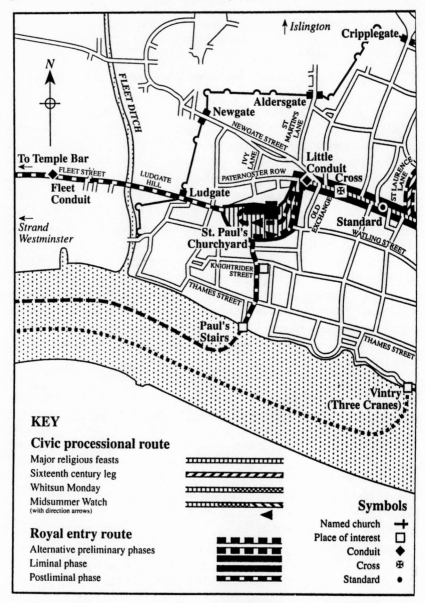

5. Lawrence Manley's map of processional routes for major civic ceremonies in London.

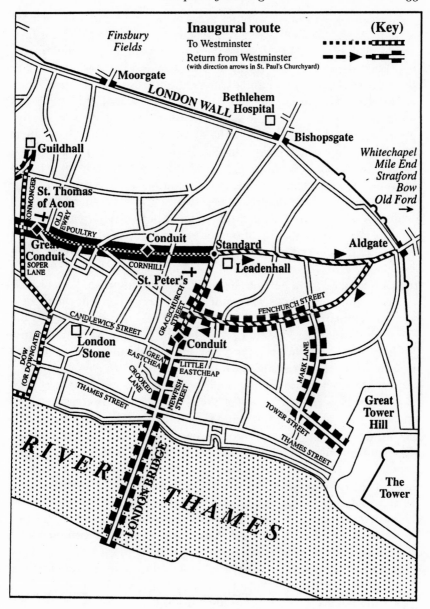

5. *(cont.)*

The title page signals two other areas of interest besides the defence of London; Edward's 'merry pastime with the Tanner of Tamworth, as also his love to fair Mistress Shore, her great promotion, fall and misery, and lastly the lamentable death of both her and her husband'.[6] Both these stories, of the tanner and Mistress Shore, extend the humanisation of the King. The tanner story offers a classic version of the king-in-disguise motif (see Barton, 'The King Disguised'). The King uses his disguise to ask the tanner both what he thinks of the King and how others love him. Hobs characterises the King with a jingling rhyme: 'He's a frank franion, a merry companion, and loves a wench well' (p. 44).[7] On the other hand, he tells the King that people love him 'as poor folks love holidays, glad to have them now and then; but to have them come too often will undo them' (p. 45). So the King is both ordinary and special, a man like other men and a monarch set apart. The whole tanner plot negotiates this contradiction, showing Edward on the one hand in idealised, easy friendship with the tanner, eating bag-pudding and drinking ale with him, taking a fancy to his daughter and, in pointed celebration of their common patriotism, together singing a song of how the English beat the French at Agincourt; on the other hand always one up on the tanner because Hobs does not know that this is the King, and because he (Edward) finally has the power of life and death over the tanner's wayward son, about to hang for robbery.

The idealised nature of the bond between king and tanner is most explicit in the scene where two of the King's justices try to raise a loan to finance war against the French. Where the two judges give generously according to their means, the landowning gentry and prosperous yeoman begrudge the money and are berated by Hobs the tanner, who sees the matter as one of personal loyalty. For him, the King is no mere figurehead, but 'my King', who is entitled to ask for Hobs' money as long as Hobs has any to give (p. 71). Like other plays of this period, it shows king and commoner united as honest, plain-speaking Englishmen, while those in between are suspect.[8] The rural context is conspicuously different in this respect from the civic one, where Londoners of every class, from apprentices to aldermen, are shown as united in their unswerving loyalty to the King.

Yet the King's relationship to the citizens of London is complicated by the Jane Shore plot. His liking for pretty women is demonstrated at various points, not only in the play's opening, where Edward's marriage shows him putting personal attraction before political expediency and the defence of London, but also in his expression of interest in the tanner's daughter. What is left undeveloped in that plot, however, is developed to its conclusions in the Jane Shore plot. The King's attraction to Jane Shore makes for particularly difficult viewing because of the noble light in which Jane's husband, the goldsmith Matthew Shore, is presented. Not only is Matthew Shore actively involved in the defence of the city, putting duty to king and country above the wife he loves so dearly, but he is also shown refusing, on grounds of his unworthiness, the knighthood the King offers to confer on him. When the King therefore takes active steps to pursue Jane Shore while she sits working in her husband's shop, the effect of his disguise is more problematic for the audience than in the tanner plot.

It is particularly difficult to know how to read his familiarity with London when he first appears in disguise in the vicinity of the goldsmith's shop. His speech, like earlier speeches in celebration of London, is one that requires the audience to visualise London very specifically:

> The watermen that daily use the court,
> And see me often, know me not in this.
> At Lion quay I landed in their view,
> Yet none of them took knowledge of the King.
> If any gallant strive to have the wall,
> I'll yield it gently. Soft; here must I turn;
> Here's Lombard Street, and here's the Pelican;
> And there's the phoenix in the pelican's nest. (p. 64)

(The phoenix in the pelican's nest is Jane Shore, whom he perceives at this moment.) But what kind of celebration – or not – is this? Is an audience to understand this itemisation of locations merely as setting location or as part of the King's character? And, if it is to be regarded as part of his character, does it enhance or undermine his image? It could be argued that, following the rebellion's display of the King's absence from the city at a time when his presence is required, Heywood now wants to write the King into the city, as a man indistinguishable from other citizens, equally familiar with the layout of London streets and equally likely to be challenged by a cocky gallant. On the other hand, his motive for being here is to seduce a married woman, which gives to his disguise a treacherous potential that is not present in the tanner scenes, and his willingness to yield the wall to any gallant that challenges him may suggest a cowardliness that creeps in through the inherent ignobility of his situation, demanding that he put up with insult rather than risk being recognised.

The problem here is that his disguise, rather than aligning him with the citizens with whom he seeks to blend in, identifies him as an inter-loper, intent on destroying their contentment with their way of life. In plucking Jane Shore out of the city and into the court he sets in train the circumstances for her ruin, her husband's departure from London and both their eventual deaths. Once Edward is dead, and the new King Richard is enthroned, Jane is made to retrace in reverse the route of the pageants that celebrate the mutual obligation between court and city:

> This day it is commanded by the King,
> You must be stripp'd out of your rich attire,
> And in a white sheet go from Temple Bar
> Until you come to Aldgate, bare footed
> Your hair about your ears, and in your hand
> A burning taper. (p. 161)

The moment, close to the end of Part II, recalls with cruel irony the sum-moning up of images of formal triumphant procession in Part I, at a point when the city's symbolic capital was offered as inspirational. That symbolic capital is increasingly debased not only by the progress of Jane Shore herself, for whom this penitential progress is a preliminary to being 'thrust forth the city-gates / Into the naked cold, forsaken field' (p. 158), but also by the introduction of city figures like Mistress Blage, who advises Jane to take Edward's offer of an easy life at court and then puts her on the streets when the new king condemns her, or Rufford, who petitions her when she is high in Edward's favour for a licence to trans-port corn out of England, so that, as Jane puts it, rejecting his petition, 'The poor must starve for food, to fill your purse' (p. 83).

As Part II progresses, the city comes to seem a more cruel and inhospitable place, one whose pageants are more harshly moralistic than celebratory. For Jane, both city and court are instrumental in her fall and punishment, and she expresses her wish for death in a way that brings the two together in ironic, not celebratory, mode:

> Oh, that my grave had then been made my house.
> When either first I went unto the court,
> Or from the court return'd unto this place! (p. 161)

Matthew, seeing her at this point, as her fortune turns irrevocably, explic-itly casts her life as a moral pageant:

> Oh, what have I beheld, were I as young,
> As when I came to London to be prentice,
> This pageant were sufficient to instruct

And teach me ever after to be wise.
First have I seen desert of wantonness
And breach of wedlock; then of flattery;
Next of dissembling love; and last of all,
The ruin of base catching avarice. (p. 162)

Though the speech ostensibly moralises Jane's life as a pageant, the shape of his own life, from first coming to London as an apprentice to his return now to the city after his self-imposed exile, is inextricably bound up with it; it is a shape which offers a grim alternative to the Dick Whittington model, as expressed in John Crosbie's monologue.

Not only Matthew, but Jane, too, is given the opportunity of moralising on her fate. The city is expressly foregrounded in her speech, which takes the form of a direct address to London:

Farewell to thee, where first I was entic'd
That scandaliz'd thy dignity with shame;
But now thou hast return'd me treble blame;
My tongue, that gave consent, enjoin'd to beg;
Mine eyes adjudg'd to hourly laments;
Mine arms, for their embracings, catch the air;
And these quick, nimble feet, that were so ready
To step into a King's forbidden bed,
London! thy flints have punish'd for their pride,
And thou hast drunk their blood for thy revenge. (p. 165)

London is both injured party and revenger: Jane blames herself for shaming the city with her adultery, but accuses the city of punishing her three times as harshly. This is scarcely the city so gloriously defended and adored in the scenes of Falconbridge's rebellion. It has exchanged that heroic status for a more cruel and punitive face.

The two plays of *Edward IV* are fascinated by the idea of exchange: the Mayor of London must step into the King's place to supply his absence; the King changes places with his butler to win the tanner's confidence and masquerades as a customer in Matthew Shore's goldsmith's shop to bargain for Jane Shore's favours; Jane Shore stands in as Lady Mayoress for her widowed uncle John Crosbie and exchanges her place as a citizen's wife first for the place of King's mistress at court, then for that of city beggar; and other characters inevitably change places too in consequence of these transformations. This fascination with exchanges simultaneously emerges out of a deep desire for interchangeability between loyalties to nation and city and reveals the sense of binary opposition between the two. None of these exchanges is negotiated without ideological discomfort; and though the plays in many ways seek to idealise relations between court and city, city and country, country and court, this ideality is undermined by their repeated production of such discomfort.[9] The relationships between each pair, despite the trumpeting of mutual alliance and duty, are exposed as potentially manipulative and exploitative. One may appear to do duty for another, but the performance of that duty may have a deeper affinity with the model of economic exchange than with the model of perfect love. When the Mayor does duty for the King, it is because the King puts his private pleasure first; when the King takes on the role of citizen it is because he wants to buy a mistress. The King, it is evident, constitutes the major locus of unease in the attempt to glorify the city through its allegiance to king and country. What the plays express, as the underbelly of that failed glorification, is the tension between different ways of conceiving the city: as a separate, bounded space, as a space in dialogue with and close relation to Westminster and the court, and as a space within the larger territory of the nation.

CHAPTER THREE

From retreat to display

LOVE'S LABOUR'S LOST AND THE WAR OF THE THEATRES

The theatre in which *Edward IV* was performed remains uncertain, though the title page tells us that it was performed by Derby's Men. If the play is correctly dated to 1599, it was probably played at the Boar's Head.[1] For all its ideological tensions, it is a play that seems to belong in an existing, perhaps even somewhat old-fashioned, tradition of plays glorifying either of the city of London or the English nation or both, a tradition going back through Heywood's own *Four Prentices of London* (1594) to the plays of Robert Wilson in the 1580s (see prologue, pp. 4–5 above). But at the same time as *Edward IV* was being staged in London, within this broadly conservative and celebratory dramatic tradition, a newly fashionable kind of theatre was emerging at the recently revived children's theatres and the Globe. Its starting point, I wish to argue, is in Shakespeare's *Love's Labour's Lost* (c. 1595).

In thinking about the coexistence of these two kinds of theatre it is helpful to return to Stow's *Survey*, a product of the same cultural moment and a text that displays cultural tensions through its combination of novelty and resistance to change. For Stow the word 'commodity' means primarily 'good' or 'benefit'. When he uses it, for example, in lamenting the enclosure of open land for gardens and private summer-houses, the phrase 'common commodity' has something of the sense of the old phrase 'common weal'. Such enclosures, he argues, are 'not so much for use or profit, as for show and pleasure, bewraying the vanity of men's minds, much unlike to the disposition of the ancient citizens, who delighted in the building of hospitals and alms-houses for the poor, and therein both employed their wits, and spent their wealths in preferment of the common commodity of this our city' (*Survey*, vol. II, p. 78).[2] 'Profit', too, in context here, is a word in which the moral sense out-weighs the economic sense. Even when he uses the word 'commodities' in the plural, in the context of praising the benefits of commerce, its sense is usually distanced from that of more modern usage, where economic connotations take precedence over moral ones: 'Other the benefits that merchandise bringeth, shall hereafter appear in the general recital of the commodities that come by London, and therefore it resteth that I speak a word of retailers, and finally show that much good groweth by them both' (vol. II, p. 210). The 'commodities that come by London', which he goes on to recite, are not moveable objects or saleable products but 'the commodities of the furtherance of religion, and justice: the propagation of learning: the maintenance of arts: the increase of riches, and the defence of countries (all which are before showed to grow generally by cities, and be common to London with them)' (vol. II, pp. 210, 212).

Stow's usage of this term, like so much else about his project, stubbornly resists change. Though Stow was familiar with the use of the word to mean material objects, as shown in his description of the Royal Exchange (p. 28 above), the very context of its occurrence there has much to say about the grounds of Stow's resistance. The Royal Exchange monumentalised precisely that devotion to buying and selling, to the accumulation, possession and transfer of capital that Stow deplored. His on-going lament is that people nowadays put their business and their private pleasures above their concern for their neighbours and the common good. The difference between Stow's values and those of some of his contemporaries, however, emphasises the ambivalence of emergent capitalism. In a work published just nine years after Stow's *Survey*, Richard Johnson plagiarises Stow in order to rewrite his moral stance. Writing in the persona of a country gentleman addressing a London citizen in a dialogue called *The Pleasant Walks of Moorfields*, Johnson first turns Stow's condemnation into congratulation: 'The citizens I perceive ever carried gallant minds, and to this day (I see) they continually strive to beautify this famous city, for what fair summer-houses with lofty towers and turrets are here builded in these fields, and in other places, the suburbs of the city, not so much for use and profit, as for show and pleasure, bewraying the nobleness of their minds' (sig. B1).[3] Stow's view, however, is accommodated, though not shared, in the citizen's reply: 'Many of our ancient citizens sir have far more worthier dispositions, and chiefly delights in the repairing of hospitals, and building almshouses for the poor and therein employ their wits, spending their wealths to the common commodity of this our city.' Johnson thus turns both pursuits into laudable ones, implying that however citizens spend their money, they do so in the public interest and for the greater glory of the city. Perhaps Johnson intended his audience to recognise the quotation from Stow and thereby consciously to revise Stow's teaching. In any case, his intention to accommodate the pursuit of luxury, pleasure and show within an ethic of civic usefulness as opposed to condemning it, as Stow does, for opposing civic duty, is clear.

Both the fact and the nature of the Royal Exchange, standing at the intersection of these opposing views, bring together the influences of the market and the court. The need for a building in place of the previously rather casual customary use of an open street for business transactions signals an expansion of the market and a different conception of its cultural place. The expansion of the market itself both represents and produces a growing demand for consumer goods indicative of an increasing preoccupation with possession and display; and this preoccupation can be seen in turn as a product of both the conspicuous presence of the court and the expanding market itself. The city and the palace, as argued in chapter 1 above, are not separate units, but closely interdependent.

Space is differently conceived in this emergent culture. The pulling down of eighty houses crowded into narrow alleys to make space for the planned, shapely orderliness and palatial dimensions of the Royal Exchange seems to stand as emblematic not only of the engulfing of living space by the marketplace but also of the privileging of display over use. In a sense, of course, display is itself a kind of use – goods need to be displayed in order to be sold, and the better the display the better the sales and the higher the prices that can be demanded – but that concept of use is a more mediated one, tied to the sale of goods rather than more directly to the goods themselves.

The Royal Exchange was not just a place *for* display; it was also a place *of* display. Though the necessity for a building was prompted at one level by the inconvenience of the Lombard Street arrangement, the conception of the building was not primarily functional but grounded in a different kind of necessity: the need to construct a visible marker of the power and international prominence of London's market. The plan was conceived from the start within the contexts of both civic pride and international awareness: Gresham's promise was 'to build and plant within this City a burse to be more fair and costly builded in all points than is the burse of Antwerp' (Imray, 'Origins of the Exchange', p. 27). Evelyn's diary demonstrates the pride in the Exchange still felt by one Londoner over seventy years later. In his eyes the Exchanges of Amsterdam, Paris and Venice failed to come up to the standard of 'ours

6. Exterior view of the Royal Exchange by Franz Hogenberg, c. 1569.

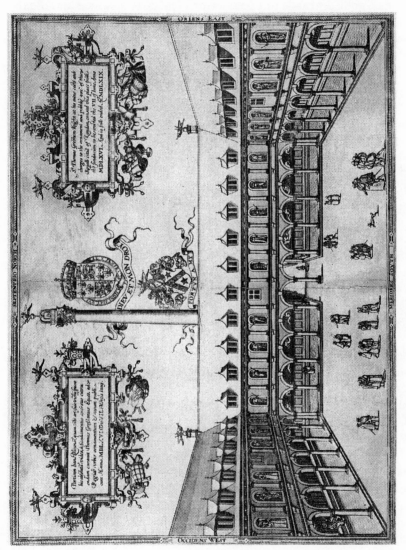

7. Interior view of the Royal Exchange by Franz Hogenberg, c. 1569.

in London' (the diary entries are quoted more fully in Saunders, 'Organisation of the Exchange', p. 96). The symbolic status of the building is clearly indicated in Stow's account of the ceremonial laying of its foundations: Sir Thomas Gresham himself laid the first brick with a piece of gold, and each of the aldermen who accompanied him did the same (*Survey*, vol. I, pp. 192–3). Nothing could better signify the importance of putting wealth on show. Though the action is useless or wasteful in the strictest sense, it is clearly functional in the sense that it deliberately enhances the status of the newly founded building.[4]

It is no accident that the first theatre buildings were going up at the same time. Their existence establishes the permanent presence and commercial availability of show in the city. And while the symbolic display of the Royal Exchange is very different from the commercial spectacles offered in the theatres, both, as chapter I above argues, recognise the pleasure and importance of looking and signal the development of a culture that puts a high premium on glitter, spectacle and conspicuous expenditure. It is well known that the entrepreneurs of theatre in this period spent far more on costume than on paying actors or playwrights (as scenes like those listed on p. 44 above serve to confirm). If there was going to be a show, then it had to be worth looking at.

This emphasis on show is more widely evident in both court and city, but it brings with it a sense of unease about the relationship between the visible and the non-visible. The more glittering the surface the more doubt it created about the nature and quality of what might be 'below' it; and this translated into an anxiety about people as well as objects and buildings. It is notable that theatre in the latter half of the 1590s becomes particularly interested not just in performing fictions but in performing performance. The figure of fashion, who stages his own persona as a carefully manufactured display of collected fragments, becomes a focus of interest and anxiety.

As Jean-Christophe Agnew has argued, this figure is intimately related to the development of capitalism: a 'volatile and placeless market' produces a 'crisis of representation' (*Worlds Apart*, p. 59) which problematises the process of representation itself, so that the kinds of characters the stage now chooses to represent are conscious performers, inhabiting multiple identities without embodying any one of them. 'Just as London's Exchange enforced an ideal of financial liquidity, so London's theaters enacted a vision of this new sociological and psychological fluidity' (p. 98). '"Protean man"', as Agnew calls him, 'the plastic, polymorphous, performative figure that is both the ideal and the nightmare of modernity', must be understood to be 'the collective dream work of commodity culture' (p. 14). Clearly the growth of a 'commodity culture', where objects are valued 'not so much for use or profit as for show and pleasure' (Stow, above) produces anxieties for those who inhabit it. Cultivation of the surface shapes concern over what, if anything, lies below, and the notion of identity comes to seem increasingly precarious.

Guy Debord, like Agnew, sees consumption and spectacularisation as necessarily linked to each other and as mutually supportive of capitalism. 'The world of consumption', he argues,

is in reality the world of the mutual spectacularization of everyone, the world of everyone's separation, estrangement and nonparticipation . . . Outside of work, the spectacle is the dominant mode through which people relate to each other. It is only through the spectacle that people acquire a (falsified) knowledge of certain general aspects of social life . . . The relation between authors and spectators is only a transposition of the fundamental relation between directors and executants. It answers perfectly to the needs of a reified and alienated culture: the spectacle-spectator relation is in itself a staunch bearer of the capitalist order. (Knabb, *Situationist International*, pp. 307–8)

Though Debord is analysing capitalism in a much later phase of its development, his remarks are also applicable to the early modern period, when social relations under capitalism seemed so new and unfamiliar.

The sense of alienation and reification in early modern London is linked to place as well as time. City life is bound almost by definition to produce a tension between personal or individual imperatives and collective imperatives. The 'accommodation of the One to the Many', as Gail Paster writes, 'is a central urban theme and a practical urban problem' (*Idea of the City*, pp. 33–4). According to Stow, 'common weals, cities and towns, were at the first invented, to the end that men might lead a civil life amongst themselves', and it is via this 'nearness of conversation' that city dwellers 'are withdrawn from barbarous ferity and force to a certain mildness of manners and to humanity and justice; whereby they are contented to give and take right, to and from their equals and inferiors, and to hear and obey their heads and superiors' (*Survey*, vol. II, p. 197). This, of course, is an idealist picture of the city. Though the governors of any city might yearn for an urban body as mild and obedient as Stow describes, in practice the effects of city life were rather different, as the authorities knew to their cost. Particularly in times of pressure, when jobs, housing and food are insufficient for the whole city, as they were in the 1590s, individuals tend to seek to protect their own interests at the expense of the collective interest. As many historians have pointed out, the late Elizabethan and early Jacobean period was the age of the monopoly and the projector, of systems that privileged the protection of private interests. From the latter part of Elizabeth's reign there were signs of a waning interest in activities that were in the collective interest: Michael Berlin notes such features as absenteeism at the livery halls, unwillingness to take on onerous civic offices and refusals to contribute to civic enterprise, all trends that became even more visible in the early seventeenth century ('Civic Ceremony', p. 24).[5] For Stow, the swallowing up of open, common space by private ownership was a sign of individual interests taking precedence over the common good; for King James, the flocking of country gentry to London was another, since gentlemen thereby neglected their duty of hospitality on their own estates. The only kind of public project likely to inspire enthusiasm was one aimed at enhancing private profit. As Berlin points out, London citizens may have been unwilling to contribute to the rebuilding of the St Paul's spire after it was damaged by lightning in 1561, but they were enthusiastic about such projects as the building of the Royal Exchange and the development of the New River ('Civic Ceremony', p. 21), from which they stood to benefit more materially.

Love's Labour's Lost is a play that concerns itself very directly with the tension between individual and collective impulses; yet more than one critic has noted Shakespeare's persistent rejection of a London setting for any of his plays (Paster, *Idea of the City*, p. 178; Barton, 'London Comedy', p. 160). This makes him, as Anne Barton notes, almost unique among contemporary dramatists; and Barton goes further, to argue that 'Shakespeare's comedies deliberately bypass the teeming life, not only of contemporary London, but of cities generally. They are filled with evasions of the urban' (p. 160). In terms of settings, this is certainly so; but plays do not have to take up their concerns in a direct or explicit way. An 'evasion of the urban' may still have an important bearing on the urban. Drama, like poetry, often adopts 'the evasive mode' (Martines, *Society and History*, p. 106); this play's characteristically courtly facades mask their own identifiably urban foundations.

The play is set entirely in the court of the King of Navarre and opens with the King's declaration of his intention to establish his court as 'a little academe, / Still and contemplative in living art' (1.i.13–14).[6] The king and his three fellow-courtiers are to devote themselves to study, to conquer bodily needs and desires and effectively to step out of time. In establishing their academy as 'the wonder of the world' they will spite 'cormorant devouring Time' and make themselves 'heirs of all eternity' (I.i.12, 4, 7). The two concepts dominating the establishment of the academy are pause and retreat – the retreat from the body, from women, from 'the huge army of the world's desires' (I.i.10) and the creation within that retreat of a prolonged pause, a life out of time, 'living art'. The space of the court is thus constructed as a fetishised space that seeks to enclose and distance itself from the ordinary distractions of a social life.

Within the context of the 1590s, when Shakespeare was writing, it might be argued that this creation of a retreat is a response to the rush and noise of the expanding city. Numerous plays and fictions of the 1590s demonstrate the tendency to seek a green place, to quit the bustle of court or city for the liberating tranquillity of a pastoral dream (which often turns out to be not quite so tranquil or liberating after all). The retreat in *Love's Labour's Lost* is conspicuously fettered and untranquil, rigidly enforced through statutes, oaths and signatures and constantly subject to intrusion and disruption. The academy is not a free or open space, but a tightly enclosed and regulated one, oddly resembling the city it seeks to reject. Like apprentices binding themselves to their masters, these courtiers sign an agreement for a fixed term (here three years), during which time they must live with their master, work hard and for-swear the company of women (apprentices' indentures bound them to live in their master's house, work for him for a fixed term, usually seven years, and postpone marriage until the completion of that term).

From the start, the play admits the knowledge, voiced by Berowne, that such a project is doomed to failure. Berowne reminds the King that he is already bound to break the prohibition against seeing women if he maintains his agreement to meet with the French king's daughter, who is on her way to negotiate the surrender of Aquitaine. When the Princess arrives, she pointedly rebukes the King in terms similar to proclamations soon to be issued with wearying regularity by King James, urging gentle-men who have flocked to the fashionable city to return to their country houses:

> I hear your grace hath sworn out housekeeping.
> 'Tis deadly sin to keep that oath, my lord,
> And sin to break it. (II.i.103–5)

The academy, despite its members' protestations that what they do is by way of duty and a renunciation of pleasure, is thus recast by its noble guest as neglecting duty in pursuit of private ends.

The key concept underpinning the academy gradually emerges as not learning but fashion, the desire to set trends rather than follow them and to be recognised as 'singled from the barbarous' (v.i.71–2),[7] dazzling the riff-raff with a display of fashionable accomplishment. The terms are both reminiscent of, and contradictory to, Stow's notion of the origin of cities. Though cities are designed, he says, to exclude the barbarous, so that 'good behaviour is yet called *urbanitas*' (*Survey*, vol. II, p. 198), they aim to do so collectively. By implication, the 'single' or individual cultivation of exclusiveness works against the virtue of civility, producing isolated and alienated modes of being.

This is evident in the play's concern with different kinds of excess, particularly linguistic excess. Language is constructed in the play as a fashionable object, revelling in its own novelty value at the expense of its use value. It is language commoditised, its materiality so foregrounded that its usefulness, or referentiality, disappears under the excessive weight of its self-reference;[8] the multiplicity of linguistic abuses on show in the play calls attention to a deeply fragmented relationship between speakers and their words, which impinges on the integrity of both. The following exchange between Moth and Costard conceives of first words and then their speakers as loose scraps (Moth is speaking of Armado and Holofernes):

MOTH. They have been at a great feast of languages, and stolen the scraps.
COSTARD. O, they have lived long on the alms-basket of words. I marvel thy
    master hath not eaten thee for a word, for thou art not so long by the
    head as *honorificabilitudinitatibus*.[9] (v.i.35–40)

The exchange stands in emblematic relation to the play. Not only are characters identified and described by their linguistic habits, but words are a self-consciously acknowledged currency. Speakers (both characters and, consequently here, actors) do not merely utter words; they taste them, chew them, roll them round in the mouth. They conceive their relation to the world in terms of words. This observation might seem to be applicable to very different kinds of characters on stage before the 1590s (figures like Tamburlaine or Faustus, for example); but the nature of the relationship to rhetoric is quite different. When Tamburlaine speaks Marlowe's mighty lines, they are invested with expressiveness, emotional affect and identity. Though some of them may seem detachable from plot, like rhetorical flowers in an anthology ('What is beauty, saith my sufferings, then?'), they are not detachable from the spectator's affective investment in the figure of Tamburlaine, but rather designed to heighten it. In *Love's Labour's Lost*, by contrast, the play with *copia* is precisely that: play. Language here is more a matter of effect than affect. It is uninvested, playful and packaged; and it is 'for sale' to the spectators like a set of fashion accessories. Words here come with designer labels, and characters are fashion victims rather than expressive entities.

Underpinning attitudes towards this linguistic extravagance is the same model of opposition between functionality and excess that underpins Stow's preference for alms-houses over summer-houses and so much urban and Protestant discourse, from sermons to popular pamphlets, moralised biographies and handbooks for the citizen. The image of 'a great feast of languages' that affirms its own wasteful extravagance via the 'scraps' it leaves highlights its own attachment to materiality and display at the expense of function. Language as densely ornamental object celebrates its own pointlessness, its determination to 'waste' rather than 'use' time.[10] Hence the set-piece quality of so much of the play's speech (Costard's meditation on 'remuneration' at iii.i.132–8, for example, or Armado and Holofernes on 'the posterior of the day' at v.i.81–4).

Clearly, material like this invites an audience to enjoy the extended savouring of particular words, and there is some evidence that audiences applauded individually striking speech-acts. Luscus, in Marston's *Scourge of Villainy*, is described as one who has

> made a commonplace book out of plays,
> And speaks in print, at least whate'er he says
> Is warranted by curtain plaudities. (Satire xi, lines 43–5)[11]

This suggestion of a set of relations between performers and spectators whereby the individual 'turn' is the highlight, and engagement with continuous narrative is happily sacrificed in favour of dazzling moments, finds an analogy in music hall, and it is some such model of performance that we need to bring to *Love's Labour's Lost* in order to appreciate its appeal to a contemporary audience. A bastardised derivative of music hall in fact suggests quite a precise analogy: in the 1960s television show, *The Good Old Days*, the presenter, Leonard Sachs, who introduced the various turns, made himself into a turn by the simple device of speaking in a thickly textured, arcane and alliterative register, isolating each long and special word by a combination of pause and voice inflection, in a way that encouraged the audience to roar its outrage or approval. Such a dialect, like the dialects of *Love's Labour's Lost*, might well be described as speaking 'in print'.

The very phrase points to a kind of language that elicits applause by parading its 'writtenness' in spoken form, and thereby marking its own cultivation of conspicuous inappropriateness. To speak in a way that gratuitously undermines spoken register (that is, without a recognisable context for doing so) is to mark the word as alienated. It is not only to mark it, but to market it, to construct it as a commodity, to display it for admiration as goods are displayed in the luxury shops of the Royal Exchange. Certainly, within *Love's Labour's Lost*, on-stage listeners seek to take possession of new words, making lists of those that take their fancy. Speakers acquire and display their new possessions with sensuous obsessiveness, and both the buying and the selling of the word-object are acquisitive acts of love. Thus Holofernes expends five adjectives on Armado: 'He is too picked, too spruce, too affected, too odd, as it were, too peregrinate, as I may call it'; and Sir Nathaniel takes out his notebook to acquire (by writing down) the object of his choice, 'peregrinate', which strikes him as 'a most singular and choice epithet' (v.i.12–15).

The sheer length of time taken up in uttering catalogues of polysyllabic words like this, or even individually long words like '*honorificabilitudinitatibus*', allows the play to create particular kinds of time and space which differ from those of earlier plays. *Love's Labour's Lost* circles narcissistically around the fabric of its own design, reflecting on the modes of speech and performance it speaks and performs. The plot, such as it is, is little more than a framework within which speech and performance may take place. The purposive movement of time generally signalled by narrative is almost overwhelmed by a devotion to the pleasures of the moment, drawn out at self-indulgent length, and the thrill of the beautiful fragment is offered in place of the satisfaction of wholeness. Pause and retreat, the declared aims of the academy the courtiers seek to establish at the opening of the play, are precisely the play's own modes of operation. It invites its audience to experience the theatrical event as a retreat from the rush of the city outside and to savour its dedicated triviality as an extended, aesthetically pleasurable pause.[12]

Music hall, however, while it may suggest a model for understanding the pleasures of a show that seeks to dazzle through a sequence of *tours de force*, does not offer to moralise its own highlights as this play does. Even Holofernes, word spinner *extraordinaire*, is made a mouthpiece for the condemnation of the tendency to prefer sound over sense, or 'the thread of . . . verbosity' over 'the staple of . . . argument' (v.i.16–17).

The image draws together many of the anxieties around commoditised speech: the sense of its material tricksiness, the feeling that it is not quite delivering what it promises, the worry that its glittering surface is a substitute for functionality and that it is somehow fraudulent or inauthentic. And the same moral viewpoint is also coded into the structure of the play, which ends with the women's rejection of the men's elaborate speeches and Berowne's well-known abjuration of 'taffeta phrases' (v.ii.406). Ways of passing time which have previously seemed to celebrate the notion of leisured diversion are now offered up for moral judgement and found wanting. Suddenly the plot, apparently a mere framework up to now for enabling the perpetuation of this extended triviality, claims a new kind of status for itself and lashes out against its own previous languishment. The moral imperative of social duty invades first in the form of Marcade's message from outside the court and then in the imposition of tasks to be fulfilled (withdrawal to a hermitage, jesting in a hospital) before marriage can take place. The closure approaches a sternness remarkably like Stow's, insisting on the priority of hospitals and alms-houses over, as it were, private summer-houses.

Yet the structure of rejection and Berowne's recognition of its truth are somehow fraudulent themselves, since this is not finally a play that celebrates plainness. Berowne's opposition feels literary even as it is spoken. What the theatrical experience of the play is offering its audience as pleasurable is precisely elaboration, not transparency; and what it is struggling with is that model of usefulness versus wastefulness which seems so damaging to theatre itself, yet to which theatre keeps returning in order to validate itself. Sixteenth-century attacks on theatre constructed it as dangerous because it wasted time, substituting its non-productive pleasures for the useful functioning of, say, sermons; and theatre's defenders, whether in treatises or plays, found it difficult to avoid becoming locked in the terms of the attack. So at one level what *Love's Labour's Lost* is negotiating is the tension between a theatrical understanding of how to give an audience pleasure and an intellectual recognition of the moral paradigm that positions pleasure without purpose as wasteful and in need of correction (see further Shepherd and Womack, *English Drama*, ch. 3, esp. pp. 53–62).

Interestingly, there has always been an urge on the part of the present academy to position *Love's Labour's Lost* as a coterie play, demanding a special and exclusive place of performance, despite absence of evidence

8. Paul's Walk. Reproduced from William Dugdale's *History of St Paul's Cathedral* (1658).

for such a view. What little evidence there is works against this imagined special space for the play. G. R. Hibbard, in his introduction to the play, cites a poem by a certain Robert Tofte, published in 1598, describing a visit to see *Love's Labour's Lost* at what sounds very much like a public theatre (pp. 1–2). The title page of the first Quarto (1598) states that the play was performed before the queen 'this last Christmas', while that of the second Quarto (1631) informs us that it was acted at the Blackfriars and the Globe. Furthermore, as Alfred Harbage has noted, there is no evidence that any company during Shakespeare's lifetime ever performed a play specially commissioned for private performance. Surviving evidence suggests that plays privately presented on special occasions were taken from the existing public repertories (Harbage, '*Love's Labor's Lost*', pp. 19–20).[13] In any case, whatever the location of its first performance, *Love's Labour's Lost* quickly became popular in the public theatre.

The critical resistance to seeing it as a public-theatre play surely stems from the play's own attempt to distance itself from the city. Yet its preoccupation with the fashionable and constructed persona was soon to emerge as very much a concern of urban life and popular theatre. A group of plays associated with the company responsible for *Love's Labour's Lost*, the Chamberlain's Men, and with the recently revived children's companies at St Paul's and the Blackfriars, became especially preoccupied with fashion and excess around 1599–1601. Many of these plays, though not all, were part of what has come to be known as the 'War of the Theatres' or 'poetomachia'.[14] Like *Love's Labour's Lost*, they are self-referentially about language and theatre before they are about anything or anyone else. The city is central to the performance auspices of most of these plays, though sometimes still occluded from their fictional settings.[15] They aim to attract regular audiences to particular theatres and to construct a specific product identity for each theatre.[16] Though the poetomachia may not have been manufactured *only* as part of a publicity campaign on the part of the theatres, self-publicising was certainly part of the function of these plays. As Andrew Gurr has noted, the six-year duopoly of the Chamberlain's and Admiral's Men was facing particularly fierce competition around the turn of the century, with both Derby's and Worcester's Men jostling for position in the public theatres and the revival of the children's companies in the private hall-theatres (*Shakespearian Playing Companies*, pp. 243–4, 265–6). Hence the plays are full of in-jokes about the theatre and blatant or coded references to the city of London.

The fascination with linguistic decorums and excesses also becomes a source of mutual cross-reference and joking, part of a shared culture both on stage and off and of the construction of a shared audience.[17] Hence Chrisoganus' learned, philosophical register in *Histriomastix*, performed at the Middle Temple (Act i; vol. iii, p. 249), becomes Clove's absurd discourse in *Every Man Out Of His Humour* at the Globe (iii.iv.21–30). Place, both performance place and fictional location, are of course crucial to the tone with which each is heard. What may be uttered and received entirely seriously in an allegorical location and an elite performance space makes quite different meanings when the imagined place is the middle aisle of St Paul's and the performance space a Bankside theatre. It is the fact that Clove's speech is quite literally out of place that defines it as 'fustian', a favourite contemporary term for exotic speech. As John Hoskins, himself a member of the Middle Temple, argued at about the same time, it is 'purpose' that renders particular rhetorical modes either elegant or ridiculous (*Directions for Speech and Style*, pp. 50, 15, and cf. 111).

Class and class origins of speakers are also central to the tone attaching to elegant speech. The innovative list of dramatis personae that Jonson supplies with *Every Man Out Of His Humour*, for example, is insistent on distinctions of class: Puntarvolo is a knight; Fastidius Brisk, a courtier; Deliro, a citizen; Clove and Orange, 'an inseparable case of coxcombs, city-born; the Gemini or twins of foppery'. But the satiric point is that all these representatives of different classes strive to display the latest fashions in language and clothes. *Cynthia's Revels* dissects the meeting of classes through fashion with vitriolic specificity. Amorphus, a well-born traveller, is keen to be introduced to Asotus, a citizen's son, and ponders at greath length how to address him, whether with 'some choice remnant of Spanish, or Italian' or with 'some encomiastic speech upon this our metropolis',[18] before finally hitting on the ideal point of contact: ''Tis a most curious and neatly-wrought band, this same, as I have seen, sir' (I.iv.94–5). Fashion is the common currency between courtier and citizen.

Just as Shakespeare's Sir Nathaniel and Marston's Balurdo detach and collect remarkable words in their notebooks to drop into their own discourse, so the plays of this period isolate, inspect and circulate particular choice terms in a highly self-conscious way. Chapman's *An Humorous Day's Mirth* (1597), for example, has a scene satirising vacuous courtly manners in some detail and drawing attention to the word 'compliment' (I.ii), which Marston develops further through a character called Puff in *Jack Drum's Entertainment* (Act III; pp. 209–13). The joke is picked up and carried on in *Cynthia's Revels*, which has a reference to the character of Anaides as 'a strange arrogating puff' (III.iii.26),[19] and is then extended by Dekker, who appropriates the whole four lines in which the phrase is embedded in *Cynthia's Revels* and turns them into a reference to Crispinus and Demetrius in his own *Satiromastix* (I.ii.153–6), two characters themselves appropriated from Jonson's *Poetaster*. The later stages of the joke gain extra purchase from the fact that the characters who speak or are the subject of these utterances are impersonations of some of the dramatists concerned. But though criticism of these plays has usually concentrated on decoding the correlations between theatrical characters and real-life counterparts, this is only part of the point. The joke is as much about urban fashion-mongering and the vacuousness of a society in which language has become a collectable item, unhinged from sense and context; the on-going commentary on language use by characters themselves highlights this thrust:

It is my custom in my common talk to make use of my reading in the Greek, Latin, French, Italian, Spanish poets, and to adorn my oratory with some pretty choice extraordinary sayings. (Gullio, in *The Return from Parnassus*, lines 1134–7)

Your pedant should provide you some parcels of French, or some pretty commodity of Italian to commence with, if you would be exotic and exquisite. (Amorphus, in *Cynthia's Revels*, III.v.79–81)

Amorphus' very name is representative of the socially fluid persona who seeks to establish his own presence by speaking 'in print'; it is no surprise to find such a speaker using the word 'commodity' in its later sense (the one Stow resists) quite naturally and in relation to language.[20]

The War of the Theatres could be said to be a dispute about the proper place of theatre and theatricality in the city. The plays are fascinated not only by linguistic excess, but by the theatrical implications of staging and focusing on that excess. At the heart of these plays is a conundrum: the affectations this theatre seeks to expose may be described as fashions, humours, or the games people play; but, in using the stage to expose those affectations as games, the plays themselves become part of a similar fashionable game. The ritual unmasking to which these plays almost necessarily lead is predicated on a morality that denounces masking by definition as guile; but the medium of denunciation is itself a mask. It is a reformulation of the old problem of theatre addressed by its attackers, from Lollards to Puritans, the problem that theatre is constructed on pretence; but the problem is now posed in particularly urgent relation to the developing city, with its heightened awareness of the 'look', its push towards a notion of the self as no more than the sequence of its multiple social stagings.

The very structure of these turn-of-the-century plays highlights their self-reflexivity. Just as so much of their spoken dialogue is about itself as linguistic object, so their shapes, like that of *Love's Labour's Lost*, are predominantly circular rather than linear. They willingly devote whole scenes to linguistic play which is barely attached to plot, thereby playing with questions about what drama is, and what it is to be on stage at all.

They seem to drive towards a staging of the moment that will encapsu-
late the visibility of pretence and pretentiousness almost emblematically
rather than seeking to advance a narrative, and, as in *Love's Labour's Lost*,
there is often a pointedness to the absence of any narrative to advance,
since narcissistic characters who play with words for pleasure as opposed
to meaning are thereby constructed as by definition going nowhere. Yet
the sense of purposelessness does not merely operate as a negative
hermeneutic attaching to certain characters within the fiction of the
play; it also expresses some radical doubts about what performance is
and how theatrical performance intersects with social performance.
This kind of drama seems to want to strip the theatre of as many elements as it can in order to see what resists that stripping. It pushes against
theatrical form, seeking to find whether there are any limits to that form,
in order to test whether there is anything that may be defined as 'core',
in relation to either theatre or the human self. If such a 'core' could be
isolated as germane to one rather than the other, the worry about the
resemblance between the two would be resolved.

Sometimes the attempt to incorporate exploration of the parallel
between social and theatrical performance is dizzying in its self-reflex-
iveness, as when Mercury and Cupid decide to disguise themselves as
pages in *Cynthia's Revels*. Mercury urges on Cupid the need to *practise* the
right speech and behaviour in order for them to pass themselves off as
'cracks' ('pert boys'): 'since we are turned cracks, let's study to be like
cracks; practise their language and behaviours, and not with a dead
imitation: act freely, carelessly, and capriciously, as if our veins ran with
quicksilver, and not utter a phrase but what shall come forth steeped in
the very brine of conceit, and sparkle like salt in fire' (II.i.3–8). The word
'cracks' here is a reminder that the speakers of these lines are precisely that already, since this is a Chapel Children's play. So the boy-
actors, or 'cracks', speak for characters who are 'turned cracks' and who
must therefore 'study to be like cracks'. The layers of self-reference work
to expose and problematise the gap between performer and role, since
they simultaneously show performers constructing roles while reminding the audience that 'selves' too are performed.

It is hardly surprising that this kind of drama has sometimes been suggested to be unperformable. Anne Barton, writing on the plotlessness of
Every Man Out Of His Humour, for example, argues that none of the extant
editions of it represents a performable text (*Ben Jonson*, p. 65). She notes
the prominence of set-piece descriptions of character 'designed more, it
seems, for readers than for theatre audiences' and speculates on the

probability that such descriptions were cut or abbreviated in performance (pp. 69–70). Admittedly the early quartos of Jonson's *Every
Man Out* explicitly state that they contain 'more than hath been publicly
spoken or acted'; but is it legitimate to read back from these statements
a fundamental unperformability attaching to this particular mode of
speech? The kind of speeches Barton identifies as unperformable are not
mere occasional hiccups in the texts, but deeply embedded in and essential to the nature of these particular plays. As with *Love's Labour's Lost*, a
different model of performance is necessary, one committed to recognising the highly fashionable status of these supposedly unperformable
speeches in this particular theatrical mode.

But, again like *Love's Labour's Lost*, these plays seek to moralise their
own most characteristic excesses. As Cupid's comment on the practised
speech of cracks suggests, the plays are characteristically hung between
admiration for speech that sparkles 'like salt in fire' and disapproval of
cultivating sparkle for pure effect. The critical tone emerges most clearly
in the trio of adverbs qualifying the verb 'act': 'freely, carelessly, and
capriciously'.[21] This notion of careless whimsicality implies a familiar
moral take on the surface–depth binary; it carries the suggestion that
cultivation of the surface is fraudulent, inauthentic and amoral. The
issues theatre confronts in confronting the conditions of its own representation are, as Agnew has shown, the same as those of the market:
'authenticity, accountability, and intentionality' (p. 11, above).

Cupid's moral stance is even clearer in his explicit disapproval of the
courtiers' folly. It is he who speaks the condemnation of flamboyant
speakers who, 'when they have got acquainted with a strange word,
never rest till they have wrung it in, though it loosen the whole fabric of
their sense' (II.iv.15–18). But this moral frame of disapproval, like the
closure of *Love's Labour's Lost* with the ejection of the courtiers from their
leisured display into earnest work, functions in tension with the play's
own dedication to displaying that same exhibitionism of which it dis-
approves. The pleasure of shared jokes, collective play and stylishly conscious performance encounters the fear that such celebration of the
surface covers up emptiness. The dramatists reflect on the fragments
pieced together to dazzling effect and worry about the consequences of
working with fragments and surfaces. This worry manifests itself as a
moral discourse that upbraids the dialect that wallows in the surface of
the sign as evidence of cultural bankruptcy. Figures who seem to fashion
their social personae 'freely, carelessly, and capriciously' are presented as
decentred beings. A society that seeks to cultivate the sign at the expense

of the referent, it is implied, is idolatrous, irresponsibly unconcerned about its own inner state.

The problem is deeply related to what theatre understands its role to be. Now that it is firmly established 'for sale' in permanent theatre buildings in and around the city, it has truly entered the marketplace. These plays respond to market demand by developing a particular kind of flamboyant set-piece in response to audiences' expression of approval for this kind of thing; but they also feel the need to reprove the audience for enjoying such display for its own sake. The dramatists respond to the commodification of their product with ambivalence, giving the audience prolonged and conspicuous displays of the verbal glitter it likes, but seeking simultaneously to position such displays as invalid or excessive. Even as the theatre displays the excesses of fashion that audiences clamour for, it registers discomfort about its own complicity with the market. At the same time as it begins to understand itself to be a fashionable commodity, it seeks to reject that status and to validate its own authenticity via its capacity to recognise the theatrical forms that need to be disowned.

CHAPTER FOUR

The place of dirt

PLAYS AT WAR

Numerous contemporary satirists, both inside and outside the theatre, comment on the necessary link between satire and the city. Everard Guilpin's Satire v, for example, begins with a plea for the solitary calm of enclosure in the study: 'Let me alone I prithee in this cell, / Entice me not into the city's hell; (lines 1–2; *Skialetheia*, p. 82). But the plea is undercut by the tension in the next line: 'Tempt me not forth this Eden of content'. As the satire proceeds, it becomes ever clearer that the study does not in fact produce content, but a state of restless desire, forever struggling to resist the temptation of the world outside. Even in describing the pleasures of the study, the satirist is in fact describing the pleasures of the city as medi-ated through books. In place of real walks to Westminster or real visits to playhouses, the study offers imaginary ones. The study is the poet's sub-stitute for the city, his 'Exchange' (i.e. Royal Exchange; line 24). All the energy of the satire pours into the description of what is supposedly rejected: the city, with its bawds, porters, car-men, whores, beadles, sergeants and its many variations on the role of 'Don Fashion' (line 126).

The tendency to pile up objects of contempt in tumbling sequence is characteristic of the genre and registers the seeming justification for satire. If abuses are as rife and varied as they are in the city, how can satire be avoided?

> For whose gall is't that would not overflow,
> To meet in every street where he shall go,
> With folly masked in divers semblances?
> The city is the map of vanities,
> The mart of fools, the magazine of gulls,
> The painter's shop of antics.   (lines 63–8)

The justification has classical origins, as indicated, for example, by the opening lines of *2 Return from Parnassus*: '*Difficile est, Satyram non scribere, nam quis iniquae / Tam patiens urbis, tam ferreus ut teneat se?*' (lines 84–5).[1] Ingenioso is reading and quoting from Juvenal's first satire. Translated, the Latin means 'It is hard not to write satire, for who could be so tolerant of the wicked city, so iron-willed as to hold himself back?' Thus the Elizabethan satirist claims classical authority, justifies the violence of his writing as an unavoidable necessity and identifies the city as the environment producing this necessity.

The beginning of the vogue for satire in the theatre is often dated quite specifically to 1599, the year in which Archbishop Whitgift imposed a ban on printed satire and called in numerous existing printed satires for burning. The ban on publishing satire, it is argued, produced a shift to the theatres, where satire could be performed without infringing the ban. The signs of a theatrical interest in satire, however, were there before 1599. Not only Shakespeare's *Love's Labour's Lost* (*c.* 1595), but also Chapman's *An Humorous Day's Mirth* (1597) and Jonson's *The Case Is Altered* (1597–8) and *Every Man In His Humour* (1598) predate the so-called point of origin. The Admiral's Men began the vogue for humours comedy with *An Humorous Day's Mirth*, performed at the Rose. Little is known about the first performance of *The Case Is Altered* other than that Jonson sold it to Henslowe,[2] but *Every Man In* was written for the Lord Chamberlain's Men and performed in a public theatre (the Curtain), and *Love's Labour's Lost* (also a Chamberlain's Men's play), as discussed in chapter 3 above, was probably in the public theatres by 1598, if not before. The spread of the fashion for satire across several theatrical companies was encouraged by playing conditions around 1599–1600, a time remarkable for the conspicuous newness and competitiveness of several theatres, as suggested in chapter 3 above. First, the timbers of the old Theatre were taken down and transported across the Thames to build the Globe in the winter of 1598–9; by the end of 1599 Paul's Boys had probably reopened (see chapter 3, n14 above); by 1600 the Chapel Children had reopened in a new building at the Blackfriars; and in the same year the Admiral's Men opened at a new playhouse, the Fortune, in an attempt to fight the competition of these other new theatres. The conditions were right for the development of a new, fashionable drama at new, fashionable theatres, and some of those dramatists who were to become well known for satirical writing developed ties with the re-established children's companies at this point: Marston wrote for Paul's Boys from the time they reopened in 1599; Jonson began to write for the Chapel Children on their reopening; and Dekker moved from a long association with the Admiral's Men to write for Paul's Boys in 1601.

This context may begin to explain why satire emerged in theatre at precisely the time it did, but does not explain why satire, theatrical or otherwise, should be so closely associated with the city, which is central to verse satire of the 1590s and becomes an increasingly conspicuous presence in dramatic satire from the turn of the century. As chapter 3 above suggests, the London location is crucial in establishing the tone of Jonson's *Every Man Out Of His Humour*. Clove's display of fustian is recognisable as satire at least partly because it is spoken in the middle aisle of St Paul's. *Every Man Out* is still unusual at this stage amongst the other poetomachia plays in insisting on an urban setting so exact and explicit, but the other plays of the 'war' share its subtle and developed sense of social class and social setting without its specificity of location, and both point in the direction of theatre fashion for the next decade, which brings city comedy to prominence.

Why, then, is the city so important to satire? The question may be approached via comparison with another literary genre, that of pastoral. As Raymond Williams has shown, the key to understanding a pastoral structure of feeling is the contrast between the country on the one hand and the city and court on the other, a contrast which depends on 'the suppression of work in the countryside, and of the property relations through which this work is organised' (*Country and the City*, p. 46). The same binary construction permits analysis of a satiric structure of feeling, which homes in on everything that pastoral rejects in its conception of the country, and attributes it to the city. A city environment, Williams argues, merely makes blatant economic and social processes that are occluded in a pastoral setting. It is because those processes, which underpin society as a whole, are so concentrated in a city environment that they seem specific to that environment. In fact, it is merely a question of visibility. What the satirist sees is 'dirt' that the pastoralist does not wish to see; and dirt is most recognisably dirt in the city.[3]

Particular circumstances also combined to heighten the visibility of economic and social processes in late sixteenth-century London. The population of Elizabethan London was expanding at great speed, and images of dirt and disease are recurrent in descriptions of the city's growth (see chapter 1, pp. 21–3, including note 2, above). This growth, as discussed in chapter 1 above, was also putting traditional understandings of social hierarchy under pressure. Falling from, or pushing into, one class or another was registered by many writers as increasingly common, and establishing the boundaries of social class was accordingly vexed and problematic. Verse satire, when it first appeared in the 1590s, was particularly associated with the Inns of Court, an environment that had experienced the characteristic Elizabethan expansion especially strongly, with admissions growing by 30 per cent in the final quarter of the sixteenth century and forcing considerable building and renovation amongst the Inns. Though the residents of the Inns remained predominantly the landed classes, the wealthier members of the citizen and yeoman classes were beginning to send their sons to be educated there.[4]

Geographically located between the city and the court, and socially more fluid than previously, the Inns produced young men fitted for a future in either court or city or a return to landed rural wealth. Sir John Fortescue said the Inns were called Inns of Court 'because the students in them, did there, not only study the laws, but use such other exercises as might make them the more serviceable to the king's court' (Finkelpearl, *John Marston*, p. 3); but in many ways a double affiliation to city as well as court was more characteristic of their culture. The model of learning was a cross between a university and a city company: though the mode of residence resembled that of a university, there were no fellows or teachers. The 'students' were in a position analogous to that of apprentices to the older qualified members, who were all practising lawyers with an additional obligation to provide tuition. Even the Inns' Christmas revels showed them looking towards both court and city, demonstrating how firmly their London location differentiated them from students at either of the two universities. While the students of St John's College, Cambridge, for example, performed *2 Return to Parnassus* privately inside the college over the Christmas of 1601–2, the Gray's Inn revels of Christmas 1594–5 included a mock royal progress from Chancery Lane to Bishopsgate Street ending with dinner at the lord mayor's house (4 January); a triumphal ride through the city on the return of the Prince of the revels, following the standard royal-entry route from the Tower to Ludgate and pausing, as Queen Elizabeth had done in 1559 and as King James was to do in 1604, for an oration by one of the children of St Paul's School (4 February); and a concluding Shrovetide masque performed at court. Rather than representing the community of Gray's Inn as a private and enclosed one, the revels took that privileged little world out into the city and the court and acted out its relations with both.[5] The environment of the Inns was a limited world self-consciously at a social crossroads, a world that cultivated amongst its students 'a sense of belonging to an elite of wits in a world of gulls' (Finkelpearl, *John Marston*, p. 73). Inns of Court men sneered; but were as likely to sneer at courtly affectation as at citizen values. Disaffection, almost regardless of the target, was the hallmark of their sense of superiority.

The War of the Theatres plays were also associated with this environment in several ways. One of the new theatres, the Blackfriars, was next door to the Temple, the location of two of the Inns of Court, and both the children's theatres were particularly likely to attract an audience with a large Inns of Court component on account of their exclusive pricing policy as well as their western location. Two of the dramatists involved also had links with the Inns: Marston was a member of the Middle Temple, while Jonson associated with a group of Inns men and dedicated *Every Man Out Of His Humour* to 'the noblest nurseries of humanity, and liberty, in the kingdom: the Inns of Court'. Marston's decision to write professionally for the theatre to some extent enacts the ambivalent placing of the Inns at this time. It was, as Finkelpearl points out, unprecedented for a well-born and wealthy young man to make such a career move. His choice demonstrates the degree of fluidity in a social situation where city and court were both active, and indeed interactive, factors.

The city's dirt seems to have been especially visible as such to Inns of Court men, perhaps because of their special position both inside and outside the city. The war plays show the same fascination as the earlier verse satires with exposing excesses and abuses through images that define the practices in question as a kind of dirt. This is true of the focus on fashionable language, which is represented in the plays as conspicuously material, almost object-like (see chapter 3 above). Underpinning this representation of fashionable language as thick and physical is an implied notion of a pure language, which has to be, by contrast, invisible, or transparent. In the implied pure language, sound and sense are one, and words mediate meaning without obtruding their own presence. Dirty language, by contrast, is insistently present, privileging sound over sense, composed of grotesque or distorted fragments that are often literally alien (made up from borrowed bits of foreign languages). The implied polarity is between a language of the mind and a language of the body.

This polarity can be seen emerging in the earliest of the plays in this group, in Juniper's interaction with other characters in *The Case Is Altered*. Juniper cultivates a language so absurd that no one understands him. Valentine challenges his use of the word 'hieroglyphic', and asks him directly what it means. Jonson's disapproval of the severance of sound from meaning in such strained speech is audible in Juniper's reply, consciously manufactured to foreground this split: 'Mean? God's so, is't not a good word, man? What? Stand upon meaning with your friends. Puh, *absconde*' (1.iv.7–8).[6] Valentine is mocked by both form and content: Juniper not only dismisses his concern for meaning but does so in Latin. When Valentine again comments on Juniper's strange language, it is to the audience: 'Oh how pitifully are these words forced. As though they were pumped out on's belly' (lines 15–16). The image directly associates this densely material and extravagant language with the body, and in particular with the body's ejected dirt.

It is an image Jonson returns to memorably and climactically in the prolonged final scene of *Poetaster*, which fashions a staged gestus out of the image of the pumping belly. A pill is administered to Crispinus (Marston) that makes him vomit up each of his ridiculous words in turn into a basin, allowing the onlookers to note and repeat it. Latinate words are tumbled together with vernacular nonsense as Crispinus vomits up anything from 'glibbery – lubrical – defunct' to 'quaking custard' (v.iii.426, 474) over a stretch of about a hundred lines. Jonson here invents the perfect device for holding the pleasures of excess and the morality of its disempowerment in tension: he milks the gestus for maximum effect over a prolonged period of stage-time and at the same time positions the audience to disapprove of the same verbal absurdities that entertain them. The sheer length of the event, furthermore, allows the pleasures of excess to verge on punishment for the audience.

Predictably, but also pleasurably, the vocabulary is made to comment on its own faultiness – and bodiliness:

> CRISPINUS. O – 'barmy froth' –
> CAESAR. What's that?
> CRISPINUS. – 'Puffy' – 'inflate' – 'turgidous' – 'ventositous'.
> HORACE. 'Barmy froth', 'puffy', 'inflate', 'turgidous' and
>   'ventositous' are come up.
> TIBULLUS. Oh, terrible, windy words!
> GALLUS. A sign of a windy brain.   (lines 446–52)

Even in the single word 'windy', Jonson manages to combine both a joke and a judgement. Windy words are a joke about different kinds of wind (breathing and farting), but the body releasing its waste also functions here as an image of moral condemnation rejecting the same windy words from which Jonson has gained so much theatrical mileage. Jonson made the same moral judgement explicit, speaking in his own person in his *Discoveries*: 'Wheresoever, manners, and fashions are corrupted, language is. It imitates the public riot. The excess of feasts, and apparel, are the notes of a sick state; and the wantonness of language, of a sick mind' (Herford and Simpson, ed., *Ben Jonson*, vol. VIII, p. 593). Like the justification for satire that *2 Return from Parnassus* quotes from Juvenal, this piece of moralising also has classical precedent. As Tom Cain notes, citing the passage from *Discoveries* above, it is translated from Seneca, whose account of the 'hunt for novelties in speech' could stand as a summary of precisely the kind of speech that the War of the Theatres ridicules: 'now it summons and displays obsolete or old-fashioned words; now it coins even unknown words or misshapes them; and now a bold and frequent metaphorical usage is made a special feature of style' (introduction to *Poetaster*, pp. 25–6).

Jonson's determination to have it both ways, to give stage time and space to verbal absurdities at the same time as condemning them, is characteristic of the satirist's position. By definition satire depicts what it rejects and wallows in the very dirt it exposes. Even the recurrent, self-congratulatory image of the satirist as healer not only ties the satirist again to the image of the body, but makes him responsible for forcing the body to release its corrupted fluids. Satire, in fact, typically depends on a divided conception of the body. On the one hand, the naked body must be understood to represent truth, and satirists typically depict themselves as peeling off the outer layers (of clothes, cosmetics, affectations, hypocrisies, and so on) to reveal the 'truth' of the unmasked body. On the other hand, however, the wounded, infected or discharging body is a central metaphor for the individual or the state in all its imperfections. Given that all the energy of satire is concentrated on what is exposed as imperfect, the tainted body is much more prominent in the satiric genre than the imagined, referential body of unadorned truth, and its prominence affects the image of the satirist. Ingenioso's expression of approval for the satiric healer, for example, exposes the contradiction (the quotation follows on immediately from his citation of Juvenal, quoted above):

> Ay, Juvenal: thy jerking hand is good,
> Not gently laying on, but fetching blood;
> So, surgeon-like, thou dost with cutting heal,
> Where nought but lancing can the wound avail.
> (*2 Return from Parnassus*, lines 86–9)

The healing surgeon may be the technical centre of the image, but the language dwells on the violence of 'jerking', 'cutting' and 'lancing' and fetishises the open and discharging body.[7]

Marston's pseudonym in *The Scourge of Villainy*, one of the verse satires called in for burning following the condemnation of 1599, is Don Kinsayder, and Marston published several early poems under the name of 'W. Kinsayder'. The name 'Kinsayder' puns on 'Mar-stone', and means 'one who castrates stray dogs'.[8] Like the image of the physician, this associates the satirist with the body, but takes the potential damage of the association further by virtue of the fact that the body in question here is a dog's. Satiric playwrights responding to one another's plays in the War of the Theatres, however, recognise the satirist's kinship with the objects of his abuse when they turn images of the body against other satirists. Hence Don Kinsayder is addressed in *2 Return from Parnassus* as a pissing dog rather than a castrater of dogs: 'What Monsieur Kinsayder, lifting up your leg and pissing against the world? Put up man, put up for shame' (lines 267–8). Marston himself, furthermore, registers awareness of the possible reversal of dog and dog catcher in 'The Author in Praise of his Precedent Poem', a piece of verse introducing *Certain Satires*, where he portrays the satirist via the image of a dog:

> Thus having rail'd against my self a while,
> I'll snarl at those, which do the world beguile
> With masked shows. Ye changing Proteans list,
> And tremble at a barking satirist.
> (lines 43–6; *The Poems of John Marston*, p. 66)

The word 'cynic' is also derived from the Greek *kunikos* (dog-like, currish), as Marston may have been aware.

Picturing the satirist venting open abuse as a dog pissing in a public place conveys ironic recognition of the satirist as complicit with the objects of his abuse: in attacking practices he conceives as dirt, the satirist displays the extent to which he is imbued with the characteristics of what he condemns. Indeed the work of constructing the objects condemned as dirt, mess or trash is precisely effected by the material language of the satire that inveighs against them. Horace, Jonson's spokesman for clear-sighted rejection of others' excesses in *Poetaster*, is made to express his rejection not in moderate or reasonable terms but with the violent excess of the satirist. Trapped by the unstoppable verbiage of Crispinus, the speaker who is later made to vomit up his excesses in front of the audience, Horace expresses furious outrage:

> Death! I must crave his leave to piss anon;
> Or that I may go hence with half my teeth:

I am in some such fear. This tyranny
Is strange, to take mine ears up by commission,
Whether I will or no, and make them stalls
To his lewd solecisms, and worded trash. (*Poetaster*, III.i.91–6)

There is a symmetry about this satiric construction whereby one excess meets another excess and the first excess is brought into being as 'trash' by the virulent 'trashing' of the second. The very fact that Horace speaks of the need to piss yokes his language with the bodily language the play seeks to outlaw. It is as though he cannot construct Crispinus' speech as physical waste matter without bringing his own bodily functions into his speech. Thus the satirist, whether speaking publicly of the need to piss or categorised by others as a pissing dog, demonstrates his complicity with those who vomit their trash in the same openly offensive way. Pissing and vomiting as visible urban practices and as functions of the satiric speaker are co-dependent. They interact to defile public space.

The language of satiric abuse does not need to speak directly of the gutter in order to resemble the language it attacks. Its stylistic modes are rhetorically similar with or without the shared bodily content. The satirist, like the *flâneur*-figure he satirises, accumulates words and phrases, revels in the sound and materiality of words, distorts and alienates his language. Immediately following Judicio's attack on Monsieur Kinsayder as a pissing dog in *2 Return from Parnassus*, Ingenioso offers this description of Judicio's characteristic verbal style:

Methinks he is a ruffian in his style,
Withouten bands or garter's ornament.
He quaffs a cup of Frenchman's Helicon,
Then royster doyster in his oily terms,
Cuts, thrusts, and foins at whomsoever he meets
And strews about Ram Alley meditations. (lines 269–74)[9]

The description, especially with its reference to the 'cup of Frenchman's Helicon', is not so different from other descriptions of how fashionably affected speakers carry on. The rough tone singles out the satirist (as 'ruffian')[10] from other verbal showmen, but many of the features of his vocabulary are comparable with those of other affected styles.

D. Allen Carroll, drawing on an Elizabethan wordplay, describes satire as 'a grab bag, *sated* with *ire* . . . in which are collected the satirist's effects, loosely thrown together' (introduction to Guilpin, *Skialetheia*, p. 24). Carroll is writing on verse satire, but the same principle holds true for these dramatic satires, which are very loosely plotted and similarly 'stuffed' with a variety of objects of abuse. The fragmentedness that is

so frowned on in fashionable characters and their speeches (see chapter
3 above) is also part of the satiric mode itself. So too, ironically, is the
concern for fashion. The satirist rails against fashion, but railing itself is
thereby made a fashion. The plays demonstrate awareness of this
paradox, as they demonstrate awareness of other features the satirist
shares with his targets. When Lampatho Doria, in *What You Will*, denies
the charge of railing, for example, Quadratus comments drily: "tis now
grown fashion; / What's out of railing's out of fashion' (ii.i.580–1). And
though Lampatho Doria denies the charge here, he acknowledges the
fashionability of railing later in the play:

> This is the strain that chokes the theatres,
> That makes them crack with full-stuff'd audience.
> This is your humour only in request,
> Forsooth to rail; this brings your ears to bed,
> This people gape for; for this some do stare;
> This some would hear, to crack the author's neck;
> This admiration and applause pursues.
> Who cannot rail? (iii.ii.1142–9)

As late as 1606, the induction to John Day's *Isle of Gulls*, a satire on the
court, registers the continuing popularity of railing. 'But what method
observes he in his play', a gentleman asks of the Prologue, 'is't any thing
critical? Are lawyers' fees, and citizens' wives laid open in it: I love to
hear vice anatomised, and abuse let blood in the master vein' (lines 52–5).
And a year or two later, Heywood is savage in his condemnation of this
same 'railing' (also his term), condemning 'the liberty, which some arro-
gate to themselves, committing their bitterness, and liberal invectives
against all estates, to the mouths of children, supposing their juniority to
be a privilege for any railing, be it never so violent'.[11] Railing, like any
other fashionable speech, as the theatre best knows, is yet another
'humour' available to be staged on demand.

The placing of this puncturing self-awareness is important to the
effects of these plays. Quadratus' comment on the fashionability of
Lampatho's discourse follows on one of Lampatho's more hysterical
outbursts of righteous self-justification:

> Dirt upon dirt, fear is beneath my shoe;
> Dreadless of racks, strappados, or the sword,
> Maugre informer and sly intelligence,
> I'll stand as confident as Hercules,
> And with a frightless resolution
> Rip up and lance our time's impieties. (iii.ii.1121–6)

As elsewhere, the fetishistic focus on 'dirt' and the thick, excessive language show the satirist's complicity with the *flâneur*. The distancing effect of Quadratus' remark merely confirms what the excesses of Lampatho's speech already reveal.

This perspective coexists uneasily with the satirist's claim to singular superiority, the position embraced by the content, if not the texture, of Lampatho's words. Despite its intermittent recognition of underlying parallels between the satirist and his objects, satire constructs a polarity of 'above' and 'below', which seeks to remove the satirist from the mire of the city. This is evident, for example, in the 'apologetical dialogue' appended to the Folio text of *Poetaster*, where the persona of 'the Author' claims a position of superior isolation, distances himself from the excesses of the city and heaps scorn on 'the stuff'd nostrils of the drunken rout' who approve the 'base, and beggarly conceipts' of his contemporaries (lines 205–8). The printed text is itself at pains to emphasise the singularity of the apologetical dialogue: it was, the printed address to the reader tells us, 'only once spoken upon the stage'.[12] This highlighted, 'once-only' quality appropriately mimics the exclusivity of the authorial persona who speaks. Like those in *Love's Labour's Lost* who seek to be 'singled from the barbarous', he proudly calls attention to his cultivated isolation from the crowd: 'if I prove the pleasure but of one, / So he judicious be; He shall b'alone / A theatre unto me' (lines 226–8). Asked by Polyposus to answer the libels of his detractors, his position is insistently absolute and uncompromising:

AUTHOR. No.
POLYPOSUS. Nor the untrussers?
AUTHOR.   Neither.
POLYPOSUS.   You are undone then.
AUTHOR. With whom?
POLYPOSUS.   The world.
AUTHOR.   The bawd!   (lines 152–3)

Yet the audience is positioned paradoxically, since it knows, as Jonson knows, that the play was specifically written to answer the slanders of the world (in the shape of his fellow-dramatists). Though 'the Author' claims lofty isolation, Jonson is really 'down there' in the city dirt he claims to transcend. The very terminology that separates the author from 'the world' is a visibly necessary fabrication on the part of the persona. Even as *Poetaster* abuses the writing of Jonson's fellow-dramatists as 'beggarly, and barren trash' written to 'tickle base vulgar ears' (v.iii.357–8), the audience knows that this play too is part of that same specific theatre culture, where one dramatist gets laughs at another's expense. For the audience, the pleasure seems to lie in holding that knowledge in tension with the satisfaction of engaging with the excessive terms in which an impossibly complete individuality is expressed.

This is so even when those excessive terms take the form of abusing the audience, a speciality of satire. Satire condemns its audiences not just by implicating them in the behaviours it condemns, but more directly, for wanting this fashionable railing at all. This is again a feature of verse satire as well as plays. Everard Guilpin's epigram, 'Of a railing humour', mocks its readers for craving abuse:

> (Good Lord) that men should have such kennel wits
> To think so well of a scald[13] railing vein,
> Which soon is vented in beslavered writs,
> As when the colic in the guts doth strain,
> With civil conflicts in the same embrac'd.
> But let a fart, and then the worst is past. (*Skialetheia*, pp. 40–1)

Reading satire, the epigram implies, is taking pleasure in other people's farts. The audience, then, is made as complicit with the satirist as the satirist is with the objects of his abuse.

Plays also play games with different audiences (the paying audience and the licensing authorities) by carrying statements that blame the audience for 'falsely' wrenching topical applications out of supposedly innocent material. According to Virgil, prime spokesman for moral authority in *Poetaster*, it is irresponsible audiences, not satirists, who endanger the body politic:

> 'Tis not the wholesome sharp morality,
> Or modest anger of a satiric spirit[14]
> That hurts, or wounds the body of a state;
> But the sinister application
> Of the malicious, ignorant, and base
> Interpreter: who will distort, and strain
> The general scope and purpose of an author
> To his particular, and private spleen. (v.iii.118–25)

Again the trope of the body is evident in negotiating the relationship between satire and its object, but here the negative connotations of 'spleen' are projected on to the audience. The body politic is here in the process of definition by way of a discourse that seeks to exclude 'malicious, ignorant, and base / Interpreter[s]' from the body that is in need of protection. Yet the definition is highly unstable, since it is based on a set of binaries that depend on each other rather than on any point of reference outside the discourse. Wholesome morality is defined only by its opposition to sinister application, speaking in the public interest only by its opposition to private spleen. What emerges from the speech is less a definition of the state than an indication of how powerful the need to set up such an opposition is.

This is because membership of the body politic is conceived not as natural or necessary but as selective and conditional. Jonson wants to define the state in such a way as to exclude its 'dirt'. So too does Marston, whose condemnation of the state of Venice in *What You Will* as 'young, loose and unknit', relishing 'naught, but luscious vanities' (II.ii.916–17), implies a possible state not so disordered, and explicitly names the disorder as 'dirt' (line 920). The satirist's need to divide the body in two to provide tropes of both purity and dirt is symptomatic of his engagement with a dual image of the body politic, as either healthy or infected. Nor are satirists alone in seeking to construct the state according to this binary of health and infection. The strategy is precisely analogous to the move implicit in contemporary official discourses of the city, which attempted to insist on fixed boundaries while demonising all that lay outside them (masterless men, unruly suburbs and so on). But part of the strategy here is a refusal of the term 'city'. The terms 'state' and 'body politic' represent an attempt to come to terms with the messy and difficult city by endowing it with the coolness and neutrality of 'universal' terminology and excluding its materiality. The abstract vocabulary of political theory seeks to remove the notion of civil society from its local habitation and name, as does the historical and geographical removal to ancient Rome. It allows the conception of the public good to be removed from the very material public space in which dogs piss and turgid speakers vomit their waste matter.

Jonson, most conspicuously among these dramatists, makes a bid to be free of the shaping discursive interaction between the satirist and the dirt of the city. One of his strategies is to try to insist on a distinction between the true and the false poet. He always prefers to describe his own function, even in dramatic works, as that of a poet. While 'poet' is the routine term for 'playwright' in the period, Jonson goes out of his way to create a distance between the 'poet' and the mere hack dramatist. His depiction of Anthony Munday as the city pageant-poet Balladino in *The Case Is Altered* shows a writer determined to write whatever will bring in the money, regardless of its artistic merit, while the scene between Captain Tucca and the player in *Poetaster* (III.iv) is used as an opportunity to run down various hacks who will fill an actor's mouth with rant for forty shillings. His extraordinary decision to publish his works in folio, and to include plays under the term 'works', are indications of this same attempt to rehabilitate, or authenticate, plays (commonly regarded, in Sir Thomas Bodley's phrase, as 'riff-raffs') as 'true' works of art. There is evidently an on-going project here to rehabilitate some drama (his own) as art, by way of setting it against another drama portrayed as trash. 'True' poets and 'true' art cannot be made to be recognisable without 'false' counterparts against which to measure them.

Both *Every Man In His Humour* and *Cynthia's Revels* present sons who seek to be poets in the face of their fathers' disapproval, while the corrective figures in all Jonson's plays within the group examined in this chapter either know how to value true poetry or write it themselves. The title of *Poetaster* highlights this concern as its dominant subject. No fewer than eight of the characters are poets (Barton, *Ben Jonson*, p. 81), and the various plots all return to the subject of poetry. Central to the definition of the true poet for Jonson is the question of his relation to the state. Ovid's choice of a poetic career is carefully positioned in opposition to his father's choice for him of a career in law. This opposition is not set up to suggest that the poet should detach himself from matters of state, but rather to suggest that the state is more in need of poets than of lawyers, provided that 'true difference' is established "twixt those jaded wits / That run a broken pace for common hire, / And the high raptures of a happy muse' (i.ii.213–15). The 'false' poets, naturally, must be recognised and rejected so that the 'true' poets can be elevated to their rightful role at the centre of government. Three poets, Ovid, Horace and Virgil, present themselves as candidates for the category of true poet. Ovid's status is high at the point where he recites over forty lines of classical lyric verse in English translation at the end of the first scene (i.i.39–80), but drops when he becomes too closely associated with vulgar citizen-types and is lured into licentious dramatic revels. Play-acting is here presented as licensing its participants to indulge in folly, seduction and oath-breaking (iv.v.10–37). And this denunciation of theatre as frivolous at best, degrading and potentially treasonous at worst, is of a piece with the extraneous scene that brings together Captain Tucca and a player (iii.iv) at least partly in order to create space for Tucca to address the player in an on-going stream of abusive terms ('player, rogue, stalker . . . twopenny tear-mouth . . . stinkard . . . slave', etc.). Lurking in here is a radical discomfort with theatre, a fear that plays are by definition 'false', or inauthentic, poetry.[15] Ovid is a true poet as long as he is reciting lyric verse, but a false one when he turns to plays.

Horace is presented not as a lyric poet but as a satirist. Caesar's attitude towards Horace represents the ideal relationship between the governor and the true poet: he values Horace's honesty, indeed thanks him for his 'free, and wholesome sharpness' (v.i.94). Lupus, on the other hand, who accuses Horace of treason on the basis of having misinterpreted one of his emblems as a slur on Caesar, represents the ignorant multitude. Again the body politic is constructed as an exclusive alliance between elites, while the mass of citizens is dismissed as misguided and unnecessary, showing its true colours in cheap dramatic shows and fit only for banishment. On the other hand, as Tom Cain has noted, of the three poets Horace is the most firmly tied to the city: 'whereas Ovid recites alone, behind his philistine father's back, and Virgil reads in a formal, hieratic setting, Horace is first seen composing while walking through Rome' (introduction to *Poetaster*, p. 18). He is not, however, associated with foolish citizens, and his attachment to the city is mediated through his poetic activity, not through indulgence in trivial and characteristically urban pursuits. It is necessary, too, that the satiric poet should retain some kind of link to the city if he is to cleanse it of its filth. If the poet is to advise the governor on the purification of the body politic he cannot be cut off completely from that body, but must maintain an idealised relation to it which allows him to be identified with its civilised potential yet free of the taint of its excesses.

The third poet, Virgil, is depicted with extraordinary reverence in a way that distances him from the city proper but implies his authority over it. He appears only in the court, but is looked to by the whole court as one who restores harmony by inspiration rather than by direct intervention. His poetry represents the benchmark of what Ovid calls 'high raptures'; his poetic voice carries the note of authenticity by which other poets are to be judged false. A whole scene in Act v is given over to his public reading to the court from his *Aeneid* at Caesar's request and, at the Emperor's insistence, from Caesar's chair. The speech as printed takes up forty-three lines (v.ii.56–97), but the last line of the extract ends with an 'etc.', which leaves the length of the recitation unspecified.[16] The forty-odd lines here, then, are apparently a minimum, and the performer may have tacit licence to prolong the recitation as appropriate. The filling of dramatic time with extended recitations of verse is symptomatic of the dilemma of Jonson's drama. While from one angle these recitations represent a hijacking of theatre for poetry which seeks to idealise this kind of theatre as 'true', from another they look more simply like boring theatre. The distinction between 'true' and 'false' poetry (or theatre) is in constant danger of imploding: as soon as this theatre aspires to the condition of poetry by which it seeks legitimation it runs the risk of destroying its success as theatre. 'True difference', such as Ovid (and Jonson) want, is simply not available as a pre-existent or absolute index of value; like the opposition between wholesome morality and sinister application, it works only as a relational structure, fabricated by poets who need it.

Whether these plays are examined from the angle of the fashionable excesses they condemn (chapter 3 above) or from the angle of the satiric viewpoint of that condemnation (as here), the arguments point in the same direction, towards a theatrical impasse. Within the context of a wider anxiety about the changing relationship between court and city, the theatre worries about its own role inside that developing dynamic. The War of the Theatres represents an extended encounter with questions about the place of theatre in the city, often distorted into a shape that puts those questions in terms of the place of poetry in the ideal state. The morally and politically elevated role that Jonson claims for the poet in the ideal state is seen as inflated pretension by Marston and Dekker, who see Jonson and themselves as primarily city dramatists drawing on and constructing city fashions. Their own plays caricature poets who seek higher social roles. The very title of Dekker's *Satiromastix, or The Untrussing of the Humorous Poet* pointedly laughs at the solemn judgement of *Poetaster*, which warns Crispinus and Demetrius (caricatures of Marston and Dekker) against 'affecting the title of the untrussers, or whippers of the age' (v.iii.605). Jonson's attempt to cast them in the role of false poets to his true provokes a mischievous parody of the self-styled true in *Satiromastix*, which not only appropriates and remoulds the character of Jonson's Horace, but makes a fool of him by giving him Jonson's own lines to quote within a quite different play-world.

Yet it would be wrong to suggest that Jonson's self-righteousness provokes only good-humoured parody from Dekker; it also stimulates further excess, verbal dirt that besmears the dramatic enterprise of both parties. When Horace begins to utter the satirist's classic defence of his viciousness, citing his loathing for 'the general leprosy of sin', Tucca interrupts him with this version of what the self-righteous satirist really does: 'you did it ningle to play the bugbear satyr, and make a camp royal of fashionmongers quake at your paper bullets; you nasty tortoise, you and your itchy poetry break out like Christmas, but once a year, and then you keep a revelling, and arraigning, and a scratching of men's faces, as though you were Tiber the long-tailed prince of rats, do you?'

(*Satiromastix*, v.ii.199–206). Healing physician or 'bugbear satyr'? Wise counsellor or 'fashionmonger'? True poet or false showman? These are the polarities that shape the warring and playing of these uncertain, exploratory and highly fashionable plays.

CHAPTER FIVE

Placing the boundaries

THE KNIGHT OF THE BURNING PESTLE

As the seventeenth century moves on, theatre begins to satirise the city not merely as the location for occasional fashion-conscious excess, but more widely as a place that fosters charlatans, liars and frauds. Greedy shopkeepers, roguish apprentices and scheming gallants become the staple content of numerous comedies between 1600 and 1610. *The Knight of the Burning Pestle*, first staged at the second Blackfriars Theatre in 1607, takes a step beyond most citizen comedy in deciding to mock shopkeepers and apprentices for their very status rather than for any vices that might be associated with such status, and in doing so it also mocks those earlier plays like *Edward IV*, many of which were still popular at the Red Bull, that celebrate citizen values.

Even *The Knight of the Burning Pestle*, however, for all its sophisticated distance from the citizens it mocks, demonstrates serious concerns about the city and about relations between city, court and theatre. The play opens with a Prologue highlighting the symbolic importance of the city boundary:

> From all that's near the court, from all that's great
> Within the compass of the city-walls,
> We now have brought our scene –[1]

The precise meaning of these opening lines is ambiguous in print. Hattaway's punctuation suggests that the play brings its scene away both from all that's near the court and from all that's great within the city walls to another location (the liberty of the Blackfriars). Alternatively, since the Blackfriars was situated geographically within the city walls, the lines might be taken to mean that the movement is from all that's great (near the court) to a location within the city walls (see, for example, Andrew Gurr's punctuation in his edition of the play, which places a comma after 'great' instead of after 'city-walls'). Performance would no doubt have made this clear. Either way, however, it is evident that the opening lines centre on the distinction between the worlds within and without the walls and that it is the Prologue's allusion to this distinction that provokes the Citizen to intervene at this point.

Evidently much is at stake. Cities, as Braudel emphasises, want to be worlds apart, and their investment in marking and policing boundaries is enshrined in law and ritual as well as in the building of physical defences. Yet the boundaries are never as firmly fixed as cities want them to be, and individuals experience the spaces of city and not-city in ways that are more fluid than walls, laws and rituals might seem to indicate. As anyone who has ever played the game of standing with one foot on either side of a notional boundary knows, there is a fundamental arbitrariness about attempting to draw lines in space. Lines are for maps. Space, as Lefebvre's work highlights, is experienced socially, psychically and ideologically as well as physically. The play is centrally interested both in marking boundaries and in playing across them. Its teeming references to London and its environs are carefully insistent on the distinction between city and suburbs ('I believe thou hast not thy fellow within the walls of London; and I should say the suburbs too I should not lie' (II.39–40)), but its action repeatedly explores what it feels like to cross these arbitrary lines.

The location of the Blackfriars Theatre is crucially implicated in producing the meanings made by the play's negotiation of city limits. The Blackfriars district was a liberty on account of its former monastic status, which rendered it free of the jurisdiction of the city, despite being physically enclosed within its walls (see chapter 1 above). Though London's official discourse chose to construct the liberties as places of riot and disorder, the boltholes of those on the run from authority, the liberties need not be read in the city's terms. The official discourse may equally well be read as the city's attempt to purify its own self-conception. Though the city authorities demonised the liberties as riot zones, they knew very well that many of the participants in suburban riots had come from within the city limits.[2] If the liberties look like the interstices where the city's dirt collects, it is primarily because that is how the city, with its desire for clearly marked boundaries, wants them to look.

But to see them in this way is to fall for the city's rhetoric. In practice their status was much less clear-cut. Both city and state were looking to draw fixed boundaries and to identify, if possible visibly, those who put themselves beyond the pale. Schemes like badging the poor or branding criminals and vagabonds were attempts to make visible on the body the distinction between belonging and not belonging. But those who lived outside the boundaries of civic rule might include the exclusive as well as the excluded. And this was especially true of the Blackfriars. Whereas other theatrical locations outside full city jurisdiction were subject to county authority (the manors of Holywell and Finsbury, for example, were subject to the control of the Middlesex Justices of the Peace, while the Southwark liberties were under Surrey jurisdiction), there were apparently no officials in charge of order in the liberties of Blackfriars and Whitefriars. A Privy Council order of 1597 makes this clear in a reference to 'the said liberty of the Black and White Friars, which being grown more populous than heretofore and without any certain and known officer to keep good orders there, needeth to be reformed in that behalf'.[3] On occasions of disorder it would seem that the Privy Council, or someone delegated on its authority, was responsible for maintaining control.

These liberties were a safe haven not only for immigrants and vagabonds, but also for Puritans and other non-conformist groups to pursue their desired form of worship and, of course, for players to establish their theatres. And although certain kinds of discourse had vested interests in equating players with vagabonds, the London theatre companies were clearly not made up of vagabonds. Even within the boundary of the city the players could successfully defy its authority;[4] there is no better evidence for the ambiguous status of the liberty of the Blackfriars than the disputes concerning the theatre in its midst.

The Blackfriars Theatre stood in tense relation to both the city and the surrounding liberty. James Burbage's first plans for a playhouse in the Blackfriars in 1596 encountered protest from the residents. Interestingly, among the arguments marshalled against a playhouse in their petition to the Privy Council of November 1596 is the fear that it will lead to 'the great resort and gathering together of all manner of vagrant and lewd persons that, under colour of resorting to the plays, will come thither and work all manner of mischief'.[5] Clearly this is not the collective voice of a vagrant population, but rather the closing of middle- and upper-class ranks against the possible invasion of barbarian hordes. Among the signatories to the petition were Lady Russell, a Puritan; Stephen Egerton, a preacher; Richard Field, who published Shakespeare's poems; and George Carey, Lord Hunsdon, the new patron of Shakespeare's company following the death of his father, the lord chamberlain, in July 1596. (Unlike his father, who acted as guarantor of the safety of that player who refused to come at Recorder Fleetwood's command (see note 4 above), this Lord Hunsdon could not be relied upon to support the players.) The name of Lord Cobham, the newly appointed lord chamberlain, also a resident of Blackfriars, does not appear, since he was himself a member of the Privy Council (and in fact also specifically responsible for regulating playhouses) (Gurr, 'Money or Audiences', pp. 6–7).

The slipperiness in the use of the term 'liberty' (which might mean the freedom of or freedom from the city; see chapter 1 above) illustrates the distance between the city's desire for clearly marked boundaries and the contradictoriness of actual social practice. It represents an ideological clash between two different conceptions of what it meant to be free. The city, via the structure of the livery companies, effectively regulated the behaviour of its members by dangling before them the prospect of eventual 'free' status. Being 'free of' the city effectively meant accepting certain restrictions and controls in return for certain rights and privileges, some of which might turn out to be as burdensome in fact as the restraints. Only the elite of what the play knowingly refers to as 'the twelve companies of London' (II.200–1), for example, were eligible for the offices of alderman and mayor (see chapter 1 above), but these positions, while undoubtedly conferring high social status, could also bring financial ruin. Nevertheless, at least to the end of the sixteenth century, it would appear that civic freedom looked sufficiently attractive and sufficiently attainable, broadly speaking, to allow the companies to maintain their own particular style of hierarchical social order.[6]

By the first decade of the seventeenth century the ideology of community which had bound London so strongly through much of Elizabeth's reign was showing evident signs of strain, and the emphasis on the city wall as fixed boundary may be read as a sign of that strain rather than of real fixity. The practical overlap between city and not-city was becoming ever more visible. The city was trapped between unwillingness to have its authority compromised by the existence of the liberties within its very walls and unwillingness to take on the burden of responsibility that would fall on it if the liberties were to become fully incorporated into the city. As Valerie Pearl argues, 'its desire to act as a magistracy in the liberties with some supervisory control over the out-parishes did not imply a desire to exercise complete responsibility for preserving law and order there' (*London and the Outbreak of the Puritan Revolution*, p. 31). Hence the city was willing to pay a very high price indeed (the cost of King James' new banqueting hall) in order to secure jurisdiction over various areas, including the Blackfriars, granted to it by

James' second charter of 1608, but accepted the charter's preservation of certain privileges for the residents of these ancient liberties that distanced them from full incorporation into the city.[7] They were exempt from certain taxes and from serving in the lowliest offices of the ward, but were to be eligible for all the elite offices of the city.

The Knight of the Burning Pestle is not the only Blackfriars play to show a particular interest in the city limits in this decade, though it is the most insistent on the subject. Of the three *Ho* plays, all of which have plots centring on departure from and return to the city, *Westward Ho* (1604) and *Northward Ho* (1605) were both staged by Paul's Boys, and *Eastward Ho* (1605) by the Blackfriars Children. *Ram Alley* (Children of the King's Revels, Whitefriars, 1607–8), closely contemporary with *The Knight of the Burning Pestle*, is similar to *The Knight* not only in its compulsive interest in the distinction between city, suburbs and liberties, but in its repeated naming of London streets and districts. It is notable that all of these plays were performed by children's companies in 'private' playhouses. Whitefriars was a liberty (outside the walls, but inside the bars) incorporated into London at the same time as the Blackfriars, while the Paul's playhouse, also located in an ancient ecclesiastical liberty within the walls, would have stood in analogous relation to the city up to 1608, when the other two liberties were incorporated.

The date and place of performance of *The Knight of the Burning Pestle* situate the play right at the heart of this redefinition of the space called London. It speaks from within the Blackfriars just before that liberty is ambiguously incorporated into the jurisdiction of the city, and seems deliberately to stage the tensions between the city and the various different kinds of space that encroach upon it. It is utterly knowing about its own theatrical location; indeed it is precisely the interplay between the Blackfriars Theatre and the city of London that it wants to stage. The play is made up, as many critics have noted, of three interlinking plays, and all of them pointedly transgress significant boundaries. The play of *The London Merchant*, which the Prologue announces the intention to stage, centres on a polarity between London and not-London and is dominated by a tension between mobility and staying put. It opens with the eponymous merchant turning his apprentice Jasper out of the house for daring to love his daughter Luce. Luce, on the other hand, vows that she will only accept a man who is bold enough to steal her away from her home. Jasper's mother, meanwhile, jumping to the conclusion that Jasper has run away from his master, condemns him as a vagabond (1.343). When Jasper's father, Old Merrythought, gives him ten shillings to 'thrust [himself] into the world' (1.395–6), his mother simultaneously decides that she and her younger son Michael must leave home too if they wish to keep her savings out of the hands of her husband and elder son. Thus most of the characters in this plot end up 'some ten miles off, in the wild Waltham Forest' (II.59), while the two fathers remain safely within the city walls, the location to which the plot must finally return for resolution.

Rafe, apprentice-hero of the play the Citizens substitute for *The London Merchant*, gets out of London even faster than Jasper. Though Rafe is first shown, as the stage direction says, '*like a grocer in's shop*', this image of civic rootedness is immediately discarded in favour of a life of romance outside London. 'What brave spirit could be content to sit in his shop with a flappet of wood and a blue apron before him, selling mithridatum and dragon's water to visited houses, that might pursue feats of arms?' (1.248–51), Rafe asks rhetorically, and promptly shuts up shop. When he next appears the location is, yet again, Waltham Forest, or, more properly, 'Waltham Forest', the always-framed, impossible, outside space, perpetually in dialogue with the materiality of London and the Blackfriars Theatre.

The prologue's reference to the city is the trigger for both the second and the third play. If the second is Rafe's quest, the third is that of the Citizen and his Wife, who are so anxious to replace the Prologue's proposed play with the romance in which their apprentice Rafe stars. Theirs is yet another play staging the collision between London and not-London, and one which is located on the Blackfriars stage itself. As soon as the incomplete third line is out of the Prologue's mouth he is interrupted by a performer placed amongst the audience, playing 'a member of the noble city' (induction, 10), further identified as a freeman and a grocer (12–13). George, the Citizen, fears for the honour of the city and rightly distrusts the players' readiness to offer proper respect towards London. In place of a play on the potentially satiric topic of a merchant, he wants one on a fail-safe topic such as Dick Whittington or Sir Thomas Gresham. When this proposal is received mockingly by the Prologue, he and his wife Nell try to impose their will on the fiction by literally colonising the playing space. They not only transgress the boundary between audience and stage by climbing on to the stage, but invade the personal space of the gentlemen already seated on the stage by requiring them to 'make a little room' and even to get up and lend a hand to help the Wife up. George and Nell then demand their own stools, making clear their intention of continuing to occupy the stage-space, and order Rafe to come up with them. They intrude further, into the privacy of the tiring house, by asking for one of the players' costumes for Rafe, and can only be persuaded to sit down and stop interfering for a moment by the Prologue's agreement to bring the Southwark waits across the river to provide the music. Throughout the play they attempt to control the players' rights to the space, directing their entrances and exits so that Rafe is brought on as often as possible. ('Go thy ways, Rafe'; 'I prithee come again quickly, sweet Rafe' (I.301, 305, etc.)).

At the same time as they colonise the stage-space, however, they completely misunderstand its distinctive quality *as* stage-space, a space whose virtue is to be 'not there', but rather transformable into other, imaginary spaces. Instead they bring to it a mindset that never leaves the Blackfriars playhouse or the city that encircles it. For Nell, the Citizen's Wife, the boy-actors are always primarily London boys, and her instinct is to try to place them within a specific London location (St Paul's School): 'I pray you, brother, with your favour, were you never none of Master Monkester's scholars?' (I.96–7).[8] When Jasper exits with his mother's casket, Nell reminds her husband that 'here are a number of sufficient gentlemen can witness, and myself, and yourself, and the musicians, if we be called in question' (II.162–4). And when Jasper appears to threaten Luce's life, Nell urges her husband to send for the watch like a good London citizen (III.92–3). Meanwhile, Rafe, in the role of grocer errant, is laboriously explaining to his squire and dwarf the process by which theatre transforms actual space into imaginary space. All they have to do, he says, is 'call all forests and heaths "deserts"' (I.275–6).

The fact that this instruction is given while the stage still represents Rafe's shop confirms the foregrounding of the mechanics of representation. Space, the play emphasises, is occupied by minds as well as bodies, and the treatment of physical boundaries may call into question conceptual ones. The question that young Michael asks in *The London Merchant*, 'Is not all the world Mile End, mother?' (II.69), speaks for the collision in all three plays between London and not-London. Mile End was a mile beyond Aldgate, the easternmost of the seven gates in the city walls, and would have been familiar to Michael as the location for display battles by London's trained bands, such as the one the Citizen's Wife mentions between the English and 'the naughty Spaniels' in response to Michael's question (II.71–5) and the one she later calls for to conclude Rafe's deeds of honour: 'Rafe, I would have thee call all the youths together in battle-ray, with drums, and guns, and flags, and march to Mile End in pompous fashion' (V.57–9).[9]

The trained bands were regional armed forces that might be called upon both to defend the nation in time of war and to police local outbreaks of internal disorder, in the absence of either a standing army or a professional police force in Elizabethan or Jacobean England. Established by Elizabeth in 1573, at which time they had been summoned for training three times a year, they quickly became the butt of jokes during the first decade of James I's reign, when they were allowed to fall into abeyance until general musters were reinstated in 1612. Notably, mock battles were very much a feature of seventeenth-century, as opposed to Elizabethan, musters, and may suggest something of the emphasis on show as against real training in the later period. Certainly *The Knight of the Burning Pestle* is not the only Jacobean play to present the trained bands in derisory terms: *The Roaring Girl* (1611) also makes reference to 'a company of Mile End milksops' (II.i.190–1).[10]

Nevertheless, there is a more sinister aspect to this mockery too. Mile End, though geographically outside London, is the place where the city stages its forces of control. To mistake all the world for Mile End is to suppose that the controlling presence of the city is everywhere, even beyond the city. Michael's question is thus at one level yet another of the 'girds at citizens' (induction, 8) for which the Blackfriars was well known, a sneer at the kind of uncritical admiration for the city to be expected of a freeman's son, but it also speaks of the fear inspired by the encroaching city, seeking to extend its powers beyond its jurisdictional limits.

The play across the boundary between physical space and fictional space is closely linked to the anxiety around the boundary between London and not-London. The Citizens' crossing of the boundary between audience and stage is directly analogous to Jasper's move out of his master's household or Rafe's move out of his grocer's shop; and in each case the move is presented as a focus for anxiety. It is an anxiety that could be described as centring on people out of place. Each of the three sub-plays shows its protagonists moving away from the fixed point with which they are identified. Errancy is constructed as aberration, though the tone is mocking. Punishments vary from the trivial to the grotesque: the risks of travel range from getting chilblains to having to fight a giant. Even apparent rewards for the successful negotiation of risk are rejected in favour of the satisfactions of home: Rafe is stern in his rejection of the Lady Pompiona of Moldavia for Susan the cobbler's maid in Milk Street. The wonderfully comic and apparently irrelevant moment when Nell recalls how her child nearly drowned because it strayed alone to Puddle Wharf (11.344–9) becomes emblematic of the anxiety the play both mocks and displays.

What, then, is the cultural context for this anxiety about people out of place? Why does the play need to engage with questions of mobility and stability or, to put it another way, freedom and restraint? The question demands to be answered in relation to both national and local perspectives. Jasper's response to being banished from his master's household offers an insight into the wider context: Luce's love, he says, is 'all I have to keep me from the statute' (1.48). His loss of place is a source of worry not only because he now has no job and no place to live, but because the law of the land constructs such a position as deviant. As Michael Hattaway notes in his edition of the play, the reference to 'the statute' could be either to the Statute of Artificers of 1563, which required all young men to be apprenticed and specified imprisonment as the punishment for any that left their master's parish without licence, or to the Act against Vagabonds of 1572 (updated in 1597 and 1604) laying down even harsher penalties for masterless men (see chapter 1 above). As Roger Manning remarks, 'the law made little distinction between labour mobility and vagabondage' (*Village Revolts*, p. 159).

The savagery of the measures taken to control the problem of vagrancy is an indication of the level of anxiety the problem provoked, rather than of the 'true' size of the threat. Though the numbers of masterless men arrested and punished increased significantly in late Elizabethan and early Jacobean London, the fear in which they were held was out of all proportion to their numbers. There is no firm evidence for the existence of an organised underworld of masterless men speaking its own secret language and threatening to bring down the established social order, as presented in various plays and pamphlets of the time.[11] The literature of roguery tells us more about Elizabethan fears and fantasies than about actual social conditions. It was not really either numbers or practical dangers that made vagabonds the object of such anxiety, but rather the fact that they occupied a conceptual space *outside* the regulating structures of family, household and ward, while at the same time invading the physical territory of groups within those structures. The threat they offer is that of barbarians crossing over into civilised territory. While the city tries to define itself by excluding them, they insist on returning to haunt it.

Other statutes besides these two also attempted to keep people literally in their places of residence, as sumptuary law had long attempted to keep them in their social places. An act of 1593, for example, forbade recusants to go more than five miles from their place of abode without licence, while poor laws routinely ruled that poor relief should only be available to residents of the parish, sometimes with a minimum residence qualification. Those seeking poor relief outside their home parish were treated as vagrants and subject to the same penalties. The first concern of parish authorities was to return non-residents to their place of origin, and thus to protect and maintain the boundaries of existing communities defined precisely by their exclusion of the homeless 'hardcore poor'.[12] A statute of 1589 attempted to restrict the squatters' rights permitted by earlier law by requiring that cottages built on commons must have no more than one family in them and no less than four acres of land attached to them. Though enclosure acts strove to regulate or proscribe the practice of fencing off common space into individual properties, the general drift of legislation throughout the late Tudor and early Stuart period nevertheless underlines an attempt to insist on very clear boundaries. The law strengthened the rights of those within the enclosures it demarcated and in doing so provoked in turn those very behaviours it most feared. Enclosure riots were especially frequent in the two decades between 1590 and 1610, and the first performance of *The Knight of the Burning Pestle* probably took place within a few months of the Midland Revolt in the spring of 1607.[13]

Reference to civic controls, however, is far more frequent in the play than reference to the statutes of national government. Characters seem to think of calling the watch or a constable when any threat presents itself. The Citizen's Wife, as we have seen, wants to call the watch to Luce's aid when Jasper threatens her, and Luce herself teases Humphrey following his declaration of love by suggesting that she may need to 'send for a constable and raise the town' if Humphrey's 'strange passion' cannot be restrained (1.137–8). Her response in this vein, moreover, is prompted by the very terms in which Humphrey chooses to express his love. 'My valiant love', he claims, 'will batter down / Millions of constables, and put to flight / Even that great watch of Midsummer day at night' (1.139–41). The very language of love, it seems, is shaped by the forces of control within the city of London. And, like Michael's innocent question about Mile End, this language displays a real anxiety at the same time as it holds the speakers up to ridicule.

Humphrey's reference to the midsummer watch brings together images of celebration and control. The midsummer watch, as briefly discussed in chapter 1, had, like the Mile End musters, changed in status within living memory. During the course of the sixteenth century it had gradually come to be replaced by the more purely civic ceremony of the lord mayor's show. Midsummer rituals represented an older tradition: they incorporated religious and secular elements, including the military display of a 'marching watch'. According to Stow, the festival was cele- brated in its traditional form up to 1539, after which the 'marching watch' (the processional element) was suppressed, despite attempts to revive it in 1548 and 1585 (*Survey*, vol. I, pp. 101–4). A city government keen to repress the traditional disorderliness of carnival both reduced and appropriated carnival in this instance. On the one hand, the lord mayor's show, with its own elaborate procession, effectively took over the place formerly occupied by the midsummer festival, thus replacing popular festival with civic ceremonial, while, on the other hand, the increasing dominance of military show in the midsummer festivities reduced it to an occasion more closely resembling a general muster. Indeed as early as 1567 a certain William Pelham, lieutenant-general of the Ordance Office, was explicitly suggesting the substitution of military shows for traditional festivals: his plan was to finance a company of royal harquebusiers by substituting such training displays for the recognised entertainments of 'Robin Hood' and 'Midsummer lords and ladies' and charging the public to watch the training displays (Boynton, *Elizabethan Militia*, p. 59). Furthermore, the gradual combining of ritual military activity with so-called 'privy' watches (real action as opposed to show) against particular offenders at midsummer transformed the festival, ironically, into a training ground for policing itself.[14] In place of the world turned upside down the city put a display of the forces it could summon against such disorder.

But London's insistence on the display of its forces of control at mid- summer also highlights the particular problems of control that made such a display necessary.[15] Its conspicuous need for more emphatic self- definition through both law and pageantry suggests a mounting pressure on its boundaries. The most obvious and literal pressure on its space was that of population, and the tripling of London's population during the course of the sixteenth century, with most of that growth occurring during the Elizabethan period, created a double sense of people both pouring into the city and bursting out of it. That pressure on the bound- aries from both inside and outside the city stimulated a need to insist even more firmly on the distinctions that seemed to be in danger of col- lapsing, between the city, the liberties, the suburbs and the open spaces.

The double pressure inwards and outwards is echoed in the plot shapes of *The Knight of the Burning Pestle*. The tendency of each of its interwoven plots towards errancy, the crossing of boundaries and the negotiation of wild or unfamiliar spaces, has already been noted; but equally prominent is the drive to conclude each plot by returning to the safe point of departure. The closing in of space is almost suffocating in *The London Merchant*. Luce has to be not only fetched home to London by her father, but locked in, before the problems of her elopement can begin to be resolved. Jasper gets himself into Luce's house by enclosing himself in a coffin, then hides in Luce's closet while she is conveyed out of the house in the same coffin. The tighter the space, it seems, the closer to resolution. Parallel with the return of Jasper and Luce to the city is the return of Merrythought's wife and younger son. And they return home to find Merrythought again literally locked into his own house and forbidding them entry. The task they are required to perform to be allowed readmission is to sing a song; yet this is no festive release dissolving the anxieties of the play. Merrythought's own following song warns precisely against such release: 'You shall go no more a-maying' (v.226).

Rafe, whose return to London becomes the excuse for two ostentatious celebrations of the city, simultaneously problematises the traditional festive release of comedy. Though Rafe, as Lord of the May, invites his fellow-Londoners out a-maying to Hogsdon or Newington, the occasion is nevertheless dedicated to the 'honour of the city' (interlude iv.15). Their collective excursus from the city effectively takes the city with them, as they march out crying 'Hey for our town' (interlude iv.53). The second celebration of the city's honour presents Rafe as captain of the musters at Mile End, and is similarly displayed as an occasion which, again located outside the walls, shows the city imposing itself on the suburbs. Rafe's rousing speech to his men appropriates the discourse of Shakespeare's Henry V before Agincourt, except that it substitutes London for England. He addresses his soldiers as 'men, valiant men, and freemen' (v.140) in a transparent piece of rhetoric that clearly makes Rafe the unconscious vehicle for lampooning the climactic place of the city in this corporate self-definition. Required to stage the Mile End musters by Nell, the citizen-wife who so enthusiastically embraces the subject position offered by the hegemony of London, the play neatly calls attention to the conspicuously constructed quality of this image of civic glory.

Rafe's farewell, with its allusion to his own past participation in the traditional Shrove Tuesday apprentice riots, positions Rafe as a rioting apprentice, crossing the city limits to wreak havoc in the liberties:

Farewell, all you good boys in merry London;
Ne'er shall we more upon Shrove Tuesday meet
And pluck down houses of iniquity. (v.321–3)

It presents an image in outright contradiction to the preceding picture of Rafe as noble captain of the musters, trained to police exactly the kind of disorder he now admits to joining. Nell's position is similarly undercut: her complaint about the gentlemen smoking on stage gives way to her inviting the same gentlemen back to her house for wine and tobacco. This is the play's revenge on the city propaganda the Citizens have required it to stage. Rafe and the Citizens may have appeared to colonise the stage-space, just as the London authorities were poised to incorporate the Blackfriars, but the play disempowers them by exposing them as complicit with the transgressiveness they seek to police.

On the other hand, however, as with old Merrythought's song, these images are no simple emblems of a triumph for festive release. They also work in reverse, to expose apparent festive release as already-policed. Though the agents of control are made to look foolish, their involvement in the pleasures they condemn is in fact more sinister than their exclusion would be. The controlling city may be exposed as hypocritical, even ridiculous, but its framing authority nevertheless continues to push ever further beyond existing city limits. All the world, or at least the world around London, in a sense really is Mile End.

Finally, the play's reiterated exposure of the mechanisms of representation constructs a sceptical viewing position for the audience from which they see the actors more clearly than the characters. And the play, disliked as it was by its earliest audience, who may or may not have failed to note 'the privy mark of irony about it', as its first publisher claims they did, is a victory for actors. Though the actors play city characters who negotiate boundaries in different ways, they do not themselves speak from a space shared with the characters. Nor is this merely a matter of speaking from the liberty of the Blackfriars rather than the city of London. Geographical and jurisdictional space are finally made to give way to theatrical space. Though the play displays and examines different kinds of control, these controls are all subject to the control that the theatre has over the fiction it presents. Those who do the playing occupy a space that here celebrates its own freedom.

CHAPTER SIX

The place of accommodation

THE ROYAL ENTERTAINMENT AT THE NEW EXCHANGE

Between the court and the western boundary of the city's jurisdiction following the new charter of 1608 there were as yet no permanent the-atres;[1] but in 1609 a remarkable piece of theatre was staged at the New Exchange in the Strand. The New Exchange was the brainchild of Sir Robert Cecil, Earl of Salisbury, Secretary of State since 1596 and Lord Treasurer of England since the spring of 1608. (Arthur Wilson describes him as 'that great engine of the state, by whom all wheels moved' (*History of Great Britain*, p. 55.) As Sir Thomas Gresham had wished to monu-mentalise the city in a building worthy of its flourishing economic status, so the Earl of Salisbury wished to raise a monumental building in the city of Westminster. The rivalry between the two institutions was explicit from the outset. The lord mayor spoke on behalf of protesting shopkeepers in the Royal Exchange when he wrote to Cecil pointing out that the proposed new building would draw trade away from the city; and Cecil, while disclaiming any intention to damage the city's interests, expressed the wish to leave 'some such monument as may adorn the place, and haply derive some effect of present benefit and future charity to the whole liberty' in terms that echoed Gresham's own declared intent with regard to the Royal Exchange.[2] For both Gresham and Cecil, busi-ness interests were inextricably tied up with the more personal matter of reputation. Both stood to make a financial profit by their investment in these buildings, but both must also have expected to enhance their own present and future honour by giving their business interests architectural magnificence and quasi-charitable status.

The careers of both men show commercial and courtly interests coming together, though Gresham's roots are in the city, while Cecil's are at court. It is Cecil, however, whose project represents the more unfa-miliar phenomenon for the time. For the city to imitate the court was not

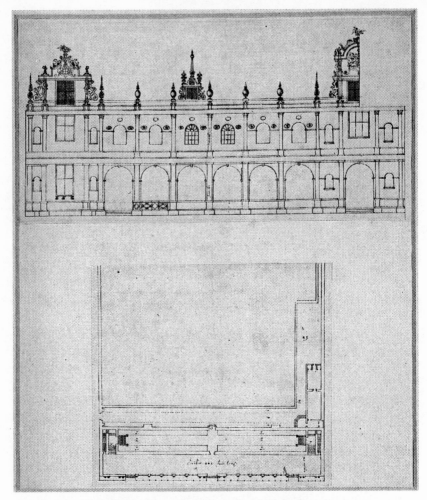

9. John Smythson's drawing of the New Exchange, *c.* 1618–19.

new; but the court's imitation of city enterprise did signal a new
dynamic. What is new about the New Exchange, as pointed out in
chapter 1 above, is its courtly location and connections; and it is precisely
the cachet of this unprecedented location, as the lord mayor recognises,
'being near unto the court of Whitehall in the midst of the nobility and
where much of the gentry lodge and reside as also in the highway by
which all termers pass to Westminster', that makes it such a threat to the
Royal Exchange in the city.[3] Cecil does not deny that his new building
will compete to some extent with the Royal Exchange; indeed rivalry

between the two institutions seems to have been widely recognised as implicit in the intention of the later undertaking. Arthur Wilson's *History of Great Britain*, published in 1653, summarises the move thus: 'The Lord Treasurer erected out of the rubbish of the old stables of Durham House, a goodly fabric, to be rival to the Old Exchange' (p. 48); while Stow's *Survey* notes the visible parallel in the design of the two buildings: 'Some shape of the modelling, though not in all respects alike, was after the fashion of the Royal Exchange in London, with sellers underneath, a walk fairly paved above it, and rows of shops above, as also one beneath answerable in manner to the other and intended for the like trades and mysteries' (Stow, *Survey*, 1633, p. 494).[4] The New Exchange, then, was to be like the Royal Exchange, but more fashionable.[5]

The building was erected on the site of Durham House, one of the few Strand palaces still occupied by a prelate, the Bishop of Durham. Most of the others had been taken over by members of the nobility following the Dissolution. Only York House stood between Durham House and Whitehall to the west, while the site was adjoined by Cecil's own recently constructed Salisbury House on the east. The New Exchange occupied the northern perimeter of the Durham House site, fronting on to the Strand and overlooking the outer court of Durham House from the rear. Like the Royal Exchange, the New Exchange consisted of a ground-floor arcade, which served as a meeting place for business, with shops above;[6] but where the Royal Exchange was built around a quadrangle, the New Exchange was a long narrow building resembling any one side of the older building and borrowing various elements of its design. Cecil employed the most fashionable craftsmen of the day to ensure a luxury building that would call attention to itself.[7]

Three features stand out in the Venetian ambassador's brief description of the New Exchange: its location, its magnificence and the huge profit it is likely to bring in. 'Hard by the Court', he reports, 'the Earl of Salisbury has built two great galleries, decorated, especially outside, with much carving and sculpture. Inside each of these galleries, on either hand, are rows of shops for the sale of all kinds of goods. These will bring in an immense revenue.'[8] The location and decoration were part of the design to appeal to a shopping elite, resident in the court, the Inns of Court and the fashionable houses beginning to spring up west of the city (see chapter 1 above). Everything possible was done to maintain that elegance. Strict regulations sought to control noise levels and unruly behaviour and to keep all unpleasantness out of view.[9] The shops did not in fact sell 'all kinds of goods'. Luxury and variety were cultivated only

10. Inigo Jones' unexecuted design for the New Exchange, 1608.

within exclusive parameters, and leases were restricted to traders in goods likely to attract a specifically high-class clientele. Most of the earliest leases went to milliners, linen-drapers and haberdashers. The leases were expensive, however, and take-up was slow. The 'immense revenue' projected by the Venetian ambassador, and presumably by Cecil himself (who spent £10,760 on the building, having already expended a large sum in acquiring the lease of the Durham House site; see Stone, 'Inigo Jones and the New Exchange', p. 118) failed to materialise. Less than one-third of the shops were occupied in the early months; finding new tenants when the leases ran out after eleven years proved even more difficult; and in 1627 a decision was taken to replace many of the shops with flats. It was not until the 1630s, well after Robert Cecil's death in 1612, that the shops really began to bring in significant profits (Stone, 'Inigo Jones and the New Exchange', pp. 116–19).[10]

All this was unforeseen, however, when Cecil invited the king and his family to a royal entertainment to name his new building in April 1609. This was prior to the Exchange opening for business, which did not take place until the summer. For the occasion of the king's visit Cecil, as the Venetian ambassador points out, 'fitted up one of the shops very beautifully' and erected above it the motto 'All other places give for money, here all is given for love'. The motto is as anomalous and multilayered as the fact of a royal entertainment in a shopping mall is in itself. At the same time as making explicit the relationship between elements whose apparent distance from one another it was normally ideologically necessary to insist upon (court and trade; gifts and purchases; patronage and the sale of services), it also tries to blur that explicitness with virtual denial. Evidently, this is precisely a place where all will be 'given' for money; it is on this occasion alone that gifts will be given 'for love'. And that 'love' is in any case economically determined, not only by virtue of being indistinguishable from self-interest (the minister must demonstrate his 'love' for his sovereign in order to maintain or advance his position), but by the fact that, in order to be satisfactorily displayed as 'love' at this elevated social level, it needs to be underpinned by serious money. The gifts that are given on this occasion are the climax of the spectacle, as the ambassador's account makes clear: 'To the King he gave a Cabinet, to the Queen a silver plaque of the Annunciation worth, they say, four thousand crowns. To the Prince he gave a horse's trappings of great value, nor was there any one of the Suite who did not receive at the very least a gold ring.' These sentences, cataloguing the gifts and estimating their economic value, represent virtually all the ambassador has to say about the event. And Cecil was wise enough in the ways of state to know this and plan for it. Over half the cost of the entertainment went on the items to be given away at its finale. 'It would seem', as Scott McMillin concludes, 'that Jonson's plot about a shopkeeper, an apprentice, and a keykeeper was little more than the focal point for a display of international gift-giving at Westminster's new center of commercialism' ('Jonson's Early Entertainments', p. 166). As with any apparent generosity surrounding a new commercial venture then as now, the 'gifts' are always in fact investments made in the expectation of recouping more than their worth in the response they stimulate.

The ambassador's report of the occasion contains one final detail: 'The King named the place Britain's Burse.' If the jamboree of free gifts is the Earl of Salisbury's contribution to shaping the meaning of the occasion and the institution, the naming is, at least in part, the king's opportunity for intervention. The name, pointing as it does to James' pet project for the unification of Britain, suggests his personal stamp of approval. On the other hand, this does not necessarily mean that James first proposed it. Cecil, or someone else, may have suggested the name to the king by way of flattering him and thereby enhancing his good will towards the enterprise. Certainly the name resembles the motto in its determination to dress up commercial enterprise as a noble endeavour fitting for courtiers. It also identifies the Exchange as an emblem not merely of Cecil's and Westminster's standing, but also of the greatness of the nation (strategically named here as Britain rather than England). Thomas Wilson, the skilful manager of Cecil's business affairs, displays in playful form exactly the aspect of the enterprise that must not be named. A piece of writing in his hand amongst the state papers, headed 'An idle discourse about naming the new building at Durham House', portrays figures such as godparents suggesting a variety of names and offers as his own proposal 'Mercurial, because Mercury is the god of merchants and of craft and cunning' (Brushfield, 'Britain's Bourse', p. 41). Such naked signalling of the project's real underpinning knowingly pinpoints exactly the element of the building that must remain vague and inexplicit, thereby highlighting the element of ideological masquerade in the celebratory naming event. The role of the spectacle is as much to mask economic relations as to stimulate economic success.

Others concerned in mounting the show on 11 April were equally familiar with the unwritten rules of manufacturing shows for political ends. Ben Jonson, commissioned to write the text, was experienced in producing both urban and royal spectacle as a writer of city entertainments and court masques. Inigo Jones, the designer, had been collaborating with Jonson on court masques since 1605. The actors were established professionals in the private theatre, and one of them, Nathan Field, was already a recognised star.[11] As in the design, construction and decoration of the building, Cecil hired the best in the field, men who not only knew what they were doing, but whose reputations would enhance the status of the entertainment and the occasion, and thereby, of course, his own status. Both Jonson and Jones, furthermore, had been commissioned by Cecil to produce royal entertainments on his behalf on three previous occasions, twice at Theobalds in 1606 and 1607 (the latter the occasion of celebrating Cecil's gift of his country estate to the king) and once at Salisbury House, possibly in celebration of Cecil's appointment as lord treasurer that year.

Letters and bills from Hatfield House indicate that Cecil was fairly prescriptive about what the content of the entertainment should be, and that he kept a close eye, through Wilson, on how Jonson and Jones developed his basic 'conceit'. Wilson's letter to Cecil of 31 March 1609 indicates in just how much detail Cecil wished to be kept informed:

The design is to have three persons only actors, according to your conceit. The first shall represent the keeper, who from the foot of the stair to the place of show shall give entertainment by familiar speech, in discoursing upon the place and what it is, and what it is not, thereupon taking occasion to tax the divers idle comments that have been upon it since it was begun, which doubtless the King had heard of: and by this time he shall come to the place. At the first opening, they would have loud music of cornets and such like, to erect more the intendment. Then the other two *personati* shall begin to play their mountebank tricks, first in talking one to another after their fashion, and then to discourse upon and distribute their trifles . . . Whilst these toys are in hand they would have the mountebank to have a vizard as they use to have, and all this while those things of price to be covered with curtains. When their turn comes to be spoken of, he shall unmask as a merchant that sells not *merces adulterinas*, and then shall make a presentment of them as the things and persons deserve. This is shortly the subject which according to your invention they have framed theirs, and promise . . . to make it an admirable and pleasing spectacle. The conclusion they would have with soft music and a song in the middle window next Durham Yard, as the King shall return that way.[12]

According to Wilson, then, the 'invention' of the subject is Cecil's, which Jonson and Jones have merely 'framed'. Presumably the task of 'fram[ing]' included deciding how the building was to be used for the event, although here too Cecil may have been directive about what he wanted. It seems evident that the entertainment had both a promenade and a fixed element, beginning with a welcome at the door, progressing upstairs, pausing for music of cornets in the first 'opening' to announce the transition to the fixed part of the show, moving to the luxuriously fitted shop for the interaction between the shopkeeper and his boy, and incorporating a song in the rear middle window, overlooking Durham Yard, as the royal party made their way back out of the Burse.[13] The event, then, carefully showcased the building, making entry to the building itself a feature, highlighting the fitted shop as the centre of attention, and building in a pause for song at a decorative point (perhaps one of the armorial windows?) to mark the leave-taking of the royal party.

Until recently these details, as supplied by Wilson's correspondence and the Venetian ambassador's account, together with brief accounts in the later continuations of Stow's *Annals* and *Survey*, and some bills at Hatfield House, were all that was known of this entertainment. In February 1997, however, James Knowles published his discovery of the text amongst papers at the Public Record Office. Though Knowles cautiously refrains from making an absolute claim that this text is to be equated with the text of the royal entertainment of 1609, there can be little doubt about it, given the strength of the circumstantial evidence, which Knowles presents clearly and forcefully. Access to the spoken text of the show makes it possible now to compare the ideological aims laid bare in Wilson's letter with the event as scripted.

The Key Keeper (played by Nathan Field) welcomes the royal guests into the new building with an emphasis on the topos of discovery which is to run right through the proceedings: 'I think you scarce know, where you are now nor by my troth can I tell you, more than that you may seem to be upon some land discovery of a new region here, to which I am your compass' (lines 9–13). The Key Keeper's 'discoursing upon the place and what it is, and what it is not' (Wilson's description) is designed to show that the present function of the building far exceeds any other kind of function others might have wanted for it. Though Cecil clearly knew from the start what kind of enterprise he was constructing, the conceit here is of numerous parties proposing possible uses for the new building, including a bank, a pawnshop, a store house, a private library, or even 'a fair front, built only to grace the street, and for no use' (lines 60–1).[14] Against these various other projects of low status or restricted usefulness, the combination of openness and elitism offered by the present building is made to look self-evidently preferable.

The shop fitted up especially for the occasion of the show proves to be, not surprisingly, a China shop, selling a range of exotica, as the Shopboy's harangue immediately advises the royal party:

What do you lack? What is't you buy? Very fine China stuffs, of all kinds and qualities? China chains, China bracelets, China scarves, China fans, China girdles, China knives, China boxes, China cabinets, caskets, umbrellas, sundials, hourglasses, looking-glasses, burning-glasses, concave glasses, triangular glasses, convex glasses, crystal globes, waxen pictures, ostrich eggs, birds of paradise, muskats, Indian mice, Indian rats, China dogs and China cats? Flowers of silk, mosaic fishes? Waxen fruit, and porcelain dishes? Very fine cages for birds, billiard balls, purses, pipes, rattles, basins, ewers, cups, cans, voiders, toothpicks, targets, falchions, beards of all ages, vizards, spectacles? (lines 73–85)

China houses, selling oriental goods generally, not merely porcelain, were the height of fashion. They are twice mentioned in the same breath as the New Exchange in Jonson's *Epicoene* (first performed within a year of the opening of the New Exchange), as places frequented by ladies and gentlemen of the town (I.iii.32–3; IV.iii.22–3), and Mistress Otter is referred to as 'the rich China-woman, that the courtiers visited so often, that gave the rare entertainment' (I.iv.23–4). (China houses became known as what the *OED* calls 'houses of assignation'.)

Cecil himself, as Knowles points out, helped to create the fashion for Chinese objects by making them a central feature of his growing private collection.[15] Displaying such items in his own home and giving spectacular gifts to the king and court helped to stimulate the desire for possession of such items among the fashionable elite who aped the court (though, within the mutual dynamic discussed in chapter 1 above, it is clear that the urban economic forces of developing trade with the East created the conditions for such courtly pursuits; Cecil's nickname of 'parrot-monger' suggests a more satiric perspective on his pursuit of exotica). Cecil was furthermore a close friend of Sir Walter Cope, whose cabinet of wonders was noted in such detail by Thomas Platter (chapter 1 above), and Cope had helped to direct Cecil's taste, for example, over the furnishing of Salisbury House (Cecil, *Life of Robert Cecil*, p. 167). The bills for China ware for the entertainment at the New Exchange are signed by Cope, which leads Knowles to propose the probability that some of the objects on display were in fact supplied from Cope's *Wunderkammer* ('Cecil's Shopping Centre', p. 15). There is an ironic appropriateness about the crossover between these two new and parallel developments in fashion, the shopping mall and the *Wunderkammer*, both centred on accumulation and display. The items listed in the

Shop-boy's harangue might belong equally to the learned and leisured sphere of collecting or to the commercial transaction in luxury goods. And it is striking that so many of the same items also figure in Dekker's description of the Triumph of Apishness in his *Seven Deadly Sins of London* (1606):

Apishness rides in a chariot made of nothing but cages, in which are all the strangest outlandish birds that can be gotten: the cages are stuck full of parrots' feathers: the coach-man is an Italian mountebank who drives a fawn and a lamb, for they draw this gew-gaw in winter, when such beasts are rarest to be had: in summer, it goes alone by the motion of wheels: two pages in light coloured suits, embroidered full of butterflies, with wings that flutter up with the wind, run by him. (p. 44)

Clearly caged birds, feathers, rare beasts and butterflies are already characteristically recognisable as the height of useless fashion and vain display even before the establishment of the New Exchange.[16]

Jonson evidently understood that highlighting the oriental origins of numerous items simultaneously paid compliment to Cecil's interests and set up the conditions for desirous gazing that were to impress the royal guests and thereby to create the fashions for court and town and the stimulus for avid shopping. Hence the first rhetorical device conspicuous in the Shop-boy's speech is the sheer insistence on the word 'China'. From insistence on 'China' it moves through two miscellaneous items, 'umbrellas' and 'sundials', to 'hourglasses', and thence to privilege the variety of glass items. Miscellaneity, however, is as important a principle as categorisation or the attraction of particular categories like glass or Chinese goods. One of the things the list seeks to stress is sheer difference. In indicating the range of objects on view the rhetorical strategy is deliberately to emphasise disconnectedness, not merely in terms of category but in terms of relative expense. So, a fine birdcage is not only very different in kind and status from a toothpick or a 'voider' (used to collect the dishes and debris from a meal), but also much more expensive. And even the most elaborate toothpick or voider would remain very different in terms of potential luxury status from items for display purposes only, like mosaic fish and waxen fruit.

The list, like the whole entertainment, with the exception of the songs, is in prose. This differentiates it from Jonson's other royal entertainments, which are predominantly in verse. Though some contain prose passages, these are understood within a verse framework, which creates a very different effect from a dramatic piece entirely in prose.[17] This feature of the entertainment becomes especially worthy of comment at this point because it is evident that the Shop-boy's speech plays on the edge of prose and verse, adapting certain features of verse at particular moments. Hence rhyme, in rhythmic patterns, for example, becomes briefly conspicuous in the middle of the speech: 'Indian mice, Indian rats, / China dogs and China cats? / Flowers of silk, mosaic fishes? / Waxen fruit, and porcelain dishes?' (slashes mine). This is no doubt partly a way of interrupting the potential tedium of an undifferentiated, unstructured catalogue, and of highlighting the climactic effect of listing single nouns one after the other in the last sentence, but it also has the effect of reminding the listener of the stylistic mode that the entertainment as a whole refuses, of tacitly prompting the question of why this entertainment, in this particular place and time, is wholly in prose.

That question is further implied by the fact that the Master's first speech interrupts the boy's speech to comment on its inappropriateness ('Peace sirrah. Do it more gently') before himself turning to address the royal visitors: 'What lack you nobilities? Please you to take a nearer view of these excellencies' (lines 88–90). In effect, the Master's speech undercuts the list-form of the Shop-boy's harangue, exposing it as vulgar and excessive. The ideological contradictions of a royal entertainment in praise of shopping seem to surface here, showing the tension between the requirement to celebrate commodities for sale, essentially a shopkeeper's activity, and the requirement to welcome and entertain royalty, an inherently higher-status activity that seeks a more indirect and mediated relation to subjects like cost and value, which only the vulgar (those selling goods rather than purchasing status) would specify. It may be that the piece is in prose because to put it in verse would have had the effect of lowering by implication the status of past and future courtly shows. Perhaps the Jonson who disowned those pieces he wrote for the city also wished to distance himself from this piece by putting it in prose as well as by excluding it from the Folio *Works* (in which, for example, his royal entertainment in celebration of Cecil's gift of Theobalds to James (in verse) was included). It is as if he works to a double project here: on the one hand, to produce the entertainment commissioned by a rich and powerful patron, who was prescriptive about what he wanted, and on the other, to signal, in a tacit and coded way, to other audiences (including future ones) his own sense of this commission as indicating a certain lapse of taste.

When the Master picks up the rhetorical device of listing single commodities, the punctuation and the context of his speech combine to create a very different impression from the Shop-boy's crude rush of advertising: 'You have divers other China houses about the town I know, and that have been honoured with the visitation of great persons, no less than this: But alas what ha' they, what rarity can they produce? Feathers? Cockleshells? Wooden daggers? Trash?' (lines 95–100). Not only do the question forms indicate a clear pause between each item, as opposed to a breathless tumble of words,[18] but the incorporation of the word 'trash' evacuates by implication the value of the other commodities. This is of course part of a deliberate project to establish the superiority of this shop and this building over all other shops in the city. Porcelain for sale elsewhere, the Master assures his courtly audience, is 'counterfeit . . . most false and adulterate'; only 'what you see on this shelf' is authentic (lines 101–4).

The opposition between the false and the true is evidently part of Cecil's conceit, as described in Wilson's letter. The shape of the entertainment, as outlined by Wilson, begins by recognising and playing out the associations that courtly visitors may bring with them to the whole notion of commercial transaction: associations of selling (as opposed to giving) with fraudulence and pressure to buy worthless objects (salesmen playing 'mountebank tricks', talking to each other 'after their fashion' and attempting to palm off 'trifles' on their custom-ers with high-pressure sales patter). But, having confronted the cheap and nasty side of commerce, Cecil's plan is to transform that image of tawdriness and deceit into one of rich authenticity. Both the merchant and the goods of real (that is, high economic) value are to be masked, literally, so that at a given moment the merchant may reveal himself as a purveyor of commodities of worth (and subsequently an acceptable giver of gifts) rather than a mountebank, and the curtains may be drawn back to reveal the 'things of price'.[19] The scene is thereby to be trans-formed from one that seems to confirm a courtly audience's prejudices against the low and adulterate status of commerce to one that corre-sponds to what the royal visitors 'deserve' (that is, expect).

This process of unmasking, however, so far as we can tell from a text completely lacking in stage directions, seems not to occur in the enter-tainment's extant form. The transition from the Shop-boy's crude sales talk to the Master's chiding of his manner and trashing of other traders seems a very pale and ambivalent version of the transformation Cecil had planned. Though the Master's vocabulary seems to make the move from the false to the true, his inflated claims for the true have the effect of casting doubt on its truth (his porcelain, for example, he assures the guests, is not merely authentic in terms of quality, it is also, he claims, capable of discerning the false from the true in terms of what touches it – it supposedly breaks or discolours if poison is put into it). The range of items he singles out for comment mixes up genuine rarity and innovation with impossible fantasy, so that the status of the 'mysteries' on display (line 150) becomes very hard to fathom.

The absence of both stage directions and any evident moment of unmasking make it difficult to know exactly how far the actual event corresponded to the one anticipated in Wilson's letter. It is unclear, for example, whether curtains were used, and if so at what point. It is also impossible to establish whether, or at what point, the entertainment moves away from the shop. The arrival at the shop is fairly clearly signalled by the Key Keeper's closing words ('Some of our shopkeepers are come here; and one or two of 'em are furnished. Especial our China man' (lines 69–71)) and by the immediate commencement of the Shopboy's speech, but it is not clear whether the proceedings do in fact move from the shop to the 'middle window next Durham Yard' for the song. The Master's introduction of the 'statue' of Apollo that sings the song follows immediately on his demonstration of previous items apparently still within the shop. Mid-sentence, he turns to introduce the statue's song, a song of transformation, flattering the king and queen as representing the qualities of wisdom and beauty necessary to 'move a stone' and 'strike . . . harmony' into 'dullest earth' (lines 292–7). Given the small size of the shops and the fact that niched statues were a feature of the building, it would seem likely that the singing statue was located, like the fixed stone statues, in a niche outside the shop, and perhaps, as Wilson indicates, in the middle window overlooking Durham Yard.[20] It is also possible that Jonson consciously chose to make his point of transformation the song, outside the shop, rather than the unveiling of rare objects inside the shop. [21] If he had any doubts, as I have suggested above, about the tastefulness of his patron's conceit, he might have here been trying to steer away from a climax which would have remained in the shop, within both the physical and the conceptual arena of commercial transaction, to one which, in moving out of the shop, could more freely celebrate qualities such as wisdom and beauty by removing them from the marketplace. In fact what the extant text does at the point of the song is what Jonson was used to doing in court masques: it reveals and celebrates the removed mysteries of sovereignty.

The real point of climax, according to the Venetian ambassador, is the giving of rich gifts to the king and queen; but what the song does is make it possible to move to that point of climax by refocusing attention away from the shop, with its goods for sale, however valuable, and on to the royal spectators and their supposed capacity to transform the material, earthbound, nature of those values into spiritual qualities that are revealed rather than permanently accessible. Where Cecil's proposed revelation would have made the building the primary object of celebration, Jonson's text follows courtly precedent in giving the king that primacy. If Cecil saw the final text beforehand (which he may not have done, since it seems to have been finished in a rush at the last moment),[22] he may simply have realised that Jonson's solution was the more politic one.

One final point regarding the staging of the entertainment concerns its capacity to trigger associations with other kinds of spaces. As James Knowles comments, the design of the shop, with its shelves and curtains, resembles the Renaissance *Kunstkammer* ('Cecil's Shopping Centre', p. 15), a comparison which keeps the shop firmly anchored to the world of physical objects, however rare or rich or curious. But a statue that comes to life within a recessed space, perhaps even a curtained recess, might more prominently suggest a theatrical discovery space. *Britain's Burse* is fixated on the notion of discovery, and the transformation is a highly theatrical one that has curious parallels with a public-theatre play performed possibly in the same year as the 1609 entertainment: *The Winter's Tale*. The climactic moment of that play, when the curtain is drawn to reveal a statue, first admired in silence as a wonder of art, then brought to life while music plays, is strikingly similar to this moment in Jonson's entertainment; and the vocabulary of both events, though the transformation is drawn out at much more length in the play, emphasises, naturally enough, the same elements: beauty, harmony, silence, wonder, nature's law.[23]

The statue that comes to life in both texts may stand as an image for the transformative power of theatre. What theatre performs – and what Cecil specifically wanted it to perform on 11 April 1609 – is the work of ideological transformation. Wilson's letter makes clear that Cecil wanted a show that would overcome such assumptions and prejudices as might already be in place concerning his new enterprise and persuade the spectators to think differently about it. From the Key Keeper's opening harangue to the motto above the shop, the imagined unmasking of the Master and the revelation of goods of great price, Cecil's agenda was clearly to transform his audience's view of Britain's Burse from one that would dismiss it as tainted by the urban 'dirt' of commercial enterprise to one that would admire it as a place of beauty, gracious living, high fashion and 'real' value. He needed to erase the memory of the smears arising out of the unseemly dispute with the city at the project's inception and perhaps even at some level out of the explicit comparison with the Royal Exchange, and to use this occasion to make the king and court reconceive the enterprise as a noble display of service and benefaction towards both the sovereign and the locality of Cecil's birth (see p. 109 and note 2 above). Jonson, even if he did not follow Cecil's plan to the letter, understood the agenda clearly, and produced a show that would do the work Cecil wanted. Displacing money with 'love' and selling with giving, it sought to highlight the elevated status of all aspects of the enterprise, from the building and location to the founder, visitors and future clientele, brushing the hard facts of buying and selling to one side for the occasion and blinding the courtly audience to that material reality through the spectacle of apparently unmeasured giving. Though the bills at Hatfield House demonstrate just how carefully the costs of the gifts were calculated and recorded, their function in the show was to be perceived as precisely excessive and immeasurably bounteous. The Venetian ambassador's reception of the event would seem to show that Cecil achieved this aim. His report suggests that the scale of the gifts stimulated intense interest in their value, setting off speculation and rumour about their cost, while prohibiting any exact assessment. Such fascination with their value was presumably exactly the effect they were intended to produce. The account of the event in Stow's *Survey* is even more explicit in its decision to imply generosity beyond even description, far less assessment, via the rhetorical trope of refusing to attempt either:

Concerning their entertainment there, though I was no eye-witness thereof; yet I know the ingenuity and mind of the nobleman to be such, as nothing should want to welcome so great an expectation. And therefore, what variety of devices, pleasing speeches, rich gifts and presents as then flew bountifully abroad, I will rather refer to your imagination, than any way come short of, by an imperfect narration. (*Survey*, 1633, p. 494)

The irony of the event is that the effect of incalculable worth is carefully calculated. Cecil knows from experience exactly how much it is necessary to spend in order to produce responses that must fail to achieve comparable precision, and are driven instead into an excess of imagination.

CHAPTER SEVEN

The masking of place

EPICOENE

Epicoene is filled with characters seeking to turn their backs on the city and to establish 'the town' as a new, distinct and fashionable location. The play was first performed in late 1609 or early 1610, within less than a year of the opening of the New Exchange, which gave the developing area west of the city a new point of focus, a public place where different levels of the elite could mix with and inspect one another at the same time as they shopped for the accessories that defined their status. The play opens in Clerimont's house, which, it soon becomes clear, is located in the town.[1] Its location is foregrounded in a brief dialogue between Clerimont and Sir Amorous La Foole, carefully calculated to exhibit the social cachet of their places of residence while at the same time exposing the greater affectation and pretension of La Foole:

CLERIMONT. Sir Amorous! You have very much honested [honoured] my
    lodging with your presence.
LA FOOLE. Good faith, it is a fine lodging, almost as delicate a lodging as
    mine.
CLERIMONT. Not so, sir.
LA FOOLE. Excuse me, sir, if it were i' the Strand, I assure you. (1.iv.2–7)

For La Foole, then, there is a fine distinction to be made between the Strand itself and the rest of the town, and at this point the Strand, location of the New Exchange and the conspicuous palaces of the aristocracy, evidently has the edge.

As the first reference to 'the town' makes clear (note 1 above), it is also, within the fictional world of the play, the location of 'a new foundation . . . of ladies that call themselves the collegiates' (1.i.70–2). And just as the newly developing town is liminally placed, between two established places, the court and the city, so the new collegiate ladies are socially placed at a point of intersection, here described as 'an order between courtiers and country madams' (72). The college has echoes of the little academe of *Love's Labour's Lost*, but differs from it in important ways. It resembles that earlier academy in that it is a single-sex foundation, whose members live together, apart from the opposite sex; but it differs from it in social and geographical location and in gender. Where the academy of *Love's Labour* is male and court-centred, this one is female and town-centred. Furthermore, where the first is seriously introduced in idealistic terms, as an institution dedicated to art and scholarship, before it breaks down, the second is never accorded any respect, even briefly. It is ironised from the start by the careful distancing of Truewit's turn of phrase. 'Ladies that call themselves the collegiates' can hardly be taken seriously when they are so described, and by a man. Furthermore, according to Truewit's account, their project does not even start out as idealistic, but is quite openly dedicated to the cultivation of trivial and fashionable pursuits: the entertainment of 'Wits and Braveries' (I.i.74),[2] the accumulation of the trappings of high living ('your coach and four horses, your woman, your chambermaid, your page, your gentleman-usher, your French cook, and four grooms' (IV.iii.19–21)) and visits 'to Bedlam, to the china-houses, and to the Exchange' (IV.iii.22–3), as well, of course, as to the theatre.

At one level, then, the world of this play is emphatically the world of the town, a world of shopping, display and spectatorship. Yet the play derives its satiric thrust partly from the insistence with which the city obtrudes itself into the consciousness of both characters and audience. Whatever the location, it seems, there is no escape from the city. Morose, for example, lives in the city, as the conversation at I.i.140–57 indicates, but is obsessively determined to draw a firm boundary between the interior and the exterior of his dwelling-place. His aim is to blot out all awareness of his noisy urban surroundings, and to that end he makes agreements with street traders to keep out of earshot, pays the city waits to stay out of his ward and lives in a street 'so narrow at both ends that it will receive no coaches nor carts nor any of these common noises' (I.i.158–60). Yet, though he attempts to close his ears to it, he cannot banish it from his mindset, and it continues to shape his thinking inexorably, whether as a term of abuse, a form of punishment or a potential penance. He compares the noise of those who invade the peace of his house after his marriage to that of 'an ill May-day, or when the galley-foist is afloat to Westminster' (IV.ii.111–12);[3] yet in order to get rid of his wife he would perform 'supererogatory penance in a belfry at Westminster Hall, i'the Cockpit, at the fall of a stag, the Tower Wharf (what place is there else?), London Bridge, Paris Garden, Billingsgate, when the noises are at their height and loudest. Nay, I would sit out a play that were nothing but fights at sea, drum, trumpet, and target!' (IV.iv.11–17). The parenthetical question, 'what place is there else?', after the reference to Tower Wharf functions to undercut Morose's apparent rejection of the city. Even as he curses it, he unwillingly reaffirms its dominance. The catalogue seems cumulative: the first-named locations, west of the city, have elite social status despite their noisiness; but the city locations are places of trade and traffic, associated with 'low' pursuits as well as noise. Again, as remarked in note 1 above, the boundary is as much a social as a physical one. For these purposes, though Paris Garden and its theatres are technically outside the city boundary, they are conceived as intrinsically urban, as are the citizen playhouses outside the northern boundary, where old-fashioned drum-and-trumpet plays dominate. Both are conceived in contrast to the more fashionable Cockpit-in-Court, at Whitehall, which is the playhouse the collegiate ladies visit (IV.iii.44). The Whitefriars Theatre, where *Epicoene* itself was playing, was part of the developing town, so that the joke is double-edged: Jonson mocks theatre generally, including West-End theatre, as part of a shared joke with the Whitefriars clientele, but at the same time distances them and himself from more down-market playhouses.

Mrs Otter is another city figure seeking to escape the city. The physical location of her residence is not named, but what is clear is that her origins are in the city and that she is trying to establish her house as a 'town' house by selling China goods, the exotic commodities so central to the New Exchange entertainment, from home. La Foole knows her as 'the rich china-woman that the courtiers visited so often, that gave the rare entertainment' (I.iv.24–5), and her own boast of Lady Haughty coming to her house 'to see some China stuffs' (III.ii.55) is confirmed by La Foole's opinion that 'she commands all at home' (I.iv.25–6). She attempts to affirm elegant social status by dropping fashionable turns of phrase into her conversation, but the effect she achieves is not quite what she aims for. Truewit calls her 'the only authentical courtier, that is not naturally bred one, in the city' (III.ii.25–6), thus anchoring her in the city even as he pretends to acknowledge the 'authenticity' of her courtly show. Her husband, furthermore, obstructs her attempts to establish the town credentials of their home by bringing the manners of his trade into polite company. His occupation as a bearward is one that associates him with the noise and roughness of Paris Garden, offering the lowest kind of entertainment on the social scale, as his wife's abuse outlines in bitter detail: 'I'll ha' you chain'd up with your bull-dogs and bear-dogs, if you be not civil the sooner. I'll send you to kennel, i'faith. You were best bait me with your bull, bear, and horse! Never a time that the courtiers or collegiates come to the house, but you make it a Shrove Tuesday' (III.i.2–6).[4] Like Morose, Mrs Otter cannot keep the city out, and the harder she tries to exclude it, the more insistently it returns, pursuing her in both her dreams and her waking life. In conceiving of it as an entity that offers her 'affronts', Mrs Otter allows it to come alive with a malignant, almost human agency emphasised by the very repetition of 'it' in the grammatical subject position:

It stain'd me a damask tablecloth, cost me eighteen pound at one time; and burnt me a black satin gown, as I stood by the fire at my Lady Centaur's chamber in the college another time. A third time, at the lord's masque, it dropp'd all my wire and my ruff with wax candle, that I could not go up to the banquet. A fourth time, as I was taking coach to go to Ware to meet a friend, it dash'd me a new suit all over (a crimson satin doublet and black velvet skirts) with a brewer's horse, that I was fain to go in and shift me, and kept my chamber a leash of days for the anguish of it. (III.iii.59–69)

Clerimont, tongue in cheek, comments that he would not dwell in the city 'an 'twere so fatal to me', while Mrs Otter is lampooned by her serious assurance that she is consulting her doctor as to reducing the frequency with which she dreams of it (71–3). The attempt to deny class origins is made to look both foolish and futile. It is no coincidence that the ties with the town that Mrs Otter seeks so hard to cultivate figure most prominently in her husband's abuse of her as a fabricated entity: 'All her teeth were made i'the Blackfriars, both her eyebrows i' the Strand, and her hair in Silver Street. Every part o'the town owns a piece of her . . . She takes herself asunder still when she goes to bed, into some twenty boxes, and about next day noon is put together again, like a great German clock' (IV.ii.82–9).[5]

Even Truewit, who inhabits the same leisured social world as Clerimont and Dauphine, finds the city a useful point of shared reference in pronouncing on the need to conceal art until it has reached completion: 'How long did the canvas hang afore Aldgate? Were the people suffer'd to see the city's *Love* and *Charity* while they were rude stone, before they were painted and burnish'd? No. No more should servants approach their mistresses but when they are complete and finish'd' (I.i.114–18). The allusion is to the refurbishment of Aldgate, on the city's eastern boundary, completed in 1609. The 1633 continuation of Stow's *Survey* makes reference to the two statues, there designated as Love and Peace.

The topography of the city figures almost as prominently in this play as it does in *Edward IV*, but the distance in tone and point of view between the two may be measured by the way those allusions function. Where in *Edward IV* they are part of a litany of celebration, tying identity to place with pride, in *Epicoene* they are part of a nightmare that refuses to be suppressed, a substratum that visibly underpins the manufactured concoction of the town. If the town is all artifice and pretence, the city is the 'real' on which it is erected. The pins and feathers, ruffs and fans, artificial hair, limbs and teeth with which the play is obsessed, are obtained or manufactured through either foreign or domestic trade or a combination of both. High fashion is erected on a base of labour and commerce. Morose inveighs against the obsession with 'that bodice, these sleeves, those skirts, this cut, that stitch, this embroidery, that lace, this wire, those knots, that ruff, those roses, this girdle, that fan, the t'other scarf, these gloves' (II.v.76–9) as if it were a purely female characteristic, but the affectations of La Foole and Sir John Daw make clear that the preoccupation with frivolities is not gendered. Nor is it only the most ridiculous characters who display it. Even Clerimont rejects Truewit's serious conversation with a clear instruction: 'Talk me of pins and feathers and ladies and rushes and such things, and leave this stoicity alone till thou mak'st sermons' (I.i.61–3). Social life at every level depicted in the play hinges on buying, wearing, displaying and talking about decorative commodities.

These commodified fragments, however, like the gifts offered at the New Exchange entertainment, must conceal their base origins in trade in order to function as objects of value. They must suggest immense costliness without revealing actual cost. Truewit is cynically explicit about this. A fashionable gentleman courting a fashionable lady, he instructs Clerimont, must learn the way to display 'value' without necessarily incurring significant cost: 'Let your gifts be slight and dainty rather than precious. Let cunning be above cost. Give cherries at time of year, or apricots; and say they were sent you out o'the country, though you bought 'em in Cheapside' (IV.i.106–10). The difference between the play's clever young men and its fools is that the clever young men understand that, while elegant gallantries are actually based on a chain of commercial transactions, that knowledge is not to be voiced in elite society. The vulgar and foolish reveal their social inadequacy by failing to understand this; and when their grossness intrudes into polite conversation, those in the know have no choice but to feign misunderstanding. Hence, when La Foole talks about spending money on ladies and ends by bragging how he can now 'take up at my pleasure', Dauphine is obliged to assume that he means taking up ladies, and La Foole compounds his own social error in the apparent correction of Dauphine's: 'No sir, excuse me: I meant money, which can take up anything' (1.iv.62–7). The social awkwardness of the remark is palpable.

Money cannot mask its associations with the base pursuits of commerce until it is exchanged for goods. The commodities it buys, by contrast, are all too easily accommodated in the appearance of elegant living and employed as part of the masquerade that is the public self. The vision of the public self as commoditised, a mere assembly of surfaces, is basically the same vision as was first evident in *Love's Labour's Lost* and the War of the Theatres plays, but the increasing disgust at what lies beneath the mask anticipates the pervasive tone of Restoration comedy. The opening scene of *The Man of Mode*, for example, in which Dorimant is exposed in his dressing-room with the mask of social niceties off, may well take its cue from the opening of *Epicoene*, where Clerimont is directed to come out 'making himself ready'. The constructedness of the social self is thus embedded in the first entrance. *Epicoene* does not develop the notion of exposure via Clerimont as Etherege does through Dorimant, but the concept of masking and unmasking underlies the whole scene, and indeed the whole play. It is the function of the boy, who is the only other figure on stage with Clerimont for the first twenty lines of the play, to open up the space for this perspective more fully without direct taint to the character of Clerimont. As a mere youth, this boy has access to both the gentlemen and the ladies at their least guarded, and provokes a degree of unmasking described by him in a way that is clearly meant to stimulate revulsion in the audience: 'The gentlewomen play with me and throw me o' the bed, and carry me in to my lady, and she kisses me with her oil'd face and puts a peruke o' my head and asks me an' I will wear her gown, and I say, "No". And then she hits me a blow o' the ear and calls me innocent and lets me go' (1.i.12–17).

What is revealed here, however, is not just an unpleasant vision of gentlewomen with their masks and manners off, but a new kind of masking, which manufactures not the self but others. In this passage the ladies' oiling of their own faces is made secondary to their pleasure in putting a wig and dress on the boy. If the self-fashioning discussed in chapter 3 above was worryingly empty and superficial, a fashioning effected by an agent other than the self is even more threatening, reducing people to mere playthings or puppets of one another. Sir John Daw and La Foole, with their show of learning and careful dress, may resemble the self-assembled personae of those earlier plays, but in fact they have even less dignity than that. Dauphine's devised quarrel between them can only work because they have no self-made identity strong enough to withstand assault: 'they'll believe themselves to be just such men as we make 'em, neither more nor less' (III.iii.88–90). The boast is as chilling in what it reveals about Dauphine, however, as in the way it evacuates the objects of his trickery. A world full of puppets may be a vision of futility, but a world in which puppets and makers establish themselves as one or the other through their interaction reveals a pragmatic and cynical vision of social life. Even Truewit, a character who speaks on occasion as from above the day-to-day concerns of the world he lives in, is not above bragging about his puppet-making skills in devising roles for Otter and Cutbeard to deceive Morose, and is confident that he can 'make the deepest divine and gravest lawyer out o' them two' (IV.vii.39–40).

But it is Dauphine who pulls off the real coup in an act of making concealed even from the audience. The creation of Epicoene, the man-woman, is the piece of construction on which the whole plot hinges, the full-blown development of the boy-plaything motif briefly introduced in the opening scene. The point about Epicoene is that s/he is even emptier than Daw or La Foole, Otter or Cutbeard. Silent at first, even in speech s/he gives away nothing of any self, precisely because there is no self to give away. S/he is no more or less than the sum of the roles s/he plays, whether the role is the female one Dauphine builds for her or the male one that frames it. In his male role, Epicoene remains nameless, a figure like the boy-actor of the Jacobean theatre, waiting for a role to bring identity. And in neither gender is the man-woman called upon to occupy a centre of being. This vacuity emblematises the social concerns of the whole play. When Epicoene accuses Morose of wanting 'one of the French puppets with the eyes turn'd with a wire' (III.iv.35–6) for his wife, the accusation directed at Morose also implicitly targets all those others in the play who willingly piece together empty masks for themselves and others in the hope of deluding those who look at them. Epicoene's final revelation, 'I am no man, ladies' (V.iv.40), seems to speak more widely for all those who are not what they claim to be but are not brought to such utterance.

The extent to which Epicoene emblematises a widespread and deep-rooted social disease in the play is further demonstrated by the tagging of variations on the name Epicoene to other characters. The most frequent term is 'hermaphrodite'. The first reference to the new ladies' college signals the monstrosity of the very concept through the careful placing of 'hermaphroditical'. Truewit reports that these ladies 'that call themselves the collegiates . . . cry down or up what they like or dislike in a brain or a fashion with most masculine or rather hermaphroditical authority' (i.i.70–6). Women, in other words, may claim masculine authority, but in doing so they only make themselves ridiculous. The college, like the little academe of *Love's Labour's Lost*, is revealed as absurd, but the revelation is more sneering than affectionate. Where Shakespeare's courtiers are witty if also foolish in their fashionable affectation, Jonson's ladies are grotesque. Yet his fashionable gentlemen, however they may mock the ladies, are subject to the same censure. Together the ladies ridicule men whose dedication to fashionable appearance effeminises them, men 'that have their faces set in a brake . . . and have every hair in form! That wear purer linen than ourselves, and profess more neatness than the French hermaphrodite' (iv.vi.27).[6]

Manhood and how to claim it are a worry in the play. Wherever swords or weapons are mentioned, their signifying power as indicators of both sexual prowess and military skill is evacuated, and where they appear as props they function as fashion accessories rather than indices of virility or valour. The mock duel in which Daw and La Foole are trapped exposes their swords as mere show in terms of their aptitude for deeds of arms, while the revelation of Epicoene's true sex exposes their claims to have had sexual relations with 'her' as equally empty boasts. The characteristic position of swords on this stage is lying inert, a feature emphasised by the verbal references that draw attention to them. Morose's comments on finding them in his house ('What make these naked weapons here, gentlemen?' (iv.vii.1); 'They have done all the hurt they will do' (iv.vii.10)) emphasise the fact of their inertia, while La Foole's enquiry for the missing swords elicits a dialogue that highlights the way the weapons have moved passively from hand to hand in a completely non-military exchange:

LA FOOLE. Where had you our swords, Master Clerimont?
CLERIMONT. Why, Dauphine took 'em from the madman.
LA FOOLE. And he took 'em from our boys, I warrant you.
CLERIMONT. Very like, sir.
LA FOOLE. Thank you, good Master Clerimont. Sir John Daw and
    I are both beholden to you. (v.i.1–6)

The scene in which Daw and La Foole play out their mutual unwillingness to duel with one another, witnessed by the collegiate ladies, produces a comment devastating in both its brevity and its precision. When

Madame Centaur comments that Mavis was the most deceived by the two men, having recommended them to the college, Mavis insists that she 'commended but their wits, madam, and their braveries. I never look'd towards their valors' (IV.vi.5–6). Wit, then, and fashionable adornments are openly recognised as praiseworthy features, but clearly distinguished from courage. (The multiple senses of 'bravery' as courage, bravado, elegant show and mere showiness (of any kind) are of course part of the joke here.) Both men and women are damned by the criteria of praise as much as by open abuse. Hence even the apparent attempt to attribute masculinity to Dauphine is undermined by the speakers, their criteria, and the sequence in which they offer them:

HAUGHTY. Sir Dauphine is valiant and a wit too, it seems.
MAVIS. And a bravery too. (IV.vi.7–8)

The effect is carried on in the praise of Dauphine as 'a worthy gentleman in his exteriors' (21), which then leads to the attempt to differentiate him from those effeminate men who are more fastidious than the French hermaphrodite (quoted above). The claimed difference scarcely frees Dauphine from the taint of their admiration.

As with Epicoene's crossing of genders, so the impotence of naked weapons and the implied slur on manhood is a central and emblematic concern of the play, echoed in both language and plot. As the pseudo-lawyers go through all the possible legal cases for ending Morose's marriage in one of the most extended set pieces of the play, the climactic decision settles finally on impotence as the best, named ironically in Latin as lack of '*Exercendi potestate*' (the power of raising his sword) (V.iii.222). The two concerns are of course linked: the ease with which crossing gender deludes the onlookers here implies the degree to which gender is socially constructed rather than essential.

The interplay between masking and unmasking operates very differently here and in the New Exchange entertainment. Transformation, as discussed in chapter 6 above, was what Robert Cecil was primarily concerned to have Jonson and Jones represent. Trifles and mountebank tricks, in his conception of the event, were to be unmasked as having hidden value or truth 'as the things and persons deserve'. The absence of an unmasking scene in the extant text, I suggested, might hint at Jonson's discomfort with revealing a merchant and his goods, however high-class and expensive, as having some kind of transcendent authenticity, when his own instincts would more characteristically lead to a reverse kind of unmasking, aimed at revealing tawdriness beneath the spectacle of attraction. It is almost as though *Epicoene* is written to exorcise a bitterness resulting from writing to commission against inclination in the New Exchange piece. There is plenty of unmasking in *Epicoene*, but it is not a cause for celebration or awe. On the contrary, it is an opportunity for wallowing in discomfiture. The unmasking of Daw and La Foole as impotent in love and war goes beyond the parodic display of fashionable surface in *Love's Labour's Lost* and the theatre-war plays too. Where those plays displayed a fascination with the glittering surface despite their doubts about its shallowness, the focus now is precisely on that shallowness. All is show; even, on occasion, down to apparent unmasking. Jonson revels in making Morose's first words on meeting Epicoene a request for her to unmask and providing a stage direction that makes her do so (II.v.1–2). This show of silent unmasking, which is so appealing to Morose, and so ironically delusory, cynically anticipates Epicoene's silence in the climactic unmasking of the last scene, when Dauphine takes off the simple wig that has allowed a boy to seem a woman and the beards and disguises that have allowed a barber and a bearward to seem lawyers.[7]

Truewit's anecdote in the first scene about a woman intruded on in her chamber who put her wig on the wrong way 'to cover her baldness' and was kept talking an hour 'with that revers'd face' (I.i.120–8) sets the characteristic tone. The anecdote is told precisely in order to encourage the audience, both on stage and off, to take pleasure in the slippage between the mask and the wearer. It is the knowledge that the mask is fallible that Jonson delights in. The last word of the play is Truewit's cruel reminder that Epicoene, having mixed as a supposed lady with other ladies, has plumbed the depths of all their 'mysteries' (v.iv.225). The implication throughout the play is that such mysteries (a word that features in *Britain's Burse* to suggest transcendent value), are obscene and disgusting. Again, the disgust is unmistakably established in the opening scene, not only through the boy's reference to how the women behave in private, but in Clerimont's revisiting of that off-stage scene in more detail through his description of Lady Haughty's 'piec'd beauty': 'There's no man can be admitted till she be ready nowadays, till she has painted and perfum'd and wash'd and scour'd, but the boy here, and him she wipes her oil'd lips upon like a sponge' (I.i.80–3).

Men and women alike delight in taking one another apart in verbal set pieces that precisely conceive of the individual, of either sex, as an agglomeration of fragments. Otter's anatomisation of his wife, quoted above, is one of numerous such speeches in the play, itemising bodily parts and fashion accessories, or bodily parts *as* fashion accessories – the play is obsessed with replacing real body parts with bought artificial substitutes. The dominating concern is with the constructedness of surfaces, and the characteristic linguistic form of the list, again a feature of the New Exchange entertainment discussed in chapter 6 above, functions to highlight the way language is used to fill up empty spaces. (It is worth noting that *Epicoene*, like *Britain's Burse*, is entirely in prose.) Lists overwhelm the ears, closing off the space and time for anxiety, distracting from the gap where substance is fearful, disgusting or simply absent. Their own frenetic plenitude reveals them as a symptom of the very anxiety they try to deny. As Truewit advises Otter and Cutbeard, the would-be lawyers, hard and fast talking may serve to cover up for absence: 'If you chance to be out, do not confess it with standing still or humming or gaping one at another, but go on and talk aloud and eagerly, use vehement action, and only remember your terms and you are safe. Let the matter go where it will: you have many will do so' (v.iii.13–17).

Interminable monologues also reveal the way trivia dominate the lives of the anxious and fragmented beings who care more about the social impact they make than about anything of deeper significance. The death of La Foole's brother figures as merely one element among others in a monologue in which La Foole sets out to convince his listeners of his own importance through a sequence of references that moves from the detail of his family's coat of arms, to what he eats, the company he keeps, the mad times he has had and the money he has spent. For him the most memorable feature of the day his brother died is what he was wearing at the time: 'I had as fair a gold jerkin on that day as any was worn in the Island Voyage or at Caliz' (i.iv.56–8). Where La Foole seeks to overwhelm the listeners with uninterrupted speech as a way of affirming his worth, they are overwhelmed instead by its tedium. Clerimont's response first highlights the sheer physical exertion and hence absurdity of gabbling at such length and pace ('Oh, let him breath, he has not recover'd' (64)) before dismissing the speaker as a 'wind-fucker' (72). Beaurline glosses the term as meaning a kind of hawk, but the separate meanings of the two elements, wind and fucking (assuming Jonson intended 'wind-fucker', and not 'wind-sucker', as in the third Folio), can hardly be absent. La Foole, with his narcissistic rambling, is a mere abuse of breath; and his endless talking, as the duel plot confirms, represents a metaphorical, if not actual, impotence.

As in *Love's Labour's Lost* and the theatre-war plays, words are exhibited as commodities to be acquired for purposes of display. A smattering of Latin enables Otter and Cutbeard to become instant lawyers; Mrs Otter seeks to demonstrate elegant status by dropping in words not in common use; Sir John Daw reels off 'a sack full' of classical authors' names indiscriminately in an attempt to impress (ii.iii.65); and even the imaginary wife that Truewit conjures up to scare Morose invites guests 'to hear her speak Latin and Greek' and insists that her husband 'lie with her in those languages too' (ii.ii.72–3). Most offensive of all is the literary name-dropping in common use to suggest an acquaintance with literary fashions, and Jonson's bitterness is audible in Truewit's attempt to frighten Morose with the horror of a fashionable wife who may 'censure poets and authors and styles, and compare 'em, Daniel with Spenser, Jonson with the t'other youth, and so forth' (ii.ii.110–12). Such shows deceive, of course, because most spectators have no judgement. As Truewit says of the collegiate ladies, 'all their actions are governed by crude opinion, without reason or cause; they know not why they do anything; but, as they are inform'd, believe, judge, praise, condemn, love, hate, and in emulation one of another, do all these things alike' (iv.vi.56–60).

Yet Truewit and his friends, who claim to see through such shows, are not free of the vices they condemn. They too speak in lists and extended monologues, and triviality is as much cultivated in their sphere as elsewhere. I have already shown how Clerimont rejects the turn from wit to earnestness with a plea for a return to talk of pins and feathers. Truewit's set speeches, however, repeatedly return to the topos of a lament for the times, and their recurrent anxiety is that shows and spectacles waste time and substitute for potentially more meaningful experiences. The prevalence of spectacle is the visual equivalent of the verbal catalogues. It distracts from emptiness. But it also corrupts. According to Truewit, the chances of finding a chaste wife in 'these times . . . When there are so many masques, plays, puritan preachings, mad folks, and other strange sights to be seen daily, private and public' (ii.ii.31–3) are remote; and the risk Morose runs in taking a wife is that she will 'run away with a vaulter, or the Frenchman that walks upon ropes, or him that dances the jig, or a fencer for his skill at his weapon' (ii.ii.55–7). Shows delude and attract, tempting spectators, as Stow and the anti-theatrical lobby know, to immediate pleasures that take the place of moral commitment to collective values. Nevertheless, an understanding of how masks and illusions are constructed, on which a capacity to value them at their worth is dependent, is only to be derived, according to Truewit, from much study of social spectacle. When

Dauphine, following one of Truewit's diatribes concerning how women should hide their defects, asks how he knows so much about them, Truewit advises Dauphine to get out and look about him more: 'you must leave to live i' your chamber then a month together upon *Amadis de Gaul* or *Don Quixote*, as you are wont, and come abroad . . . to court, to tiltings, public shows and feasts, to plays and church sometimes'. These are the places of spectacle to which women come 'to show their new tires, to see and to be seen' (IV.i.51–6).

The prevalence and extravagance of spectacle may be the index of a society's degradation, yet, as with the city, there is no escape from it. Nor is it merely a feature of town society, though it is so highly developed there. Numerous of the play's references to the city are precisely to its spectacles, from highest to lowest, from the lord mayor's show and the rebuilding of Aldgate to the baiting of bears and bulls and the bustle of Tower Wharf. The play's real anxiety, however, is less focused on public and occasional spectacle than it is on the importing of spectacle into everyday life, where Cheapside apricots masquerade as rare delicacies and bodies are assembled like German clocks out of manufactured parts. Whereas Cecil wanted Jonson to celebrate the transformation of base commerce into aristocratic gold at the New Exchange as quasi-miraculous, Jonson is here determined to expose as cheap trickery the alchemy whereby the spectacle masks its origins. The concentration of *Epicoene* is on the mechanism rather than the miracle of transformation.

Epilogue

Many kinds of spectacle share the same visual and verbal vocabulary of transformation, partly because so many are doing the same kind of ideological work, seeking to disguise unacceptable truths as material for celebration. Though the parallels between particular moments in *Britain's Burse* and *The Winter's Tale* are particularly close, curtains open on discoveries and statues come to life in all kinds of contemporary shows from the cheapest to the most glamorous. One of the most notable and symbolically significant shows of the reign is of course the pageant marking King James' coronation entry to London in 1604, and that event is full of such devices.[1] The first of seven triumphal arches, at Fenchurch, is covered with a curtain of silk painted like a thick cloud which is to be instantly drawn as the king comes towards it. Jonson's text makes the meaning of the allegory explicit: 'those clouds were gathered upon the face of the City, through their long want of his most wished sight: but now, as at the rising of the sun, all mists were dispersed and fled'.[2] Within the niches of the arch are statues, some of which are in fact actors waiting too for the king's approach in order to deliver their speeches. The conceit is the same as in *Britain's Burse*: the presence of the king is celebrated as having the power to breathe life into apparent stone.

Jonson's explanation of the allegory, however, seems to make indirect reference to one of the aspects of the real that the pageant seeks to transform: the city's 'long want' of the king's 'most wished sight'. When King James succeeded to the English throne in 1603 the city's planned coronation ceremonies had to be set aside because of the intensity of the plague that summer. The setting aside of that symbolic interaction between court and city may be seen in retrospect as the unwitting forerunner of a new distance between this monarch and the nation's most powerful city. In 1604 the city of London staged the postponed ceremonial event in James' honour, an event whose full title in print was to become *The Magnificent Entertainment Given to King James, Queen Anne his wife, and Henry*

11. The Londinium arch at Fenchurch for 1604 royal entry.

*Frederick the prince, upon the day of His Majesty's triumphant passage (from the
Tower) through his Honourable City (and Chamber) of London, being the 15 of
March 1603.*[3] The conceit of the city of London as the king's chamber,
incorporated in the title, runs right through the text of the proceedings.
The Fenchurch arch had 'LONDINIUM' inscribed on it 'in great capitals';
'And under that, in a smaller (but not different) character, was written,
'CAMERA REGIA: The King's Chamber' (*The Magnificent Entertainment*,
p. 37). Dutton notes that Dekker's 'smaller (but not different)' seems to

make a point of correcting Jonson's text, which describes the second script as 'less and different' (Jonson was responsible for writing the Fenchurch pageant). This precision may, however, have implications that go beyond the petty wish to cavil with a rival author. What the two inscriptions compare, after all, is the city *per se*, and the city in allegorical relation to the monarch. Clearly, it is a matter of civic pride that London's name standing alone should take precedence here; but in nit-picking over the size and appearance of the two scripts Dekker may be more concerned with clarifying the ideological work that the arches do than with getting one up on Jonson. Given that this was the first arch, the one through which the king made 'entrance into this his Court Royal' (i.e. the city; Dekker is harping on the same conceit as the title), it is crucial that the right relations should be signalled. Emphasising that the scripts are not different in kind may be Dekker's way of insisting on a symbolic compatibility between the two sides of the relationship: the city, according to his specification of the two scripts, is writ large, as the host, purveyor and arena of the day's celebrations, but it seeks at the same time to underline its essentially harmonious relations with the monarch. The pageant is the city's gift to the monarch; as such it must honour two aspects of the city's generosity, its willingness to bear the cost and its willingness to subject itself to the monarch.[4] It is hardly surprising to find that this double project creates some tension within the event and its printed records.

Of the three printed versions of the event, Stephen Harrison's is the most biased in favour of the city. He dedicates his book 'To the right honourable Sir Thomas Bennet Knight, Lord Mayor of this city, the right worshipful the Aldermen his brethren, and to those worshipful commoners, elected committees, for the managing this business', thereby celebrating all involved in the work of planning and funding the entertainment. His book, he claims, provides a permanent record of 'that magnificent royalty, and glorious entertainment, which you yourselves for your part, out of a free, a clear, and very bounteous disposition, and so many thousands of worthy citizens, out of a sincere affection and loyalty of his Majesty, did with the sparing of no cost, bestow but upon one day', and will stand as a testament to the honour of the city 'so long as the city shall bear a name' (fo. Br). He is also at pains again at the close of the volume to emphasise the exceptional generosity of the city, including 'mere citizens', not hitherto contributors to the cost of this kind of event: 'And thus much you shall understand, that no manner of person whatsoever, did disburse any part towards the charge of these five triumphs, but only the mere citizens being all freemen; heretofore the charge being borne by fifteens and the Chamber of London (as may appear by ancient precedents) but now it was levied amongst the companies' (fo. Kr).[5]

Dekker, however, continues to refine the conceit of London as the king's chamber in his subsequent text, singling out two of his own pageants as taking place respectively in the 'Presence Chamber' (the pageant at the Great Conduit in Cheapside by Soper Lane) and the 'Privy Chamber' (at the Little Conduit, also in Cheap). Dekker also gives the conceit great prominence when his narrative reaches the point at which the king leaves the city through the arch at Temple Bar: 'And thus have we (lowly and aloof) followed our Sovereign through the seven triumphal gates of this his Court Royal; which name, as London received at the rising of the sun, so now at his going from her (even in a moment) she lost that honour: and being (like an actor on a stage) stripp'd out of her borrowed majesty, she resigns [submits to] her former shape and title of City; nor is it quite lost, considering it went along with him to whom it is due' (p. 112).[6] The notion inherent in the simile of the actor here again plays down the city as it seeks to flatter James via the implication that, while the city's 'majesty' is a mere copy, the king's is the real thing.

The event as a whole is nevertheless designed to enhance the status of both parties. In the very act of gracious deferral to the king, the city seeks to present its own best face not only to the king and queen and the royal court but also to London citizens themselves, to foreigners living and working in London and to visitors to London for the occasion. There is no clear distinction to be made between spectators and participants. One side of the procession route was lined with the city companies in their liveries, 'having their streamers, ensigns, and bannerets spread on the tops of their rails before them' (Harrison, *Arches of Triumph*, fo. Kr), and this group was as much on view as viewing; while, similarly, the king himself was at once chief spectacle and chief spectator. The range of pageants aimed to include numerous specific groupings within the community and to celebrate especially symbolic locations across the city, its boundaries, its central streets and conduits, its institutions and monuments ancient and modern. The relatively new Royal Exchange, for example, is celebrated in a pageant organised by the Dutch merchants. This pageant and the next, at the Great Conduit, are particularly interesting for the way they negotiate the relationship between courtly and urban concerns. The very name of the

Royal Exchange, as pointed out in chapter 1 above, seeks to elevate commerce to the status of a noble pursuit worthy of kings and queens. It does not seek to erase or apologise for what it is, but rather to have its activities acknowledged as on a par with courtly business. There is an ambivalence about this aim, however, which simultaneously fore-grounds trade as a source of civic pride, while also seeking to validate it through a courtly system of values; and this ambivalence is characteristic of the city's stance in representing its relations with the court to itself and the court, both here and elsewhere. It is typically both humble and proud, seeking to display both respect for the monarch and self-respect; it both wants and rejects the idea of royalty for itself.

The language of Dekker's description of the third arch shows some-thing of how this operates. The Dutch pageant, he writes, 'was (as it were by Fate) laid near unto a royal place; for it was a royal and magnificent labour' (p. 58). The location is the Royal Exchange, a location that lends itself to the idealisation of relations between the royal and the civic; and the pageant is of course erected there not by fate but by design, based on symbolic precedent.[7] The arch represents the seventeen Belgian provinces displaying their devotion to the king and places the king within two lines of kingship, the biblical and the English. On the other side (which is, of course, the side towards which the courtly procession's backs would be turned as they rode through the arch) are depictions of Dutch workers weaving and spinning, buying and selling, and an inscrip-tion celebrating the openness of the London market and praying for its continued prosperity: 'That this market may celebrate its own people for their prudent industry, it sends businessmen out anywhere in the world, and humanely admits foreigners: may it increase its fame abroad, its wealth at home' (p. 63; Dutton's translation). The arch celebrates indus-try at every level, from domestic labour to trading on both domestic and international markets; but it does so on the reverse of an arch which first and foremost celebrates the king's personal greatness and his contribu-tion to making that industry possible.

Though a general tendency to prioritise the king over the city is visible throughout the entertainment, the Soper Lane End pageant reveals an undertow of resistance to this from within the city, which bore responsibility for commissioning, sanctioning and paying for all the pageants within its boundaries except the two erected by foreign mer-chants on this occasion. The song Dekker wrote for this pageant cele-brates London as New Troy, but has the unfortunate refrain:

12. The Dutch arch at Cornhill for 1604 royal entry.

'Troynovant is now no more a city'. The song is immediately followed, however, by Dekker's anxious explanation of its refrain:

Nor let the screw of any wresting comment upon these words,

> *Troynovant is now no more a city*

enforce the author's invention away from his own clear, straight, and harmless meaning: all the scope of this fiction stretching only to this point, that London (to do honour to this day, wherein springs up all her happiness) being ravished with unutterable joys, makes no account (for the present) of her ancient title, to be called a city (because that during these triumphs she puts off her formal habit of Trade and Commerce, treading even Thrift itself under foot,) but now becomes a reveller and a courtier. (p. 73)

The interpretation is even longer than quoted above, but the brackets and awkward sentence structure say it all. Dekker is struggling to justify an unacceptable conceit to hostile commentators, the conceit that London becomes a court rather than a city, or, to adopt Dekker's own mixed metaphors, a courtier rather than a citizen, on this day. Over the continuing length of 'this short apology' Dekker reveals, with more defensive brackets, 'that some (to whose settled judgement and authority the censure of these devices was referred) brought (though not bitterly) the life of those lines into question' (p. 74). Evidently some citizens found Dekker's tendency to bend lower towards monarch than towards city hard to stomach.

Dekker's contributions to the *Magnificent Entertainment*, however, are less biased towards the elevation of the monarch than Jonson's. As Jonathan Goldberg has shown, Jonson's arches, the first and last of the sequence, celebrate James in the imperial style which he chose for his own self-presentation throughout his reign (*James I and the Politics of Literature*, pp. 32–55).[8] Classical allusions abound throughout, and Latin is used with deliberate echoes of imperial Rome. The people of London become, in homage to the Roman mode, 'S.P.Q.L.' (*Senatus populusque Londinienses;* the senate and people of London), while James himself, in the inscription on the final gate, is acknowledged as '*Imp. Jacobus Max. Caesar Aug. P.P.*' (The mighty emperor James, Caesar Augustus, Father of the Country).

Yet Roman imperial absolutism is implied by the whole structure of the entertainment, not only by Jonson's pageants. The very presence of arches, as opposed to any other kind of architectural structure, makes an imperialist statement, which is further underlined by the richness, elaboration and allegorical content of these particular arches.[9] The simpler scaffolds bearing the pageants for Elizabeth's coronation entry had manufactured a space in which Elizabeth could play the part of a queen close to her people and speak directly to them with apparently spontaneous grace, but James cast himself in a very different role from the start.[10] With hindsight, the very fact that the royal progress through the city, planned as a coronation procession, did not in fact materialise in that form looks ominous. While clearly James had no control over the virulence of the plague in 1603, which prevented the progress from coinciding with the coronation, the postponement to 1604 is curiously in keeping with James' evident reluctance to participate in the actual event. Unlike Elizabeth, he appears to have remained passive and unresponsive throughout the day. No words of his are recorded, and the impression left by Dekker's account is that he barely concealed his impatience with it all. Dekker's address to the reader sounds a different note of apology from that for the Troynovant refrain, hinting at a displeasure which cannot be made as explicit as that of the city: 'Reader, you must understand, that a regard being had that His Majesty should not be wearied with tedious speeches: a great part of those which are in this book set down, were left unspoken: so that thou dost here receive them as they should have been delivered, not as they were' (p. 115). Even where Dekker notes a relatively positive response from the king, his tone hints, perhaps unintentionally, at the limits of James' interest: 'His Majesty dwelt here a reasonable long time, giving both good allowance to the song and music, and liberally bestowing his eye on the workmanship of the place' (p. 85). According to a later seventeenth-century writer, Arthur Wilson, it was only the promise of never having to endure such a day again that enabled James to play his part through to the end, even with cuts (*History of Great Britain*, pp. 12–13).

From this point on he withdrew from public appearance as far as possible and made his feelings known with 'frowns', if not 'curses', when forced to appear.[11] What James displayed to his subjects, as Goldberg argues, was 'their subjection . . . their need for him and his aloofness from them' (*James I and the Politics of Literature*, pp. 31–2). This had a wider effect on the nature of civic and court performance and the relations between them. As David Bergeron explains (*English Civic Pageantry*, p. 66), urban pageantry thrived, but in increasing isolation from the court; James' lack of interest in making public appearances helped to shift interest away from royal progress pageants, leaving a space in which the lord mayor's show, with its sole focus on London, could flourish. At the same time, the court-only performance of masques was actively encouraged, making masque a much more dominant and sophisticated form than it had ever been before. The drama of court and city hence became increasingly polarised, while over the same period the professional companies also tended to cultivate increasingly separate and distinct repertories and audiences. On the other hand, the private *Britain's Burse* and the more public *Epicoene*, by the same dramatist within a year of each other, signal a new interest developing alongside and despite that polarisation, one which was to become central to later seventeenth-century drama following the Restoration: an interest in the town as the place where court and city meet (though without total willingness to acknowledge its participation in each).

As masque, with its characteristically epiphanic display of the transformative power of the sovereign, became a central part of court life under James, so the project of giving it a place of performance that more fully expressed this same sovereign power became pressing. James first ordered the old temporary Banqueting House erected under Elizabeth to be destroyed and rebuilt in 1606, and the first masque was performed there in January 1608. The building burnt down in 1619, at which point James had yet another new Banqueting House built, to the design of Inigo Jones, Surveyor of the King's Works. Though the first Jacobean Banqueting House had some classical pretensions, displayed in its structure of Doric and Ionic columns, Jones' building was in a different league altogether. Built in stone and still standing today, this was the first neo-Palladian public building in England, giving visible permanence to the classical absolutist vocabulary of the temporary arches and inscriptions of the royal entry of 1604.[12] Less clear, however, is the question of whether the Banqueting House was conceived in isolation or as part of a project to build a new palace at Whitehall. Though when Jones first began to design the building in 1619 the primary intention was probably to replace the previous Banqueting House as a place for masque performances, Rubens had already been invited before the building was complete to paint the ceiling, a project which would necessarily put an end to torchlit performance in the hall, as Jones must have known (Harris and Higgott, *Inigo Jones*, p. 108). Once it was no longer used for masques, the Banqueting Hall became solely a throne room, a place in which to impress on spectators the full majesty of royal power.

What Goldberg calls 'the style of gods' becomes even clearer under James' successor, Charles I. Despite the assumption by the city authorities that he would enter London in the traditional grand style, Charles had no compunction about withdrawing altogether from the proposed event. First postponed in 1625, like the 1604 entry, on account of plague, this pageant was doomed not merely to the bad temper and ungraciousness of the previous event but to downright refusal at a point when preparations were already well advanced and arches in place. Charles' message to the city, conveyed via the Earl of Pembroke, ordered the pageants removed, dismissing them as an expensive nuisance obstructing the traffic and leaving the city to pick up the bill for the very substantial charges (£4,300) uselessly incurred (Bergeron, *English Civic Pageantry*, pp. 106–9). Though pageant theatre, along with other forms of theatrical entertainment, ceased by parliamentary order in 1642, such an order, as David Bergeron comments, was scarcely necessary, 'for the decline in such entertainments noted in the reign of the first Stuart persists and indeed increases in Charles' reign. The years 1625–42 are marked by a striking paucity of civic pageantry with the notable exception of the Lord Mayors' Shows' (p. 105).

Charles, however, while he may have despised the temporary structures designed to express the city's homage, had his own plans for permanent structures designed to express the glories of monarchy in a way more appropriate to his conception of his position. In 1634 he wrote to the lord mayor recommending ways of improving the city, 'being our royal chamber and the principal seat of our residence'.[13] A range of projects for cleaning and safeguarding the city was initiated, and there was discussion too of plans on the grand scale for a new Whitehall palace and a new London Bridge. Ironically, the king, having ordered the city's arches torn down in 1626, specifically requested the addition of arches to the model of the bridge put forward. Arches, as discussed above, represented sovereign power in the tradition of Roman emperors. Charles' hostility to the city's pageant arches was presumably based on his sense that mere temporary structures were a derisory expression of greatness such as his. Two years later, in 1636, the Privy Council instructed representatives of the city to meet with Inigo Jones in order to discuss plans for a permanent triumphal arch to mark the boundary between Westminster and the city of London at Temple Bar. Jones' sketch for the arch survives, but the arch was never built.[14] Construction of a classical portico on the west front of St Paul's, however, was begun in the same year and paid for by the king. 'There was', according to Harris and Higgott, 'no portico like it north of the Alps, and it too [i.e. like the design for Temple Bar] was thoroughly Roman' (*Inigo Jones*, p. 251).

The imperialist vision for both court and city shared by King Charles and his chief architect may be clearly seen in the text and design of the last masque to be staged before the closing of the theatres, *Salmacida Spolia*. Performed in January and February 1640 in the temporary Masquing Room, the text was written by Sir William Davenant, while 'the invention, ornament, scenes and apparitions, with their descriptions, were made by Inigo Jones, Surveyor General of his Majesty's Works' (lines 443–5).[15]

The masque is tied to yet another kind of arch: the proscenium arch. Like the triumphal arch, the proscenium arch's origins are classical and its embellishment is no mere decoration, but part of a visual and allegorical language in which the spectators need to be educated in order to understand the meanings it expresses. This feature of staging gains increasing importance in Inigo Jones' masques during the reigns of James and Charles, and its significance in *Salmacida Spolia* is evident in the number of lines devoted to describing what is here simply called 'the border' (line 19).[16] It is within this description of the arch that the title of the masque is explained:

In the midst of the aforesaid compartment in an oval table was written:
SALMACIDA SPOLIA.
The ancient adages are these:
Salmacida spolia sine sanguine sine sudore, potius quam
Cadmia victoria, ubi ipsos victores pernicies opprimit. (lines 56–60)

The Latin, in David Lindley's translation, reads 'Salmacian spoils, achieved without bloodshed or sweat, rather than a Cadmian victory when destruction falls upon the victors themselves'; but the text of the description goes on to 'set down the histories from whence these proverbs took their original' (lines 62–3). Having recounted the two classical stories on which the proverbs are based over twenty-six lines, the text then hammers out the conceit very explicitly, so that none can fail to grasp the point: 'The allusion is, that his Majesty, out of his mercy and clemency approving the first proverb, seeks by all means to reduce tempestuous and turbulent natures into a sweet calm of civil concord' (lines 90–2). (Throughout the masque, the text of stage directions and description takes up more space than the text of what was spoken or sung.)

The theme of the masque, then, is subjection, but subjection made to look like the spontaneous manifestation of natural harmony. The performance of the masque coincides with a time of growing difficulty for the king, seeking to quell a Scottish rebellion. The aim to subdue unruly subjects is presented, within a classical matrix, as the civilisation of barbarians. It is the king's 'fate', rather than his fault, according to Davenant's text, 'to rule in adverse times' (line 168). He is to be praised for his capacity to endure adversity, not condemned for any part in producing it:

> If it be kingly patience to outlast
> Those storms the people's giddy fury raise
> Till like fantastic winds themselves they waste,
> The wisdom of that patience is thy praise. (lines 321–4)

Following the climactic appearance of the king and queen initiating the resolution of earthly discord, 'the second dance ended, and their Majesties being seated under the state', the scene changes to depict the final picture of 'magnificent buildings composed of several selected pieces of architecture. In the furthest part was a bridge over a river, where many people, coaches, horses, and such like were seen to pass to and fro. Beyond this on the shore were buildings in prospective, which, shooting far from the eye, showed as the suburbs of a great city' (lines 408–13).[17] Into this final tableau, from above, come clouds carrying heavenly figures, 'which celestial prospect, with the chorus below, filled all the whole scene with apparitions and harmony' (lines 418–19), while the closing song celebrates 'obedience wrought / As if not forced to it, but taught' (lines 427–8).

The design of the scene, as John Peacock points out, seems to allude to the grand architectural plans for Westminster and the city of King Charles and Inigo Jones, with the elegant classical structures in the foreground representing the projected new Whitehall palace and the disorderly sprawl of buildings beyond the bridge representing the city of London. By reversing the standard terminology in order to reconceive the city as mere suburbs, 'Jones coolly suggests that the new seat of royal power would itself be a metropolis of overpowering magnitude, relegating the City to its margin. This is not total fantasy. The bridge, if built, would have been another of those interventions in the fabric of the City by which royal authority symbolically framed and contained its subjects' (*Stage Designs of Inigo Jones*, pp. 108–9).

This is absolutism overreaching itself. Retrospectively, the fact that this masque was the last to be staged, a mere two years short of civil war, seems far from accidental. Had civil war not shifted the balance of power again, relations between court and city might have followed a very different trajectory, and theatre might have been very differently incorporated into those relations. As it was, the outcome has the familiarity of legend. The establishment of the commonwealth meant the continued closure of the theatres, while the restoration of the monarchy brought with it a public theatre directly licensed by the king, drawing its audience from the two directions of Westminster and the city into the ever more fashionable location of the West End. Court theatre and public theatre came together, refusing pre-existing theatre buildings, and establishing new, wholly indoor theatres, first in converted tennis courts, and then in purpose-built theatres designed by specially commissioned architects. A changed sense of social space demanded new theatres in new locations to play out new paradigms.

Notes

1 The order is cited in part and discussed at some length by Virginia Gildersleeve (*Government Regulation*, pp. 156–8). William Ingram, however, who has examined the act within the fuller context of the city's other business over the period 1574–6, has warned against subscribing too easily to 'the Tale of the Playhouses in its Victorian form, with the stage set, the contending roles of court and City delineated, the lines drawn for the conflict to come, James Burbage and his fellows singled out for special attention, and the imminent appearance of the Theater scripted as a kind of epiphany' (*Business of Playing*, p. 122). This caveat notwithstanding, however, Ingram does acknowledge the likely bearing of the 1574 act on the building of the Theatre in 1576.

2 As Ingram points out, the patent should probably not be seen as a response to the statute, since the statute already exempted players with a noble patron from its penalties (*Business of Playing*, p. 121). Despite the patent's reference to the need to have plays approved by the Master of the Revels, there was no permanent master in post at the time, and none of the depositions given to the acting master mentions a duty to license plays. It was not until the appointment of a permanent master was confirmed in 1579 (and especially after 1581, when a royal patent greatly increased his authority; see below) that the system of a court official actively licensing plays for public performance seems to have become effectively established (Dutton, *Mastering the Revels*, pp. 35–48).

3 The order is quoted at greater length by Gildersleeve, who makes the case for dating it to 1582 (*Government Regulation*, pp. 163–5).

4 The formation of the Queen's Men followed within two months of the Paris Garden incident, when a scaffold collapsed, killing and injuring some of the spectators. It may be that the important step of establishing a company under royal protection was in part aimed at anticipating and obstructing any attempt by the anti-theatrical lobby, including the city authorities, to exploit what might appear to be the hand of God at work in order to attract more support for outlawing plays and players.

5 Only the boy companies played inside the city up to 1608, and their play-houses were free of city jurisdiction by virtue of being placed within eccle-siastical liberties. In 1608 the King's Men took possession of the Blackfriars Theatre and the city of London took possession of what had been the liberty of the Blackfriars (see further chapter 5 below; and for discussion of the term 'liberty', see chapter 1, p. 33 below).

6 Bernard Beckerman has argued that 'almost every popular pre-Globe play is distanced in time or place or both', adding that 'no matter how reminis-cent of a contemporary Londoner a character may have been, the audience reposed in the fiction that he was an Italian, a Roman, or an ancestor' (*Shakespeare at the Globe*, pp. 147, 149). I think Beckerman overemphasises the effect of this distancing. I would be inclined to put the argument the other way round and stress that, despite the fictional distancing of time or place, numerous plays invite a London audience to see their own world cutting across that apparently different time or place. The Boar's Head and Exchange locations discussed below are only two of many examples of strik-ing anachronism that serve to highlight the way contemporary London pushes through historicised fictions, and some of Jonson's Italian settings provide equally obvious examples of the tokenism of fictional place (see below, chapter 3 n15). It is worth noting too that occasional plays before the 1570s had evoked a London location at least in passing, especially in scenes showing sinful behaviour. Folly in *The World and the Child*, for example, talks of eating, drinking and gaming at the Pope's Head in Eastcheap (Bullough prints this passage in his *Narrative and Dramatic Sources of Shakespeare*, vol. IV, p. 243).

7 Dodsley's edition does not number scenes or lines, so references are by page number only.

8 Harbage's *Annals* dates the play to 1596–1600, but it is commonly dated 1588–90. I mention it here in case it is a particularly early example of its kind. The detail of the play's concern with London's topography is revealed, for example, in a dialogue between Brown and Mrs Drury concerning Anne Sanders' residence by St Dunstan's church. When Brown seeks her confirmation that St Dunstan's is in Fleet Street, she responds that, on the contrary, the St Dunstan's she has in mind is St Dunstan's in the east, near Billingsgate.

9 Michel de Certeau suggests making a clear distinction between the terms 'place' and 'space' whereby place (*lieu*) refers to a distinct or 'proper' loca-tion, while space (*espace*), in relation to place, 'is like the word when it is spoken', the effect of its multiple determining contexts (*Practice of Everyday Life*, p. 117). The problem with using such a distinction, however, is that it is purely theoretical and masks the way the two are necessarily bound up in practice.

10 The Bankside theatres are frequently described by modern critics as being outside the city boundary because they were across the river in Southwark,

but this is incorrect. It was because they were located within the liberties of Paris Garden and the Clink in Southwark that they were outside city jurisdiction. On the liberties, see further chapters 1 and 5 below.

11 Southwark, as David Johnson points out, was a fairly loose term 'virtually synonymous with the King's, Great Liberty, and Guildable Manors' (*Southwark and the City*, p. 117).

12 See e.g. Malcolm Smuts, 'Cultural Diversity and Cultural Change at the Court of James I', and Pauline Croft, 'Robert Cecil and the Early Jacobean Court'. John Norden's map of Westminster (figure 2) marks the location of the Strand palaces.

13 Smuts argues that much historical writing on the Stuart court exaggerates its separation from other cultural environments. 'No effective barriers', he insists, 'separated courtiers from other peers and gentlemen in the metropolis . . . Any attempt to distinguish sharply between the court's culture and that of fashionable London will therefore run into difficulties' ('Cultural Diversity', p. 103).

14 William Cecil's father, Richard Cecil, was a mere Groom of the Wardrobe on his death; his grandfather, David Cecil, was a Welshman of obscure origins who came to England with Henry VII and rose to the position of Yeoman of the Guard.

15 For fuller discussion of each of the different assemblies, see Pearl, *London and the Outbreak of the Puritan Revolution*, ch. 3. Common Hall was supposed to include all the liverymen of the city, though it seems to have been possible for men of lower social status to attend, and even to vote, since there was no system for checking the entitlement of those present. The Court of Common Council was much smaller than Common Hall and made up of elected representatives from the body of freemen. In practice, however, according to Pearl, 'there seems to have been a strong feeling that liverymen should be elected' (p. 54). Hence all three governing bodies of the city of London were tied to the trade guilds by definition, and two out of the three favoured the higher social ranks within the guilds. Only in Common Hall was there any question of those outside the company system having a say, and then only illegitimately.

16 Cf. Douglas Bruster's study of the functioning of props within the drama of this period as manifesting the degree to which the plays are fixated on moveable objects, and subjectivity is tied up with 'the cultural status of property'. The social world of this drama, he argues, is one 'in which subject and object seek new relationships' (*Drama and the Market*, pp. 43, 40).

17 Though this display is naturally most marked at the highest levels of society, 'no class of society, not even the most abjectly poor', Veblen notes, 'foregoes all customary conspicuous consumption' (*Theory of the Leisure Class*, p. 85).

18 On the concept of luxury and the later emergence of another offspring of capitalism, 'the *necessary* luxury', see also Ferguson, 'Feathers and Flies'.

19 Riggs selects these dates as the parameters because they are respectively the year of Jonson's birth and the year of his first recorded dramatic activity.

They coincide quite closely, however, with the arrival of dedicated theatre buildings in London and the beginning of the 'second generation' of playhouse building towards the close of the century.

20 The Shakespeare family took the motto *Non Sanz Droict* (not without right). Jonson's Sogliardo, like Shakespeare, buys a coat of arms which bears the motto 'Not Without Mustard'.

21 Thomas Middleton's usual signature was 'T. M., gent.' As Margot Heinemann rightly points out, of course, it was quite commonplace for the younger sons of gentry to be apprenticed into trade (*Puritanism and Theatre*, p. 49 and n4).

22 The record is cited in the introduction to the Cambridge edition of Webster, by David Gunby *et al.* (p. 5).

23 This speculation is offered by Gunby *et al.* (*Webster, Works*, p. 6).

24 Bernard Beckerman notes that during two weeks in November 1595 it was possible to see eleven performances of ten different plays at one playhouse, of which six were new plays, two were from the previous season and two were revivals of older plays (*Shakespeare at the Globe*, p. 7). Peter Thomson, taking a two-week period in September of the same year, finds only two plays repeated from the first week during the second week, and a total of ten different plays over the fortnight (*Shakespeare's Theatre*, p. 59). The typical lifespan of a new script, according to Beckerman's estimate, was about two weeks.

25 I am using the term 'city' loosely here. As I have made clear above, plays were not performed within the city jurisdiction after playing at city inns was banned. But performance in and around the margins of the city would draw an audience from inside as well as outside the city.

1 CITY, COURT AND THEATRE

1 Stow's *Survey of London* was first printed in 1598 and issued in a second edition in 1603. Quotations are taken from Charles Kingsford's edition, which is based on the text of 1603.

2 Ian Archer cites several instances from Stow's *Survey* in 'Nostalgia of John Stow', p. 22 and note 11. See also Fisher, 'Development of London as a Centre of Conspicuous Consumption', p. 37. The discussion of population that follows, together with much subsequent material in this chapter, is also indebted to Archer, *Pursuit of Stability*; Finlay and Shearer, 'Population Growth and Suburban Expansion'; Manning, *Village Revolts*; McMullan, *Canting Crew*; Pearl, 'Change and Stability'; and three publications by Steve Rappaport, 'Social Structure and Mobility in Sixteenth-Century London', parts I and II, and *Worlds Within Worlds*. See also Vanessa Harding's caveat about different ways of arriving at population data in 'Population of London, 1550–1700'.

3 Stow's lament for Hog Lane (vol. I, p. 127) is often cited, though it is not his only outburst of the kind. See e.g. Pearl, *London and the Outbreak of the Puritan Revolution*, p. 11 and Rappaport, *Worlds Within Worlds*, p. 65.

4 See Pearl, *London and the Outbreak of the Puritan Revolution*, p. 18 and Brett-James, *Growth of Stuart London*, pp. 75–84. A proclamation within months of James' accession in 1603 was the first of ten issued in the course of the reign (1603, 1605, 1607, 1608, etc.).

5 On the government of London see further Foster, *Politics of Stability* (esp. chs. 1 and 2) and Pearl, *London and the Outbreak of the Puritan Revolution*, ch. 2.

6 For a fuller picture of the economic circumstances underpinning vagrancy in London, see McMullan, *Canting Crew*, ch. 2. The city did take steps to control this expansion: two marshals (appointed temporarily in 1589–90 and continuously from 1595), each with six beadles, kept watch over the city gates between the hours of 7 p.m. to 11 p.m. and 3 a.m. to 7 a.m. in order to prevent the entrance of vagrants, and searches for vagabonds were regularly undertaken, sometimes by the recorder of London in person.

7 The statute of 1563 specifying that young men had to be the sons of forty-shilling freeholders in order to qualify for apprenticeship specifically excluded London from its ruling. This encouraged many of those seeking apprenticeship to move to London. The term 'apprentice', as Roger Manning notes, was used rather loosely by contemporaries, and has been argued for by Steven Smith as a distinct youth subculture (Manning, *Village Revolts*, p. 192; Smith, 'London Apprentices as Seventeenth-Century Adolescents'). The term 'alien' (or 'stranger'), it should be noted, is the usual sixteenth-century term for a non-English person; a 'foreigner' was an English-born immigrant to London who had not attained citizen status.

8 On the arguments for orderliness, see Foster, *Politics of Stability*; Pearl, 'Change and Stability' and 'Social Policy'; and Rappaport, 'Social Structure and Mobility', Parts i and ii and *Worlds Within Worlds*. On the scale and importance of disorder, see Archer, *Pursuit of Stability*; Ashton, 'Popular Entertainment and Social Control'; Lindley, 'Riot Prevention and Control'; and Manning, *Village Revolts*.

9 For a brief outline of the distinction between these terms, see Pearl, *London and the Outbreak of the Puritan Revolution*, p. 55.

10 For fuller discussion see Pearl, 'Change and Stability'. Each ward elected between 100 and 300 officers according to size, and in small wards this could mean that one in every three householders was required to serve at any one time. Rights and responsibilities went hand-in-hand: non rate-paying householders could not vote, and inmates (lodgers), vagrants, women, apprentices and servants were similarly excluded from voting rights (Pearl, 'Change and Stability', pp. 16–18; cf. Pearl, 'Social Policy', pp. 116–17). The fee for becoming a householder could amount to several weeks' wages (Rappaport, 'Social Structure and Mobility: Part ii', p. 126), but clearly aspiring householders were willing to pay both in cash and in service for the rights and status they gained in return.

11 Platter was not the only foreign visitor to record his impressions of the building. The earliest description, a lengthy account by a Frenchman called Grenade, is reproduced in translation in Ann Saunders' recently published

collection of essays on the Exchange (*Royal Exchange*, pp. 48–9). Two engravings of the building made by Franz Hogenberg around 1569–70 also survive (see figures 6 and 7). Saunders offers a detailed reading of these in 'Building of the Exchange', pointing out that they are 'the earliest known topographical engravings of any English building', and speculating on their possible association with the queen's visit to the Exchange in January 1571. The problem with the engravings, however, is that it is unclear how closely the detail corresponds to the reality. Some features of the engravings were certainly not incorporated into the actual building until the seventeenth century (pp. 40–3).

12 Manley provides a very full account of what he calls the 'syntax' of ceremonial routes, together with maps, in chapter 5 of his *Literature and Culture*. His map of major processional routes is reproduced here as figure 5. Popular rituals might also incorporate the perambulation of boundaries, as at Rogationtide.

13 The court was also becoming increasingly like the city in as far as it was itself a marketplace, selling rights and privileges in order to bring in much-needed income.

14 The ambiguity of the word 'prest' is richly functional here within the context of Stow's project of glorifying the city. It can mean either the same as 'loan', including a forced loan or imposition, or it can mean a gift. Failure to resolve its meaning in this sentence allows it to suggest the city's munificence without erasing the possibility of the crown's oppression of the city.

15 The terms were provisionally agreed between the king and Parliament in the summer of 1610, but both parties wanted to renegotiate after the summer recess, and then failed to reach agreement (see further Smith, *Emergence of a Nation State*, pp. 252–5; Akrigg, *Jacobean Pageant*, pp. 91–5).

16 Lawrence Manley points out that the mayor was commonly addressed as 'lord' mayor in internal communications from about 1535–40, but the external use of the title dates from 1545 (*Literature and Culture*, p. 267, citing Withington, *English Pageantry*, vol. II, p. 13). Other critics writing on changes and developments in ceremonies celebrated in the city of London include Berlin, 'Civic Ceremony'; Bradbrook, 'Politics of Pageantry (London)'; Knowles, 'Spectacle of the Realm'; Manley, *Literature and Culture*, esp. ch. 5; and Paster, 'Idea of London in Masque and Pageant'. Much of this writing is broadly indebted to the pioneering work of David M. Bergeron's *English Civic Pageantry* and to Charles Phythian Adams' well-known essay, 'Ceremony and the Citizen'.

17 On the appropriation of this popular festival by a civic elite see Berlin, 'Civic Ceremony'. On the specific displacement and absorption of features of the midsummer watch by the lord mayor's show, see further Manley, 'Of Sites and Rites', pp. 47–8 and *Literature and Culture*, pp. 264–6. Both Archer and Manley note Stow's conspicuous silence on the question of the lord mayor's show. Manley finds it 'surprising', and suggests that it may not have been a fully established ceremony by the time Stow's *Survey* was published

('Of Sites and Rites', pp. 47–8), while Archer reads it as conveying a probable scepticism about the authenticity of 'such recently invented traditions' ('Nostalgia of John Stow', p. 24).

18 Stow's Catholicism may partly account for his nostalgia and his lack of sympathy with the self-celebrating ceremonies of a strongly Protestant city government. (On the Puritan cast of sixteenth-century city governors, see further Foster, *Politics of Stability*.)

19 The full dedication is to 'the commonalty and citizens' of London as well as to the mayor. Edward Bonahue argues that the *Survey*'s emphasis on London and its governors leads Stow to play down the deeds of monarchs and aristocrats, so that civic presence decentres the role of kings and peers in making history ('Citizen History').

20 Lawrence Manley's anthology of writings relating to London, *London in the Age of Shakespeare*, represents a mere selection of the immense amount of available material.

21 Valerie Pearl notes that, while seventeenth-century writers used the term 'suburbs' to include outparishes and liberties as well as areas completely outside both city walls and city jurisdiction, more specificity is desirable in a modern analysis (*London and the Outbreak of the Puritan Revolution*, p. 10 n3). One of the problems of Steven Mullaney's analysis of city space in *The Place of the Stage* is his loose use of the term 'Liberties of London' (a term I discuss further below) to mean everything outside the city's jurisdiction. Mullaney also writes as though all theatre took place by definition in the 'margins' of the city from 1576 on.

22 See further Gildersleeve, *Government Regulation*, p. 142; Pearl, *London and the Outbreak of the Puritan Revolution*, pp. 23–9; and Friedrichs, *Early Modern City*, pp. 30–2. As Frank Foster points out: 'The question of the City's jurisdiction has never been treated extensively. Such a study would have to discover the special arrangements that existed between the City and each of the liberties and suburbs' (*Politics of Stability*, p. 184). The city's rights and responsibilities, he concludes, 'were ambiguous at best' (p. 185). Several critics have commented on the contradictory and overdetermined sense of words like 'freedom', 'liberty' and 'licence' in this civic context. See e.g. Gildersleeve, *Government Regulation*, p. 142; Wells, 'Jacobean City Comedy', pp. 41–2; and Mullaney, *Place of the Stage*, pp. 21–2.

23 Precisely because there was no guild of actors, boys, it would seem, could not be apprenticed to actors in their capacity as actors, but had to be apprenticed to those members of the company who were also members of existing craft guilds, hence technically becoming apprentice joiners, goldsmiths and so on. Forse compiles a useful table demonstrating how many of those in the theatre business can also be associated with other occupations (*Art Imitates Business*, pp. 8–9). The problem with this reading of the evidence, however, as Andrew Gurr points out, is that it does not account for those players who were not apparently members of any company, and yet

had apprentices. Gurr further underlines the limits of the parallel between the systems of theatre and city companies in terms of the age of apprentices. The minimum age for completing an apprenticeship was fixed by statute at 24, and the average age at which an apprenticeship began in London was 17.7; but these parameters were irrelevant to theatre companies, who needed boys with unbroken voices (*Shakespearian Playing Companies*, p. 100).

24 George Peele, the first notable dramatist commissioned to write for the city (in 1585), may not have written for the public theatres before this date, though his work had certainly been performed at court. By the first decade of the seventeenth century, however, the city was routinely employing public-theatre dramatists to write its pageants.

25 See also chapters 6 and 7 below, where Jonson's different attitude towards the 'town' (in the double sense of both elegant society and the developing area west of the city) in a commissioned entertainment and a play for public performance are discussed.

26 The concepts of use and waste are not, as Veblen notes, mutually exclusive. 'It would be hazardous', he argues, 'to assert that a useful purpose is ever absent from the utility of any article or of any service, however obviously its prime purpose and chief element is conspicuous waste; and it would be only less hazardous to assert of any primarily useful product that the element of waste is in no way concerned in its value, immediately or remotely' (*Theory of the Leisure Class*, p. 101).

27 On the phenomenon of the *Wunderkammer* see further Mullaney, *Place of the Stage*, pp. 60–4; Von Holst, *Creators, Collectors and Connoisseurs*, pp. 103–16; and Wittlin, *The Museum*, pp. 4, 52–4, 58–65. Walter Cope, it should be noted, also moved in court circles, was knighted in 1603, and was a close friend of Sir Robert Cecil (see further chapter 6 below); the distinction between courtly and urban fashion becomes characteristically blurred here.

28 The quotation is from the title page of Richard Johnson's *Nine Worthies of London* (1592). My attention was first drawn to this text by Louis B. Wright (*Middle-Class Culture*, p. 166), who offers much fuller discussion of the movement and overlap between different class cultures.

29 De Witt, visiting the Swan in 1600, is quoted in Gurr, *Shakespearean Stage*, p. 132. John Orrell also cites De Witt among others in his discussion of the contemporary tendency to see the new theatres in terms of classical precedent, noting that visitors repeatedly use the terms *theatrum* and *amphitheatrum* in their accounts of the London playhouses (*Human Stage*, pp. 45–8).

30 The cramped size of the shops also offered a marked contrast with the spaciousness of the courtyard. They measured a mere 5 feet (1.52 metres) in width and 7½ feet (2.28 metres) in depth (Staniland, 'Thomas Deane's Shop in the Royal Exchange', p. 60; Saunders, 'Organisation of the Exchange', p. 89). Staniland compares them with platform kiosks on the London Underground, and her study of the inventory of one of the first tenants to

occupy a shop in the Royal Exchange suggests that the design of the shops was fairly traditional, with a stallboard for laying out goods which was used to shut up the shop overnight. The novelty, as she notes, was in bringing together so many shops within one dedicated building.

2 THE PLACE OF EXCHANGE

1 Heywood, *Dramatic Works*, p. 87. All quotations from the play are taken from this edition, which does not number scenes or lines. In modernising spelling I have retained archaic word forms (e.g. 'thorough') where to alter them would affect the metre, and have rationalised Shepherd's 'ed' spellings to ''d' where the verse rhythm demands it. Heywood's authorship of the play is not firmly established, though it is likely he had at least a hand in it. The question of authorship is not germane to the arguments of the chapter, and I have assumed Heywood's authorship for the purposes of discussion here.

2 The stage direction for costuming Shore and Josselin, cited above, seems to suggest they are of the same rank. Heywood, however, seems to be elevating Shore above his historical rank. Stow describes him as 'a right honest substantial young man' (*Annals*, p. 456), and Holinshed calls him 'an honest citizen, young and godly, and of good substance' (*Holinshed's Chronicles*, vol. III, p. 384).

3 On the dating of *Edward IV*, see further note 1 to chapter 3 below.

4 The 'Hospital of London' is presumably Christ's Hospital, which had responsibility for orphans at this time (Archer, *Pursuit of Stability*, pp. 154–63). Edward Sugden points out that this reference is anachronistic, since Christ's Hospital did not exist as such in the reign of Edward IV (*Topographical Dictionary*, p. 118).

5 It is worth noting that Heywood allows the particularity of this moment to take precedence over the flow of the verse. Though the scene is otherwise entirely in verse, the differences in rank and name here are sufficiently important to be highlighted by their individual rhythms, just as they come in formal sequence, and unaltered by the potential demands of the verse line. The word 'up' in line 2, which Shepherd omits from his edition, makes the departure from the smoothness of verse even more conspicuous.

6 Both Alexander Leggatt and Kathleen McLuskie have emphasised the extent to which popular theatre is underpinned by the principle of variety, though McLuskie, rejecting the cultural loading inherent in the concept of the 'popular', offers to conceive of this kind of dramaturgy instead as 'professional' (Leggatt, *Jacobean Public Theatre*, pp. 37–9, 106–8; McLuskie, *Dekker and Heywood*, pp. 9–11).

7 Shepherd's edition mistakenly prints 'fanion' for 'franion'. A franion is a gallant, 'a gay reckless fellow' (*OED*).

8 See further my discussion of Shakespeare's *Henry V* and *2 Henry VI* in *Language and Stage*, chs. 7 and 8.

9 Kathleen McLuskie similarly notes unresolved tensions in the play:

> The play deals very gingerly with the dangerous contradictions of popular politics. The city, the apprentices and the crown are marshalled in support of the ideology of rightful monarchy. The allegiance works symbolically in the theatrical psycho-machia of the alarums and excursions but the overdetermined insistence of the speeches, the array of ideologically fraught reference and imagery suggest tensions in the political understanding which are far from completely resolved. (*Dekker and Heywood*, p. 58)

3 FROM RETREAT TO DISPLAY

1 Derby's Men were the first company to challenge the London duopoly of the Chamberlain's and the Admiral's Men in 1599, and the play was published in 1600. Robert Browne, who led the company in 1599, was involved in the conversion of the Boar's Head over the summer of 1599. It would seem likely, therefore, that the play was performed at the Boar's Head in 1599 or early 1600. Lord Strange's Men were also briefly known as Derby's Men between September 1593 and April 1594, when their patron became Earl of Derby a few months before his death, but there is no evidence to suggest that the play should be dated to that earlier period. Indeed the attribution of it to 1599 is strengthened by the fact that it was around this time that a rival company, the Admiral's Men, began to develop a more specialist repertory structured 'more narrowly and explicitly' around just this kind of citizen appeal (Gurr, *Shakespearian Playing Companies*, pp. 265–6, 244–5).

2 Stow has been citing Hall's account of how Londoners assembled during the reign of Henry VIII to pull down hedges erected around previously open fields (*Hall's Chronicle*, p. 568). Now, according to Stow, things are 'in worse case than ever'.

3 I quote Johnson because he is evidently familiar with, and concerned to refute, Stow's reading of the implications of luxury building in London. Before either Stow or Johnson, however, John Norden can be found writing admiringly in 1593 of similar developments in his description of Middlesex:

> This shire is plentifully stored, and as it seemeth beautified, with many fair, and comely buildings, especially of the merchants of London, who have planted their houses of recreation not in the meanest places: which also they have cunningly contrived, curiously beautified, with divers devices, neatly decked with rare inventions, environed with orchards of sundry delicate fruits, gardens with delectable walks, arbours, alleys, and great variety of pleasing dainties. (*Speculum Britanniae*, p. 12)

4 This moment is also celebrated in the public theatre in Heywood's *If You Know Not Me*, with a consciousness of myth-making revealed in Gresham's words as he performs the action:

> Here's a brick, here's a fair sovereign.
> Thus I begin; be it hereafter told,
> I laid the first stone with a piece of gold. (*Dramatic Works*, vol. 1, p. 290)

5 Valerie Pearl also notes a growing unwillingness to hold the office of sheriff from the later sixteenth century onwards, though she points out that this was partly because the expense could ruin the office-holder. Refusal to take up office, however, entailed the payment of a fine. Pearl notes the passing of an Act of Common Council in 1592 to reward the citizen who accepted the office, after refusal by all the other nominees, with a payment of £100 (*London and the Outbreak of the Puritan Revolution*, p. 65). Mumford reads the general growth of domesticity and privacy as a sign of weakening public interest. Instead of attending to the civic interest, he argues, citizens developed a new kind of useless work, 'the care of furniture' (and by 'furniture', Mumford means anything that is primarily for display rather than use: ornaments, bric-a-brac, objects that required washing, dusting or polishing) (*City in History*, pp. 437–40).

6 Quotations are taken from G. R. Hibbard's edition of the play.

7 The phrase is Armado's. Though he is not part of the academy, he represents the impulse towards fashion in its purest form. Hibbard prints the Quarto spelling, 'singuled', here in order to emphasise his view that this is Armado's own variation on the existing term, 'singled'.

8 My thinking about language here is indebted to Peter Womack's work on Jonson, which has implications for thinking about dramatic language much more widely in the period (cf. also Barish, *Ben Jonson*).

9 Reputedly the longest word known.

10 Thorstein Veblen's analysis of how and why a knowledge of the classics is important to the leisure class is potentially relevant here. He argues that it is the very pointlessness (from any functional point of view) of the dead languages that gives them their 'talismanic virtue'. It is 'their utility as evidence of wasted time and effort, and hence of the pecuniary strength necessary in order to afford this waste' that allows them to enhance the desired reputation (*Theory of the Leisure Class*, pp. 396–7). Ornamental language of any kind participates to some extent in this honorific function. Made up, as it is, of fragments (from classical languages, foreign vernaculars, learned discourse, archaism and neologism), it signals the expenditure of time, the time to have travelled, studied, conversed with many types and accumulated bits and pieces from all kinds of leisured activities.

11 I owe the reference to these lines from *The Scourge of Villainy* to a note by Reavley Gair in his edition of *Antonio's Revenge* (note to 1.iii.22).

12 Lewis Mumford conceives of 'baroque' time and space in relation to each other and within the overall context of the structure of baroque power. The mathematical organisation of space in the grand avenues of the baroque city, he argues, privileges 'the act of passage' over 'the object reached'; and in a similar way, the more mathematical conception of time, which breaks it up into strictly measurable fragments, privileges 'moment-to-moment continuum' over the *longue durée*. 'The abstractions of money, spatial perspective, and mechanical time', he continues, 'provided the enclosing frame of the new life. Experience was progressively reduced to just those elements that were

capable of being split off from the whole and measured separately: conventional counters took the place of organisms' (*City in History*, pp. 418–19).

13 Harbage quotes, by way of example, a letter of January 1605 from Walter Cope to Robert Cecil, informing him that 'Burbage is come, and says there is no new play that the Queen hath not seen, but they have revived an old one, called *Love's Labour Lost* [*sic*], which for wit and mirth he says will please her exceedingly' (p. 20).

14 The plays usually considered to constitute the 'war' are (in probable chronological order): *Every Man Out Of His Humour* (1599), *Jack Drum's Entertainment* (1600), *Cynthia's Revels* (1600–1), *What You Will* (1601), *Poetaster* (1601) and *Satiromastix* (1601). *Histriomastix* (1598–9) is sometimes added to this list as the trigger for the parody of Marston in Jonson's *Every Man Out Of His Humour* (see further below); and *2 Return from Parnassus* (1601–2), a Cambridge University play, makes reference to the theatrical rivalry of these years. *Every Man Out* was first performed by the Chamberlain's Men, as were two earlier trendsetting plays, *Love's Labour's Lost* (*c.* 1595) and *Every Man In His Humour* (1598); two more of Jonson's plays, *Cynthia's Revels* and *Poetaster*, were written for the Chapel Children at the Blackfriars, and a third, *The Case Is Altered* (1597–8), was certainly performed by them at some point after its first performance; Marston's plays from this period (*Jack Drum's Entertainment*, *What You Will* and the two *Antonio* plays) were written for Paul's Boys, while *Histriomastix* has been attributed to Paul's Boys, but was more probably written for the Middle Temple (Finkelpearl, 'John Marston's *Histriomastix* as an Inns of Court Play'). Dekker's *Satiromastix*, unusually, was performed by Paul's Boys and the Chamberlain's Men. I have not confined discussion in this chapter solely to theatre-war plays, since I believe the war should be seen in the wider context of certain other plays concerned with the same issues of fashion and fashionable language around this time. An excellent short narrative of the 'War', explaining the personal allusions encrypted in the plays, is Cyrus Hoy's account (*Introductions*, vol. I, pp. 179–97). On the other hand, as Roslyn Knutson has argued, the term 'war' almost certainly exaggerates the degree and extent of any rivalry between companies ('Falconer to the Little Eyases'). Both Paul's Boys and the Chapel Children were certainly active again by 1600, with Paul's Boys the earlier of the two to reopen. Reavley Gair states categorically that 'no children's drama was available to the general public in London until the very last weeks of the sixteenth century', though occasional private performances for invited guests may have taken place (*Children of Paul's*, p. 113). Michael Shapiro argues that Paul's Boys may have resumed playing before 1599–1600, possibly in 1597–8 (*Children of the Revels*, p. 18). Gurr assigns dates of 1599 and 1600 respectively to the two companies, and argues that scholars up to now have been slow to recognise the subsequent distinctiveness of the two repertories: 'While the Blackfriars Boys allied themselves with the gentry, lawyers, courtiers, and satirists, the Paul's company allied itself more and more with the London citizenry' (*Shakespearian Playing Companies*, p. 341).

The Blackfriars Boys, as he demonstrates, were the only company who maintained a consistently satirical repertory after the poetomachia, and Marston, who wrote the plays for Paul's Boys' first run, moved to the Blackfriars once the emphasis on citizen interests emerged at Paul's. The citizen's jibe at the Blackfriars Boys in *The Knight of the Burning Pestle*, when he accuses them of staging 'girds at citizens' for seven years (see chapter 5 below), should be understood as a way of distinguishing, 'however comically and involuntarily . . . the one boy company from the other' (p. 343).

15 *Cynthia's Revels* is entirely set at court, for example, while *Jack Drum's Entertainment* is set in the village of Highgate. Both nevertheless introduce figures whose ties to the city are heavily underlined: Asotus, in *Cynthia's Revels*, is first referred to as 'son to the late deceased Philargyrus the citizen', a fact which prompts Amorphus to ask for more detail about his background ('Was his father of any eminent place, or means?') and to lament that he is not 'more gently propagated' (i.iii.30–5; for note on quotations from Jonson, see *Conventions and Abbreviations* at the front of this volume); Mammon, in *Jack Drum*, is socially pinpointed with similar care as, from two points of view, 'a club-fisted usurer' and 'a wealthy, careful, thriving citizen' (Act I; *The Plays of John Marston*, ed. H. Harvey Wood, vol. III, p. 187. Wood's edition of Marston's plays has no line numbers, so quotations here cite act divisions and page numbers. I have cited Marston's plays in individual editions with full line numbering where available, but have had to use Wood's edition for *Jack Drum's Entertainment* and *Histriomastix*.) Jonson presents his depictions of London under transparent guises (Milan, Florence, classical Rome), though the Folio text of *Every Man In His Humour* is notable for the fact that it translates the scene from Florence (the setting in the Quarto version) to London. The fictional distancing that Beckerman notes up to 1599 (see prologue, n6 above) becomes after that date an increasingly self-conscious affair, in which contemporary London stands in joking relationship with the token setting.

16 The only real exceptions are the privately performed *Parnassus* plays. Even a play like *Cynthia's Revels*, which Jonson may have written specifically in the hopes of court performance, and which was indeed performed at court in January 1601, was first performed at the Blackfriars and advertised in this way on the quarto title page (the folio title page cited only the company, while the quarto cited both company and theatre). It would seem, furthermore, that the play was not a success at court (see Herford and Simpson, *Ben Jonson*, vol. IX, p. 189).

17 The voguishness of extravagant speech outside the theatre is implicit not only in Dekker's advice to the gallant to cultivate it (quoted at the close of chapter 1 above) but also in Jonson's prose condemnation of the linguistic deformities of the time: 'Nothing is fashionable, till it be deformed . . . All must be as affected and preposterous as our gallants' clothes, sweet bags, and night-dressings: in which you would think our men lay in, like ladies: it is so curious' (*Discoveries*; Herford and Simpson, ed., *Ben Jonson*, vol. VIII, p. 581).

18 It is worth noticing how the speech finds its real centre of interest in dilating on the city at this point, where Amorphus catalogues the ways in which he might praise the city or

> the wise magistrates thereof, in which politic number, 'tis odds but his father filled up a room? Descend into a particular admiration of their justice; for the due measuring of coals, burning of cans, and such like? As also their religion, in pulling down a superstitious cross, and advancing a Venus or Priapus in place of it? Ha? 'Twill do well. Or to talk of some hospital whose walls record his father a benefactor? Or of so many buckets bestowed on his parish church, in his lifetime, with his name at length, for want of arms, tricked upon them? Any of these? Or to praise the cleanness of the street wherein he dwelt? Or the provident painting of his posts against he should have been praetor? (i.iv.70–89)

19 The *OED* cites this occurrence in *Cynthia's Revels* as the first recorded use of the word 'puff' in the sense of 'one who brags or behaves insolently, or who is puffed up or swollen with pride or vanity', but earlier senses are clearly part of the word's force both here and in Marston's character (whose speech indicates that he also literally intersperses his words with puffs of air). In particular, the meanings given under 6a ('An inflated speech or piece of display; an empty or vain boast . . . inflation of style, bombast') and 6b ('Anything empty, vain, or insubstantial; a "thing of nought"') seem especially relevant. (Crites, it should be noted, is named Criticus in the Quarto edition of the play.)

20 I have elsewhere argued that such a figure may usefully be understood through the later concept of the *flâneur*, who is by definition a creature of the expanding city (see 'Fashion, City and Theatre in Late Sixteenth-Century London', forthcoming in a collection of essays entitled *Shakespeare and his Contemporaries in Performance*, edited by Edward Esche, published by Ashgate Press).

21 Jonson had already drawn attention to the word 'capricious' in *The Case Is Altered* (ii.vii.62–9). When Valentine first makes reference to 'a few capricious gallants', Juniper interjects to note the word as object ('Capricious? Stay, that word's for me') before allowing Valentine to continue with his disapproval of such types, who, he says, find fault with everything. Herford and Simpson note the reappearance of the word amongst those isolated for scorn in *Patient Grissil* (1600), which mocks 'those changeable silk gallants' who 'chew between their teeth terrible words, as though they would conjure'. 'Capricious' is one of several 'fustian outlandish phrases' listed here, including 'compliment' (ii.i.57–62, in *Dramatic Works of Thomas Dekker*, ed. Fredson Bowers, vol. i).

4 THE PLACE OF DIRT

1 These are the first lines of the play proper. Leishmann numbers from the beginning of the prologue.

2 The 1609 Quarto refers to performance by the Children of the Blackfriars. The company did not go by this name until 1606, though it was in existence from 1600. It is not clear which company might have performed it in 1597–8.

3 Mary Douglas' work (*Purity and Danger*) offers a full analysis, from an anthropological perspective, of how conceptions of 'clean' and 'dirty' are shaped within a given culture.

4 For a fuller picture of the Inns of Court in this period see Finkelpearl, *John Marston*, especially chapter 1, from which this information is taken.

5 The universities also celebrated Christmas revels in the tradition of misrule, electing a mock-sovereign along the same lines as the Inns, but the extant manuscript documenting this kind of celebration at St John's College, Oxford, in 1607–8 seems to indicate that student revels were confined within the college.

6 A resemblance to Shakespeare's Armado may be intended here. Herford and Simpson note that Juniper's next foreign interjection, 'What *fortuna de la guerra?*' (i.iv.13–14) echoes Armado's use of the same phrase in *Love's Labour's Lost* (at v.ii.527).

7 Gail Paster's book, *The Body Embarrassed*, touches indirectly on the relations between urban satire and the leaking body. Her first chapter, 'Leaky Vessels', concentrates on two occasions in Jacobean city comedy which represent 'women needing or failing to relieve themselves' (p. 23). Paster's primary interest is in the implications of this leakiness for our understanding of how women are constructed in Jacobean culture, but her discussion of relations between power and gender is suggestive for the context here. Preventing the body from leaking, Paster argues, becomes visible as 'the self-imposed responsibility of the patriarchal order', which in turn is driven to construct women as leaky vessels by way of shoring up its own interests (p. 63). Paster does not raise the question of why both her examples occur in city comedy; but that question evidently relates to my own specific concern with satire and its focus on the body here. I do not wish to suggest that the images of voluntary or accidental female leakage Paster discusses are to be equated with the image of fluids being forced out of the social body when the satirist lances it, but the latter also seems to mediate power relations, here between the satirist and the body politic.

8 See M. R. Woodhead's note to *What You Will*, ii.i.531 and cf. *The Scourge of Villainy*, Satire x, lines 50–7.

9 Ram Alley, running between the Temple and Fleet Street, was outside the jurisdiction of the city of London, and a known bolthole for those fleeing arrest.

10 The etymology of 'ruffian' is obscure, but the similarity in sound between 'rough' and 'ruffian' may have tended to highlight the parallel in sense.

11 As Andrew Gurr, quoting this passage, points out, railing was by 1606 'the characteristic and unique mode of the Blackfriars company' (*Shakespearian Playing Companies*, p. 351). The capacity to develop this kind of repertory should be linked, as Gurr demonstrates, to their apparent freedom from the control of the Master of the Revels and the queen's issue of a royal patent to Samuel Daniel giving him specific control over this single company.

12 The Quarto text, published in 1602, mentions the existence of an 'Apology' censored by the authorities, presumably more or less the same as the apologetical dialogue printed in the Folio.

13 The word 'scald', now obsolete, means 'affected with the "scall" or 'scabby'.

14 Modern spelling of the words 'satire' and 'satiric' masks a wordplay more evident in the early printed texts, which often print 'satyre' or 'satyric(ke)', thereby pointing up the potential equivalence between the satirist and the satyr, traditionally rough, crude and lecherous. The connection is more explicit in Dekker's use of the term 'bugbear satyr', quoted below, where it is necessary to retain spelling that makes the latter meaning primary.

15 False shows are conspicuous in Jonson's work, not only in the plays considered in this chapter, but this subject has already been fully explored by Peter Womack (*Ben Jonson*, ch. 4). See also chapter 7, below.

16 There is authority for the 'etc.' in the Folio text.

5 PLACING THE BOUNDARIES

1 Quotations are taken from Michael Hattaway's edition of the play. The play has act divisions, but not scene divisions, so references give act and line numbers.

2 Lindley, 'Riot Prevention and Control', p. 109; Manning, *Village Revolts*, p. 188. William Ingram's article 'The Globe Playhouse and its Neighbors in 1600' demonstrates that the prevailing view of Southwark as dominated by brothels and rioting is also wide of the mark. Examining various records of the parish of St Saviour's, Ingram finds no evidence that residents, including the relatively wealthy, were inclined to shun the vicinity of the playhouse despite the ease with which it was possible to move lodgings. (I am grateful to Andrew Gurr for drawing my attention to this article.)

3 Gildersleeve, *Government Regulation*, p. 145. On the government of these liberties before and after 1608 see also Pearl, *London and the Outbreak of the Puritan Revolution*, pp. 30–1. The liberty of St Paul's, however, as noted in the prologue (p. 7 above), was subject to ecclesiastical authority (though playing at the Paul's theatre came to an end in 1606).

4 See Fleetwood's letter to Lord Burghley, cited on p. 35 above.

5 The petition is reprinted in Gildersleeve, *Government Regulation*, p. 185. It is also reproduced by Andrew Gurr, to whose fuller discussion of the Burbages' plans (in 'Money or Audiences') the following discussion is indebted.

6 Rappaport ('Social Structure' and *Worlds Within Worlds*, chapters 7 and 8) provides evidence of the attractions of the system and the degree of social mobility it allowed.

7 On the city's payment for a new banqueting hall see Chambers, *Elizabethan Stage*, vol. II, p. 480. My attention was drawn to this point by Leah Marcus, who offers a persuasive reading of *Coriolanus* within the context of this tension between civic and state authority (*Puzzling Shakespeare*, p. 208). The charters of 1605 and 1608 are reprinted in Birch, ed., *Historical Charters and Constitutional Documents of the City of London*. Not surprisingly the 1608 charter led to frequent disputes. A tenant in Blackfriars refusing to pay his rent in

1614 was confident that no constable or sheriff would dare to take action against him in such a place of residence (Lindley, 'Riot Prevention and Control', p. 116 n33).

8 As Andrew Gurr has suggested to me, this joke may have been very specifically targeted, if the part of Rafe was taken by Nathan Field. Field was a leading actor with the Children of the Queen's Revels (Blackfriars Children) and had been a student of Mulcaster's at St Paul's School (Bentley, *Jacobean and Caroline Stage*, vol. III, p. 300).

9 What the play actually stages is the marching and inspection of the company. Rafe's command at the end of the scene as he and his men go off ('stand to your tacklings, lads, and show to the world you can as well brandish a sword as shake an apron. Saint George, and on, my hearts') however, and the men's answering cries of 'Saint George! Saint George!' (v.152–5), strongly imply to the audience that they exit into 'battle'. For information on the trained bands below, I am indebted to Lindsay Boynton, *Elizabethan Militia*.

10 Paul Mulholland, in a note on these lines in his edition of the play, draws a parallel with an earlier reference in *2 Henry IV* (III.ii.270ff).

11 As Ian Archer suggests, literary sources pose particular problems for the social historian. Historians cite the same examples, he points out, with suspicious frequency, and the rogue literature itself is heavily reliant on earlier literary tradition (*Pursuit of Stability*, pp. 204–13).

12 The phrase is Frank Foster's (*Politics of Stability*, p. 117). For a fuller discussion, see Pearl, 'Social Policy'. The crucial distinction is between what a preacher in 1628 referred to as 'God's poor and the Devil's poor' (Pearl, 'Social Policy', p. 130), recognised in law from 1576 (Manning, *Village Revolts*, p. 164).

13 The revolt took place from April to June. The precise date of performance of *The Knight of the Burning Pestle* is unknown, but there is now a broad consensus that it was written and first performed some time in 1607, despite earlier speculation about a later date of 1610–11. The play's decision to locate one of Rafe's adventures at the court of Moldavia may have been influenced by a visit to the English court by the Prince of Moldavia, which took place in November 1607.

14 On privy watches see McMullan, *Canting Crew*, pp. 83–7. Though called 'privy' watches because of the Privy Council's involvement in setting up the system of mass searches and hiring extra men to take part in them, a letter by William Fleetwood, then recorder of London, describing such a watch (cited by McMullan, p. 85) makes clear that the city had responsibility for giving the appropriate orders for such searches.

15 London was not alone either in experiencing problems of disorder or in transforming the midsummer festival into a military display. The mayor of Bristol in 1572 also transformed the midsummer festival into a general muster (Boynton, *Elizabethan Militia*, p. 18). The sheer size of the capital and the speed of its expansion, however, meant that it experienced problems shared by other towns on the grand scale.

6 THE PLACE OF ACCOMMODATION

1 The Whitefriars Theatre, which stood outside the city boundary up to 1608, was incorporated by the new charter.

2 The lord mayor's protest and Cecil's response are quoted in Stone, 'Inigo Jones and the New Exchange', pp. 107–8, to which, together with T. N. Brushfield's earlier article, 'Britain's Burse' (on which Stone draws), my account of the details of the building is indebted. Algernon Cecil's biography of Robert Cecil paraphrases some further detail from Cecil's letter, to the effect that he thought it 'unreasonable that he should not be allowed to benefit a locality which gave to London itself all the advantages of the proximity of the Court, which had been his father's residence, and where he himself was born' (*Life of Robert Cecil*, p. 320). Gresham's offer to provide the city with a Burse at his own cost, providing the city paid for the acquisition of the site, was welcomed as a 'gentle and very friendly offer' (records of the Court of Aldermen, January 1565; cited in Featherstone, *Sir Thomas Gresham and his Trusts*, p. 5). Several writers on Gresham associate his benefaction with his son's death in May 1563, seeing it as a wish to perpetuate his name in stone following the loss of his only heir and also within the context of further acts of public benevolence such as his establishment of alms-houses in Bishopsgate and the plans that eventually resulted in the founding of Gresham College (Teague, *Sir Thomas Gresham*, p. 15; Blanchard, 'Sir Thomas Gresham', p. 19; Saunders, 'Building of the Exchange', p. 37), but Jean Imray argues that his failure to formalise the terms of agreement with the city suggests a tension between apparently extravagant public-spiritedness and the constraints of other interests ('Origins of the Exchange', p. 34).

3 The lord mayor is quoted in Stone, 'Inigo Jones and the New Exchange', p. 107. The primary sense of the word 'termers' here must surely be those residing at the Inns of Court, which were of course very close to the New Exchange; but its meaning, according to the *OED*, may include anyone coming to London during term, whether for the law-courts, or 'for amusements, intrigues, or dishonest practices'.

4 Both sources are also cited in Brushfield, 'Britain's Burse', pp. 40, 39. Stow died in 1605, but his *Survey* continued to be revised and reissued after his death. Quotations from the *Survey* in this chapter are taken from the edition of 1633.

5 A ballad of 1658 shows how 'fashion' continues to be the keyword in the rivalry between the two institutions. The first twelve verses signal the fashionable edge that the New Exchange has over its predecessor:

> We will go no more to the Old Exchange,
> There's no good ware at all:
> . . .
> But we will go to the New Exchange,
> Where all things are in fashion;
> And we will have it henceforth call'd
> The Burse of Reformation.

Sheer range and variety of goods is the forte of the New Exchange, with its goods of all prices and all sizes. The second part of the poem, however, turns the tables, allowing the Royal Exchange to trump its rival with the superior power of money itself over changing fashions:

> We will keep our Old Exchange,
> Where wealth is still in fashion,
> Gold chains and ruffs shall bear the bell,
> For all your reformation.
> ('The Burse of Reformation'; quoted
> in Brushfield, 'Britain's Burse', p. 46)

6 Brushfield's description offers the clearest picture: 'It consisted of a ground and first floor, with a high roof pierced by a row of small dormer windows that probably lighted an attic storey. The upper floor, larger than the lower, was supported in front by a long arcade, having the entrance in the centre. Below were cellars, access to which was apparently obtained by outside steps in the rear of the main building, near the gatehouse . . . Each floor was divided into an outer and an inner walk, alley, or "range", all being lined with a series of small shops or "stalls"' ('Britain's Burse', p. 38). As Lawrence Stone comments, however, 'it is impossible to be absolutely certain about the precise appearance of the Exchange as it stood on completion in 1609' ('Inigo Jones and the New Exchange', p. 112).

7 Simon Basil, Surveyor of the King's Works, was in charge of building work; Rowland Bucket worked on the interior decoration; Richard Butler was involved in the armorial glazing; and Maximilian Colt did some of the sculptures. It seems likely that Cecil consulted more than one architect, including Inigo Jones, over the design of the building. Though Jones' design (figure 10) was rejected, it may have influenced the form of the accepted design (see further Stone, 'Inigo Jones and the New Exchange').

8 All quotations from the Venetian Ambassador in this chapter are taken from *CSPV*, vol. IX, 1607–10, no. 497.

9 The regulations are listed in *CSPD*, James I, vol. 49, no. 5. Most of these regulations are printed in an appendix by Brushfield, 'Britain's Burse', pp. 92–4). Algernon Cecil summarises the main points as follows:

Only tradespeople of reputable vocation were to have stalls there, except by special licence. Jewellers were not to ply their noisy hammers. There was to be no solicitation of customers by calling them. Beggars were to be altogether excluded. Masters were to be fined if they railed or scolded; and 'a private room' was to be set apart where noisy and quarrelsome servants and apprentices were to be whipped into good behaviour. For pickers and stealers there were to be stocks ready at hand. The amenities of the place were to be cared for by keepers who, as well as the owners themselves, would sweep the shops and see that the grass plot and gravel walks adjoining the arcade were kept smooth and tidy. (*Life of Robert Cecil*, p. 321)

Stone also notes the attempt to control sanitation problems by providing a 'pissing place' and levying fines for throwing 'any piss or other noisome thing' out of the windows ('Inigo Jones and the New Exchange', p. 117).

10 Take-up of leases at the Royal Exchange, however, had also been slow at first. Stow tells how the building 'stood in a manner empty' just before the queen's visit, until Gresham invited the few existing shopkeepers to take on 'as many shops, as they could, or would' rent-free for a year (*Annals*, p. 868). The queen's visit enhanced the fashionable status of the Exchange, however, and leases became more desirable after that, so that there was apparently a waiting list by 1597 (Saunders, 'Organisation of the Exchange', p. 90).

11 There were three actors: Nathan Field, William Ostler and Giles Gary (Ostler's apprentice). It seems probable that all three belonged to the Children of the Queen's Revels (the Blackfriars Children) at this time. See further Scott McMillin, 'Jonson's Early Entertainments', pp. 158–62. McMillin also provides more detail of the earlier entertainments at Theobalds and Salisbury House mentioned below.

12 The text of Wilson's letter is quoted from James Knowles' article announcing his identification of some papers in the Public Record Office as the text of this entertainment ('Cecil's Shopping Centre', p. 14). I am indebted to this article throughout, and to James Knowles' further generosity in allowing me access to his edition of the text of the entertainment now known as *Britain's Burse* before publication. Subsequent quotations from the text are from Knowles' edition.

13 The 'opening' was perhaps for one of the other shops, as yet unfitted. These shops were very small. Thomas Wilson describes them as 'as it were small chests rather than shops' (Brushfield, 'Britain's Burse', p. 43), and Brushfield cites a lease for one of the shops which describes it as 'containing in length ten foot of assize, more or less' (p. 82). At 10 feet (3.05 metres) wide, they were nevertheless twice the width of the shops in the Royal Exchange, though shallower, with a maximum depth of 5½ feet (1.68 metres; see above, chapter 1 n30). Just possibly, the 'opening' may have been an interior niche for a statue, though a drawing by John Smythson executed around 1618–19 (figure 9) seems to suggest that the niches were exterior, in imitation of the Royal Exchange (Stone, 'Inigo Jones and the New Exchange', pp. 112–13; Stone, however, points out the possible unreliability of Smythson's drawing).

14 As Knowles points out in a note, the building did have an elegant facade facing on to the Strand, and was notably plain to the rear. Lewis Mumford singles this out as a characteristic feature of baroque building (*Culture of Cities*, p. 128).

15 Knowles notes that 'the Salisbury House inventory of 1612 includes not only "a cabinet of China gilt all over" and a "nest of little boxes of China", but an astonishing sixty-five porcelain items' ('Cecil's Shopping Centre', p. 15). Cecil had a passion for wondrous artefacts of all kinds, not

merely Chinese ware, as G. P. V. Akrigg's description of Theobalds conveys:

There was a hall whose ceiling was a kind of planetarium with the signs of the zodiac, the stars shining by night, and the sun performing its course by ingenious mechanism by day. Flanking the walls were trees with natural bark attached, with birds' nests, and leaves and fruit so natural in appearance that when the steward opened the windows overlooking the pleasure gardens outside birds flew in and, perching on the trees, sang. (*Jacobean Pageant*, p. 20)

The fact that James coveted this house so much that Cecil finally gave it to him in 1607 indicates the degree to which Cecil's ostentatious display of his exotica might stimulate the wish to possess them. The Burse was itself, of course, based on the principle of inciting the longing for commodities via spectacular display.

16 Butterflies are not mentioned in the Shop-boy's speech, but they are listed alongside parrots' feathers in the following speech by the Master (at lines 110–11). Even before the fashion for China ware, some of the same kinds of frivolous or luxury items characterise the goods in the Royal Exchange. Stow specifies 'mousetraps, birdcages, shoeing-horns, lanterns, and Jew's trumps etc.' for sale, and mentions the presence of armourers, apothecaries, booksellers, goldsmiths and glass sellers besides (*Annals*, p. 869). Ann Saunders lists the traders mentioned in the first volume of the Gresham Repertories as having shops in the Exchange ('Organisation of the Exchange', p. 89).

17 The only one of Jonson's royal entertainments to mingle verse and prose before 1611 is the *Entertainment at Highgate* (1604), in which the figure of Mercury speaks in prose. None of his court masques includes any prose at all before 1612, when *Love Restored* employs prose for an opening which enacts a pretence of explaining that the masque will not go ahead. The prose is therefore quite separate from the masque proper, which is in verse.

18 Punctuation marks are not merely editorial, but separate each of these items in the manuscript.

19 The slipperiness of 'value', 'worth' and 'price' is both unavoidable and significant here. As Veblen argues, our notions of the beautiful are inevitably tied up with the expense represented.

20 The presence of interior niches is not proven, however (see note 13).

21 The terms 'inside' and 'outside' are somewhat ambiguous here. Given the dimensions of the New Exchange shops, it is impossible that the spectators were all inside the shop, though it is likely that the actors were. We should perhaps think of the shop as framing a recessed space somewhat distanced from the spectators, like a discovery space or a small-scale proscenium arch stage.

22 One of the Hatfield papers makes reference to Field sitting up all of the previous night writing out the text (McMillin, 'Jonson's Early Entertainments', p. 161).

23 Since *The Winter's Tale* cannot be dated with the same precision as the

Entertainment, it is impossible to be certain which came first. Simon Shepherd, dating *The Winter's Tale* to 1611, sets its transformation scene alongside another Jonson text, *The Alchemist* (1610), with its comic interest in the imagined materialisation of a fairy queen (Shepherd and Womack, *English Drama*, pp. 68–70). The point at issue, in both Shepherd's argument and my own, is not who 'borrowed' from who, but that very different meanings may be made by similar dramatic materials in different theatrical and cultural contexts.

<h3>7 THE MASKING OF PLACE</h3>

1 It is Truewit's statement that the new collegiate foundation is '*here* i' the town' (1.i.71; my italics) that establishes the location of Clerimont's lodging. On the other hand, 'the town' is as much a social concept as a physical entity, and should not be conceived too rigidly as falling outside the city boundary. Mrs Otter's china house, for example (see below), clearly aspires to be part of the town, whatever its exact location. Similarly, her husband apparently includes Blackfriars and even Silver Street within his understanding of the town when the emphasis is on the commodities with which they are associated (see p. 127 and n5, below).

2 The pairing occurs several times in the play (see e.g. 1.iii.28; 11.iii.51; iv.vi.5–6, discussed below). Sometimes the terms stand in, as here, for groups of fashionable men about town who evidently seek to display their wit and 'braveries' (fine clothes or other embellishments).

3 The first is a reference to an early sixteenth-century riot of Londoners against foreigners living in London; the second to the ceremonial of the lord mayor's show.

4 Shrove Tuesday was an especially riotous holiday. See, for example, Rafe's reference to it in *The Knight of the Burning Pestle*, quoted on p. 108 above. Jonson's strong classical sense probably indicates the presence of conscious irony (his, not Mrs Otter's) in the use of the word 'civil', which brings together an etymology rooted in the city with Mrs Otter's pretensions to be above it.

5 Though the Strand is the only one of the three named locations here firmly situated outside the city, I am inclined to think that Jonson's usage here includes the Blackfriars and Silver Street within a broad conception of the town. Blackfriars is of course geographically within the city walls but outside its jurisdiction, as discussed in chapter 5 above, and located on the city's western boundary. Silver Street is clearly within the city boundary and, though in a north-western situation, further from the developing town. Alternatively, the 'not-quite' status of Silver Street, and perhaps Blackfriars, may be part of the joke against Mrs Otter.

6 Beaurline here glosses the French hermaphrodite as King Henry III of France, 'a notorious transvestite, subject of Thomas Arthus' *Isle des Hermaphrodites* (1605)'.

7 Peter Womack has demonstrated that Jonson's 'coercive unmaskings' characteristically issue in silence, putting a distance between truth and language and bringing all role-playing to an unequivocal close (*Ben Jonson*, pp. 106–7).

EPILOGUE

1 The pageant, though planned for the coronation, was not in fact staged until a year after James' accession and eight months after the coronation. See below.

2 Quotations from *The Magnificent Entertainment* are taken from Richard Dutton's edition in *Jacobean Civic Pageantry*. The *Entertainment* is also discussed more fully in David Bergeron's *English Civic Pageantry*, pp. 71–89, and plates of all the arches are reproduced there. The two arches discussed in some detail here, the Londinium Arch in Fenchurch Street and the Dutch Arch in Cornhill, are reproduced here as figures 11 and 12.

3 No single contemporary printed version in fact provided the full text of the event. This title is taken from Dekker's version, commissioned by the city, and in print by May 1604. (The reference to the date on the title page is in old-style dating, which specified the beginning of the new year as 25 March.) This included the text of Dekker's own pageants, together with a fairly brief account of Jonson's pageants, an account which nowhere names Jonson or quotes his text. Jonson published his own part in the *Entertainment* both in a quarto that probably preceded Dekker's and again in his folio *Works* of 1616. (For discussion of the difficulties over these two publications see Herford and Simpson, *Ben Jonson*, vol. VII, pp. 67, 77–9.) Stephen Harrison, who was responsible for the seven triumphal arches, also published a folio account called *The Arches of Triumph*, including his own drawings of the arches.

4 The companies were assessed for contributions to the cost, which was substantial (the records of assessment are printed in Nichols, *The Progresses*, vol. I, pp. 400–1). Queen Elizabeth, it may be noted, took a sufficiently active interest in her own royal entry to become part-patron of the pageantry on that occasion (see note 10 below).

5 The reason Harrison mentions only five triumphal arches here is, as he goes on to explain, that the two arches erected by 'merchant-strangers' were also paid for by them rather than by the city.

6 There was one further pageant in the Strand, beyond Temple Bar, but this was paid for by the city of Westminster and the Duchy of Lancaster, not the city of London, and it was not an arch, but a tableau. As always in this kind of event at this period, the boundary between the city and the non-city is insistently highlighted.

7 The pageants for James' entry are erected in the same places as for Elizabeth's entry. The Royal Exchange, of course, was not built in 1559, when Elizabeth's progress took place, but there was a pageant located in

Cornhill before the building of the Royal Exchange. Dekker is hence exploiting a useful conjunction between tradition and modern enterprise, usefully named.

8 Cf. also Riggs' comparison of Jonson's arches with Dekker's (*Ben Jonson*, pp. 110–12).

9 As David Bergeron notes, no previous English pageant had been so dependent on triumphal arches, and these arches are 'highly embellished architectural achievements' (*English Civic Pageantry*, p. 75).

10 Elizabeth's coronation entry was a triumph of public relations, repeatedly revisited in print. In addition to the official record (issued twice in 1559 and again – significantly – in 1604), it was described by Holinshed and the Venetian ambassador and subsequently worked into popular plays. As David Bergeron has argued, Elizabeth's interest in the preparations, and her direction to the Master of the Revels to contribute to the provision of costumes for the pageants, suggest a careful concern to shape this public appearance and to exploit its potential to the full, even to the extent of bearing part of the cost ('Elizabeth's Coronation Entry').

11 Arthur Wilson is quoted at more length in Bergeron, *English Civic Pageantry*, p. 75 and Dutton, *Jacobean Civic Pageants*, p. 22. Wilson also explicitly makes the adverse comparison between King James and Queen Elizabeth in this respect.

12 On the Banqueting House of 1622 see further Harris and Higgott, *Inigo Jones*, pp. 108–9 and Akrigg, *Jacobean Pageant*, pp. 283–6. Goldberg reproduces a painting which depicts a version of this same absolutist statement: Paul van Somer's portrait of the king standing in full royal regalia, holding sceptre and orb, and framed from behind by a window allowing a view of the imposing facade of the Banqueting House (*James I and the Politics of Literature*, p. 41). David Bergeron has also highlighted the importance of civic pageantry in mediating classical architectural forms to English spectators before Inigo Jones, an argument he mounts in opposition to the work of John Peacock, cited below (Bergeron, 'Inigo Jones'; Peacock, *Stage Designs of Inigo Jones*). The Royal Exchange too, of course, is an early example of an English building showing classical influence.

13 The quotation is from Kevin Sharpe, *The Personal Rule of Charles I*, p. 404, to which the following discussion of Charles' building projects is indebted.

14 Jones' sketch is reproduced in Harris and Higgott, *Inigo Jones*, p. 253 and in Peacock, *Stage Designs of Inigo Jones*, p. 49.

15 Quotations are from David Lindley's edition in *Court Masques*.

16 For fuller discussion of the proscenium arch, see Peacock, *Stage Designs of Inigo Jones*, ch. 6, especially pp. 208–16.

17 The drawing is presumed to be by John Webb after Jones' original design. Two related drawings by Jones himself survive, one of the bridge and one of the distant parts of the city and suburbs that can be seen through the arches of the bridge. See further Orgel and Strong, *Inigo Jones*, vol. II, pp. 753–7 and Peacock, *Stage Designs of Inigo Jones*, pp. 107–12.

Bibliography

(Place and date of publication only are cited for early printed books.)

Agnew, Jean-Christophe, *Worlds Apart: The Market and the Theater in Anglo-American Thought, 1550–1750* (Cambridge: Cambridge University Press, 1986).

Akrigg, G. P. V., *Jacobean Pageant, or The Court of James I* (London: Hamish Hamilton, 1962).

Archer, Ian W., *The Pursuit of Stability: Social Relations in Elizabethan London* (Cambridge: Cambridge University Press, 1991).

Archer, Ian, 'The Nostalgia of John Stow', in Smith, Strier and Bevington, ed., *Theatrical City*, 17–34.

Ashton, Robert, *The City and the Court, 1603–1643* (Cambridge: Cambridge University Press, 1979).

'Popular Entertainment and Social Control in Later Elizabethan and Early Stuart London', *London Journal*, 9 (1983), 3–19.

Barish, Jonas A., *Ben Jonson and the Language of Prose Comedy* (New York: Norton, 1970).

Barron, Caroline M., 'Richard Whittington: The Man Behind the Myth', in *Studies in London History Presented to Philip Edmund Jones*, ed. A. E. J. Hollaender and William Kellaway (London: Hodder and Stoughton, 1969), 197–248.

Barton, Anne, *Ben Jonson, Dramatist* (Cambridge: Cambridge University Press, 1984).

'The King Disguised: Shakespeare's *Henry V* and the Comical History', in *The Triple Bond: Plays, Mainly Shakespearean, in Performance*, ed. Joseph G. Price (Pennsylvania and London: Pennsylvania State University Press, 1975), 92–117.

'London Comedy and the Ethos of the City', *London Journal*, 4 (1978), 158–80.

Beaumont, Francis, *The Knight of the Burning Pestle*, ed. Andrew Gurr (Edinburgh: Oliver and Boyd, 1968).

The Knight of the Burning Pestle, ed. Michael Hattaway (1969; rpt. London: A. and C. Black, 1991).

Beaurline, L. A., *see* Jonson, Ben, *Epicoene*.

Beckerman, Bernard, *Shakespeare at the Globe, 1599–1609* (London and New York: Macmillan, 1962).

Beier, A. L., *Masterless Men: The Vagrancy Problem in England 1560–1640* (London and New York: Methuen, 1985).

Bentley, Gerald Eades, *The Jacobean and Caroline Stage*, 7 vols. (Oxford: Clarendon Press, 1941–68).

Bergeron, David M., *English Civic Pageantry, 1558–1642* (London: Edward Arnold, 1971).

'Elizabeth's Coronation Entry (1559): New Manuscript Evidence', *English Literary Renaissance*, 8 (1978), 3–8.

'Inigo Jones, Renaissance Visual Culture, and English Outer Darkness', *Research Opportunities in Renaissance Drama*, 36 (1997), 97–104.

Berlin, Michael, 'Civic Ceremony in Early Modern London', *Urban History Yearbook* (1986), 15–27.

Bevington, David, *see* Smith, Strier and Bevington, ed., *Theatrical City*.

Birch, Walter de Gray, ed., *The Historical Charters and Constitutional Documents of the City of London*, revised edn. (London: Whiting, 1887).

Blanchard, Ian, 'Sir Thomas Gresham *c.* 1518–1579', in Saunders, ed., *Royal Exchange*, 11–19.

Bonahue Jr., Edward T., 'Citizen History: Stow's *Survey of London*', *Studies in English Literature*, 38 (1998), 61–85.

Boynton, Lindsay, *The Elizabethan Militia, 1558–1638* (London: Routledge and Kegan Paul; Toronto: University of Toronto Press, 1967).

Bradbrook, M. C., 'The Politics of Pageantry (London)', in *Shakespeare in his Context: The Constellated Globe*, vol. IV of *The Collected Papers of Muriel Bradbrook*, 4 vols. (Brighton and Totowa: Harvester, Barnes and Noble, 1982–9), 95–109.

Braudel, Fernand, *Capitalism and Material Life, 1400–1800*, trans. Miriam Kochan (London: Weidenfeld and Nicolson, 1973).

Brett-James, Norman G., *The Growth of Stuart London* (London: Allen and Unwin, 1935).

Brushfield, T. N., 'Britain's Burse, or the New Exchange', *Journal of the British Archaeological Association*, n.s. 9 (1903), 33–48, 81–94.

Bruster, Douglas, *Drama and the Market in the Age of Shakespeare* (Cambridge: Cambridge University Press, 1992).

Bullough, Geoffrey, *Narrative and Dramatic Sources of Shakespeare*, 8 vols. (London: Routledge; New York: Columbia University Press, 1957–75).

Burgon, John William, *The Life and Times of Sir Thomas Gresham*, 2 vols. (London: Robert Jennings, 1839).

Cain, Tom, *see* Jonson, Ben, *Poetaster*.

Carroll, D. Allen, *see* Guilpin, Everard

Cecil, Algernon, *A Life of Robert Cecil, First Earl of Salisbury* (London: John Murray, 1915).

Chambers, E. K., *The Elizabethan Stage*, 4 vols. (Oxford: Clarendon Press, 1923).

Chapman, George, The Plays of: The Comedies, ed. Allan Holaday (Urbana: University of Illinois Press, 1970).

Chapman, George, Ben Jonson and John Marston, *Eastward Ho*, ed. R. W. Van Fossen (Manchester: Manchester University Press; Baltimore: Johns Hopkins University Press, 1979).

Corbin, Peter, *see Famous Victories of Henry the Fifth*.

Croft, Pauline, 'Robert Cecil and the Early Jacobean Court', in Peck, ed., *Mental World of the Jacobean Court*, 134–47.

Day, John, *The Isle of Gulls*, ed. Raymond S. Burns (New York: Garland, 1980).

De Certeau, Michel, *The Practice of Everyday Life*, trans. Steven Rendall (Berkeley, Los Angeles and London: University of California Press, 1984).

Dekker, Thomas, *The Dramatic Works of*, ed. Fredson Bowers, 4 vols. (Cambridge: Cambridge University Press, 1953–61).

Dekker, Thomas, *The Seven Deadly Sins of London*, ed. H. F. B. Brett-Smith (Oxford: Basil Blackwell, 1922).

    The Wonderful Year, The Gull's Hornbook, Penny-Wise, Pound-Foolish, English Villainies Discovered by Lantern and Candlelight and Selected Writings, ed. E. D. Pendry (London: Edward Arnold, 1967).

Dillon, Janette, *Language and Stage in Medieval and Renaissance England* (Cambridge: Cambridge University Press, 1998).

Dodsley, Robert, ed., *A Select Collection of Old English Plays*, 4th edn., ed. W. Carew Hazlitt, 15 vols. (London: Reeves and Turner, 1874–6).

Douglas, Mary, *Purity and Danger: An Analysis of the Concepts of Pollution and Taboo* (1966; rpt. London and New York: Routledge, 1991).

Dutton, Richard, *Mastering the Revels: The Regulation and Censorship of English Renaissance Drama* (London: Macmillan, 1991).

Dutton, Richard, ed., *Jacobean Civic Pageants* (Keele University: Ryburn Publishing, 1995).

Eastward Ho, see Chapman, George.

Engle, Lars, *Shakespearean Pragmatism: Market of His Time* (Chicago and London: University of Chicago Press, 1993).

Famous Victories of Henry the Fifth, The, in *The Oldcastle Controversy*, ed. Peter Corbin and Douglas Sedge (Manchester: Manchester University Press, 1991).

Featherstone, Ernest, *Sir Thomas Gresham and His Trusts* (London: Blades, East and Blades, 1952).

Ferguson, Margaret W., 'Feathers and Flies: Aphra Behn and the Seventeenth-century Trade in Exotica', in *Subject and Object in Renaissance Culture*, ed. Margreta de Grazia, Maureen Quilligan and Peter Stallybrass (Cambridge: Cambridge University Press, 1996), 235–59.

Finkelpearl, Philip J., *John Marston of the Middle Temple: An Elizabethan Dramatist in His Social Setting* (Cambridge, Mass.: Harvard University Press, 1969).

    'John Marston's *Histriomastix* as an Inns of Court Play: A Hypothesis', *Huntington Library Quarterly*, 29 (1966), 223–34.

Finlay, Roger and Beatrice Shearer, 'Population Growth and Suburban Expansion', in *London, 1500–1700: The Making of the Metropolis*, ed. A. L. Beier and Roger Finlay (London: Longman, 1986), 37–59.

Fisher, F. J., 'The Development of London as a Centre of Conspicuous Consumption in the Sixteenth and Seventeenth Centuries', *Transactions of the Royal Historical Society*, 4th series, 30 (1948), 37–50.

Forse, James H., *Art Imitates Business: Commercial and Political Influences in Elizabethan Theatre* (Bowling Green, OH: Bowling Green State University Press, 1993).

Foster, Frank Freeman, *The Politics of Stability: A Portrait of the Rulers in Elizabethan London* (London: Royal Historical Society, 1977).

Friedrichs, Christopher R., *The Early Modern City, 1450–1750* (London and New York: Longman, 1995).

Gair, Reavley, *The Children of Paul's: The Story of a Theatre Company, 1553–1608* (Cambridge: Cambridge University Press, 1982).

see Marston, John, *Antonio's Revenge.*

Gildersleeve, Virginia Crocheron, *Government Regulation of the Elizabethan Drama* (1908; rpt. New York: Burt Franklin, 1961).

Goldberg, Jonathan, *James I and the Politics of Literature: Jonson, Shakespeare, Donne, and their Contemporaries* (Baltimore and London: Johns Hopkins University Press, 1983).

Grenade, L., '*Les Singularitéz de Londres, 1576*', in Saunders, ed., *Royal Exchange*, 48–9.

Guilpin, Everard, *Skialetheia, or A Shadowe of Truth, in Certaine Epigrams and Satyres,* ed. D. Allen Carroll (Chapel Hill: University of North Carolina Press, 1974).

Gunby, David, *see* Webster, John, *The Works of.*

Gurr, Andrew, *The Shakespearean Stage, 1574–1642*, 3rd edn. (Cambridge: Cambridge University Press, 1992).

The Shakespearian Playing Companies (Oxford: Clarendon Press, 1996).

'Money or Audiences: The Impact of Shakespeare's Globe', *Theatre Notebook,* 18 (1988), 3–14.

see Beaumont, Francis, *The Knight of the Burning Pestle.*

Hall's Chronicle, [ed. Henry Ellis] (London: J. Johnson etc., 1809).

Harbage, Alfred, '*Love's Labor's Lost* and the Early Shakespeare', *Philological Quarterly,* 41 (1962), 18–36.

Harbage, Alfred., ed., *Annals of English Drama, 975–1700*, revised S. Schoenbaum and Sylvia Stoler Wagonheim, 3rd edn. (London and New York: Routledge, 1989).

Harding, Vanessa, 'The Population of London, 1550–1700: A Review of the Published Evidence', *London Journal,* 15 (1990), 111–28.

Harris, John and Gordon Higgott, *Inigo Jones: Complete Architectural Drawings* (London and New York: Philip Wilson, 1989).

Harrison, Stephen, *The Arches of Triumph* (London, 1603).

Harrison, William, *The Description of England,* ed. Georges Edelen (Ithaca, N.Y.: Cornell University Press, 1968).

Hattaway, Michael, *see* Beaumont, Francis, *The Knight of the Burning Pestle.*

Heinemann, Margot, *Puritanism and Theatre: Thomas Middleton and Opposition Drama Under the Early Stuarts* (Cambridge: Cambridge University Press, 1980).

Herford, C. H., *see* Jonson, Ben.

Heywood, Thomas, *The Dramatic Works of,* [ed. Richard Herne Shepherd], 6 vols. (London: John Pearson, 1874).

Hibbard, G. R., *see* Shakespeare, William, *Love's Labour's Lost*.
Holinshed's Chronicles of England, Scotland and Ireland [ed. Henry Ellis], 6 vols. (London: J. Johnson etc., 1807–8).
Hoskins, John, *Directions for Speech and Style*, ed. Hoyt H. Hudson (Princeton: Princeton University Press, 1935).
Hoy, Cyrus, *Introductions, Notes, and Commentaries to texts in 'The Dramatic Works of Thomas Dekker', edited by Fredson Bowers*, 2 vols. (Cambridge: Cambridge University Press, 1980).
Hughes, Paul L., *see* Larkin, James F.
Imray, Jean, 'The Origins of the Royal Exchange', in Saunders, ed., *Royal Exchange*, 20–35.
Ingram, William, *The Business of Playing: The Beginnings of Adult Professional Theater in Elizabethan London* (Ithaca, N.Y.: Cornell University Press, 1992).
   'The Globe Playhouse and its Neighbors in 1600', *Essays in Theatre*, 2 (1984), 63–72.
James I, The Political Works of, introd. Charles Howard McIlwain (New York: Russell and Russell, 1965).
Johnson, David J., *Southwark and the City* (Oxford: Oxford University Press, 1969).
Johnson, Richard, *The Nine Worthies of London* (London, 1592).
   The Pleasant Walks of Moorfields (London, 1607).
Jonson, Ben, ed. C. H. Herford and Percy Simpson, 12 vols. (Oxford: Clarendon Press, 1925–52).
Jonson, Ben, The Complete Plays of, ed. G. A. Wilkes, 4 vols. (Oxford: Clarendon Press, 1981–2).
Jonson, Ben, *Epicoene*, ed. L. A. Beaurline (London: Edward Arnold, 1966).
   Poetaster, ed. Tom Cain (Manchester: Manchester University Press, 1995).
Knabb, Ken, ed. and trans., *Situationist International Anthology* (Berkeley, Calif.: Bureau of Public Secrets, 1981).
Knowles, James, 'Cecil's Shopping Centre', *Times Literary Supplement*, 7 February 1997, 14–15.
   'Jonson's Entertainment at Britain's Burse', in *Representing Ben Jonson*, ed. Martin Butler (London: Macmillan, 1999), 114–51.
   'The Spectacle of the Realm: Civic Consciousness, Rhetoric and Ritual in Early Modern London', in *Theatre and Government Under the Early Stuarts*, ed. J. R. Mulryne and Margaret Shewring (Cambridge: Cambridge University Press, 1993), 157–89.
Knutson, Roslyn L., 'Falconer to the Little Eyases: A New Date and Commercial Agenda for the "Little Eyases" Passage in *Hamlet*', *Shakespeare Quarterly*, 46 (1995), 1–31.
Larkin, James F. and Paul L. Hughes, *Stuart Royal Proclamations*, vol. 1 (Oxford: Clarendon Press, 1973).
Lefebvre, Henri, *The Production of Space*, trans. Donald Nicholson-Smith (Oxford and Cambridge, Mass.: Blackwell, 1991).
Leggatt, Alexander, *Jacobean Public Theatre* (London and New York: Routledge, 1992).

Leishmann, J. B., *see Parnassus Plays, The Three*.

Lindley, David, ed., *Court Masques: Jacobean and Caroline Entertainments, 1605–1640* (Oxford and New York: Oxford University Press, 1995).

Lindley, K. J., 'Riot Prevention and Control in Early Stuart London', *Transactions of the Royal Historical Society*, 5th series, 33 (1983), 109–26.

Manley, Lawrence, *Literature and Culture in Early Modern London* (Cambridge: Cambridge University Press, 1995).

'Of Sites and Rites', in Smith, Strier and Bevington, ed., *Theatrical City*, 35–54.

Manley, Lawrence, ed., *London in the Age of Shakespeare: An Anthology* (London and Sydney: Croom Helm, 1986).

Manning, Roger B., *Village Revolts: Social Protest and Popular Disturbances in England, 1509–1640* (Oxford: Clarendon Press, 1988).

Marcus, Leah S., *Puzzling Shakespeare: Local Reading and Its Discontents* (Berkeley, Los Angeles and London: University of California Press, 1988).

Marston, John, The Plays of, ed. H. Harvey Wood, 3 vols. (Edinburgh and London: Oliver and Boyd, 1934–9).

Marston, John, The Poems of, ed. Arnold Davenport (Liverpool: Liverpool University Press, 1961).

Marston, John, *Antonio's Revenge*, ed. W. Reavley Gair (Manchester: Manchester University Press; Baltimore: Johns Hopkins University Press, 1978).

What You Will, ed. M. R. Woodhead (Nottingham: Nottingham University Press, 1980).

Martines, Lauro, *Society and History in English Renaissance Verse* (Oxford: Basil Blackwell, 1985).

Masten, Jeffrey, *Textual Intercourse: Collaboration, Authorship, and Sexualities in Renaissance Drama* (Cambridge: Cambridge University Press, 1997).

McIlwain, Charles Howard, *see James I, The Political Works of*.

McLuskie, Kathleen, *Dekker and Heywood* (London: Macmillan, 1994).

McMillin, Scott, 'Jonson's Early Entertainments: New Information from Hatfield House', *Renaissance Drama*, n.s. 1 (1968), 153–66.

McMullan, John L., *The Canting Crew: London's Criminal Underworld, 1550–1700* (New Brunswick, N.J.: Rutgers University Press, 1984).

Middleton, Thomas and Thomas Dekker, *The Roaring Girl*, ed. Paul A. Mulholland (Manchester: Manchester University Press, 1987).

Miles, Rosalind, *Ben Jonson: His Life and Work* (London: Routledge and Kegan Paul, 1986).

Minchinton, W. E., *The Growth of English Overseas Trade in the Seventeenth and Eighteenth Centuries* (London: Methuen, 1969).

Mulholland, Paul, *see* Middleton, Thomas and Thomas Dekker, *The Roaring Girl*.

Mullaney, Steven, *The Place of the Stage: License, Play, and Power in Renaissance England* (Chicago and London: University of Chicago Press, 1988).

Mumford, Lewis, *The City in History: Its Origins, its Transformations, and its Prospects* (1961; rpt Harmondsworth: Penguin, 1991).

The Culture of Cities (London: Secker and Warburg, 1938).

Neill, Michael, *Issues of Death: Mortality and Identity in English Renaissance Tragedy* (Oxford: Clarendon Press, 1997).

Nichols, John, *The Progresses, Processions, and Magnificent Festivities of King James I*, 3 vols. (London: Society of Antiquaries, 1828).

Norden, John, *Speculum Britanniae: The First Part* (London, 1593).

Ordish, T. Fairman, *Early London Theatres (In the Fields)* (London: Elliot Stock, 1894).

Orgel, Stephen and Roy Strong, *Inigo Jones: The Theatre of the Stuart Court*, 2 vols. (London: Sotheby Parke Bernet; Berkeley and Los Angeles: University of California Press, 1973).

Orrell, John, *The Human Stage: English Theatre Design, 1567–1640* (Cambridge: Cambridge University Press, 1988).

Parnassus Plays, The Three, ed. J. B. Leishman (London: Ivor Nicholson and Watson, 1949).

Paster, Gail Kern, *The Body Embarrassed: Drama and the Disciplines of Shame in Early Modern England* (Ithaca, N.Y.: Cornell University Press, 1993).

  The Idea of the City in the Age of Shakespeare (Athens: University of Georgia Press, 1985).

  'The Idea of London in Masque and Pageant', in *Pageantry in the Shakespearean Theater*, ed. David M. Bergeron (Athens: University of Georgia Press, 1985), 48–64.

Peacock, John, *The Stage Designs of Inigo Jones: The European Context* (Cambridge: Cambridge University Press, 1995).

Pearl, Valerie, *London and the Outbreak of the Puritan Revolution: City Government and National Politics, 1625–43* (Oxford: Oxford University Press, 1964; corrected 1st edn of 1961).

  'Change and Stability in Seventeenth-Century London', *London Journal*, 5 (1979), 3–34.

  'Social Policy in Early Modern London', in *History and Imagination: Essays in Honour of H. R. Trevor-Roper*, ed. Hugh Lloyd-Jones, Valerie Pearl and Blair Worden (London: Duckworth, 1981), 115–31.

Peck, Linda Levy, ed., *The Mental World of the Jacobean Court* (Cambridge: Cambridge University Press, 1991).

Phythian Adams, Charles, 'Ceremony and the Citizen: The Communal Year at Coventry, 1450–1550', in *Crisis and Order in English Towns, 1500–1700: Essays in Urban History*, ed. Peter Clark and Paul Slack (Toronto: University of Toronto Press, 1972), 57–85.

Platter, Thomas, *Thomas Platter's Travels in England*, ed. Clare Williams (London: Jonathan Cape, 1937).

Rappaport, Steve, *Worlds Within Worlds: Structures of Life in Sixteenth-Century London* (Cambridge: Cambridge University Press, 1989).

  'Social Structure and Mobility in Sixteenth-century London: Part I', *London Journal*, 9 (1983), 107–35.

  'Social Structure and Mobility in Sixteenth-century London: Part II', *London Journal*, 10 (1984), 107–34.

Riggs, David, *Ben Jonson: A Life* (Cambridge, Mass.: Harvard University Press, 1989).

Saunders, Ann, 'The Building of the Exchange', in Saunders, ed., *Royal Exchange*, 36–47.

'The Organisation of the Exchange', in Saunders, ed., *Royal Exchange*, 85–98.

Saunders, Ann, ed., *The Royal Exchange* (London: London Topographical Society, 1997).

Scott, William, *An Essay on Drapery, or The Complete Citizen* (London, 1635).

Sedge, Douglas, *see Famous Victories of Henry the Fifth*.

Shakespeare, William, *Love's Labour's Lost*, ed. G. R. Hibbard (Oxford: Clarendon Press, 1990).

Shapiro, Michael, *Children of the Revels: The Boy Companies of Shakespeare's Time and their Plays* (New York: Columbia University Press, 1977).

Sharpe, Kevin, *The Personal Rule of Charles I* (New Haven and London: Yale University Press, 1992).

Shepherd, Simon and Peter Womack, *English Drama: A Cultural History* (Oxford: Blackwell, 1996).

Simpson, Percy, *see Jonson, Ben*.

Smith, Alan G. R., *The Emergence of a Nation State: The Commonwealth of England, 1529–1660* (London and New York: Longman, 1984).

Smith, David L., Richard Strier and David M. Bevington, ed., *The Theatrical City: Culture, Theatre, and Politics in London, 1576–1649* (Cambridge: Cambridge University Press, 1995).

Smith, Steven R., 'The London Apprentices as Seventeenth-century Adolescents', *Past and Present*, 61 (1973), 149–61.

Smuts, Malcolm, 'Cultural Diversity and Cultural Change at the Court of James I', in Peck, ed., *Mental World of the Jacobean Court*, 99–112.

Staniland, Kay, 'Thomas Deane's Shop in the Royal Exchange', in Saunders, ed., *Royal Exchange*, 59–67.

Stone, Lawrence, *The Crisis of the Aristocracy, 1558–1641* (Oxford: Clarendon Press, 1965).

'Inigo Jones and the New Exchange', *Archaeological Journal*, 114 (1957), 106–21.

Stow, John, *The Annals or General Chronicle of England*, continued by Edmund Howes (London, 1615).

A Survey of London, continued by A. M., H. D. and others (London, 1633).

A Survey of London, ed. Charles Lethbridge Kingsford, 2 vols. (Oxford: Clarendon Press, 1908).

Strier, Richard, *see* Smith, Strier and Bevington, ed., *Theatrical City*.

Sugden, Edward, *A Topographical Dictionary to the Works of Shakespeare and His Fellow Dramatists* (Manchester: Manchester University Press; London: Longmans, Green, 1925).

Teague, S. J., *Sir Thomas Gresham: Financier and College Founder* (Bromley: Synjon Books, 1974).

Thomson, Peter, *Shakespeare's Theatre*, 2nd edn (London: Routledge, 1992).

Veblen, Thorstein, *The Theory of the Leisure Class: An Economic Study of Institutions* (1899; rpt. London: George Allen and Unwin, 1924).

Von Holst, Niels, *Creators, Collectors and Connoisseurs: The Anatomy of Artistic Taste from Antiquity to the Present Day* (London: Thames and Hudson, 1967).

Webster, John, *The Works of: An Old-Spelling Critical Edition*, ed. David Gunby, David Carnegie, Antony Hammond and Doreen DelVecchio, vol. 1 (Cambridge: Cambridge University Press, 1995).

Wells, Stanley and Gary Taylor, *William Shakespeare: A Textual Companion* (Oxford: Clarendon Press, 1987).

Wells, Susan, 'Jacobean City Comedy and the Ideology of the City', *English Literary History*, 48 (1981), 37–60.

Whigham, Frank, *Ambition and Privilege: The Social Tropes of Elizabethan Courtesy Theory* (Berkeley, Los Angeles and London: University of California Press, 1984).

Williams, Raymond, *The Country and the City* (London: Chatto and Windus, 1973).

Wilson, Arthur, *The History of Great Britain* (London, 1653).

Wilson, Robert, *Three Ladies of London*, see Dodsley, Robert, *A Select Collection*, vol. VI.

Three Lords and Three Ladies of London, see Dodsley, Robert, *A Select Collection*, vol. VI.

Withington, Robert, *English Pageantry: An Historical Outline*, 2 vols. (1918, 1926; rpt. New York: B. Blom, 1963).

Wittlin, Alma S., *The Museum: Its History and its Tasks in Education* (London: Routledge and Kegan Paul, 1949).

Womack, Peter, *Ben Jonson* (Oxford: Blackwell, 1986).

see Shepherd and Womack, *English Drama*.

Woodhead, M. R., see Marston, John, *What You Will*.

Wright, Louis B., *Middle-Class Culture in Elizabethan England* (Chapel Hill: University of North Carolina Press, 1935).

Index

Printed in the United Kingdom
by Lightning Source UK Ltd.
102513UKS00002B/58